YOUR FAVORITE SCARY MOVIE

HOW THE SCREAM FILMS
REWROTE THE RULES OF HORROR

ASHLEY CULLINS

PLUME

PLUME

An imprint of Penguin Random House LLC
1745 Broadway, New York, NY 10019
penguinrandomhouse.com

Book design by Shannon Nicole Plunkett

LIBRARY OF CONGRESS CATALOGING-IN-PUBLICATION DATA
has been applied for.

ISBN 9780593474709 (trade paperback)
ISBN 9780593474716 (ebook)

Printed in the United States of America

4th Printing

The authorized representative in the EU for product
safety and compliance is Penguin Random House Ireland,
Morrison Chambers, 32 Nassau Street, Dublin D02 YH68,
Ireland, https://eu-contact.penguin.ie.

FOR MY HUSBAND AND SONS, WHO MAKE ME LAUGH EVERY DAY NO MATTER HOW STRESSED OR SLEEP-DEPRIVED I AM. YOU ARE PURE LOVE IN HUMAN FORM AND I AM THE LUCKIEST.

CONTENTS

YOUR FAVORITE
SCARY MOVIE

INTRODUCTION

cream was my first favorite movie.

I was twelve when it came out, and I watched my VHS copy so many times I had nearly every line of dialogue memorized. It terrified me, but while it caused a lifelong fear of landlines and remote wooded neighborhoods, it also sparked an appreciation for dark humor and creative storytelling.

About a year into working on this book, Kevin Williamson and I were talking about what I might write next, and he asked me what my favorite movie of all time is. It's a simple enough question, but I didn't have an answer. I still don't.

There are a lot of movies I love that have been favorites at certain points in my life, but nothing that's left a lasting mark the way *Scream* has.

Halloween was one of the first films that made Williamson fall in love with movies, and it's still his favorite, so he gets it.

"It always goes back to movies from my childhood. Those are the ones that speak to me because they have stuck with me for years and years and years, and you're always trying to re-create that magic. Not re-create those movies, but re-create the way you felt when you saw those movies," Williamson says. "I want to do that. I'm always trying to re-create those feelings for the audience. In the world of streaming, it's really difficult to make a lasting impact. That's what I love about *Scream*. It started before all that and it's still making an impact."

Wes Craven played no small part in that. He was fascinated with psychology, and his understanding of the human condition is why he was a brilliant director—and why *Scream* is such an effective movie.

"Wes always felt that fear and horror were rites of passage," explains Patrick Lussier, who edited the first three *Scream* films. "I recall him saying that the reason horror movies often had younger protagonists, and played so well to younger audiences, was that they were about people caught in the moments between childhood and adulthood. The fear they survived was a primal rite, the act of 'blooding' to prove that you were no longer innocent but a survivor. The act of going to a horror movie, to be part of a communal experience that terrifies, is really about the moments after the scares. There's often a laugh, a shared feeling of catharsis, where we can wordlessly acknowledge that we survived intact, whether the characters on screen did or didn't. *We* did. Wes thought the audience comes back to the genre over and over because they get to survive. They get the cathartic release of fac-

ing absolute terror and coming out the other side un-
scathed."

I describe Craven's pathos to John Carpenter, the idea
that audiences like horror because it creates a sense that
you can survive scary things in the real world, and I ask if
he thinks it's true.

"I don't know, but I like it," he says, pausing for a moment. "It's probably a catharsis. Isn't that what the Greeks
talk about? It's all about catharsis. You project into the
screen, into the characters. Yeah, I think it's true. I
really do."

Then he turns it around on me. "Now let me ask you a
question. You loved *Scream* as a teenager, right? Why?"

It takes me a second. Partially because no one has ever
asked me that so bluntly, but mostly because I don't want
to come off like an idiot to John Carpenter. (As if that ship
hadn't already sailed when I told him that, before our Zoom,
I rewatched *Halloween* in broad daylight because I was by
myself and have an overactive imagination.)

I start with the easiest answer: I've always been good at
solving whodunits, but *Scream* surprised me.

Then I get a little more honest.

When Ghostface killed Casey Becker it was shocking,
not just surprising, and it tapped into the fear of being a
teenage girl home alone. Because you're not afraid of being
alone, right? You're afraid you're *not* alone. If you're alone,
nothing can happen to you. If there is another person who
wishes you harm . . . that's truly scary, especially when it's
someone you know and trust.

It honestly probably would have been too much for

me, I tell him, except that it was funny too. *Scream* wasn't just trying to scare you, it was also trying to make you laugh.

That's where Carpenter stops me: "See, you don't need me. I'm serious, put that into the book. Put your soul in there. Put what you love about it in there and it'll show. Everybody will dig it."

CHAPTER ONE

REWRITING HORROR

Scream is a love letter to scary movies, written by a disenchanted admirer who knew that the genre wasn't living up to its potential. Seeing *Halloween* as a kid was a defining moment for Kevin Williamson. So, when he made it to Hollywood, he took horror into his own hands. Determined to re-create that feeling, Williamson poured his frustration and passion onto the page. The result was not just a great slasher but something truly iconic.

Scream not only changed his life and career but altered the trajectory of the horror genre. In retrospect, it's hard to imagine that anyone was surprised by its impact, but the movie that is now a global phenomenon and has sparked a billion-dollar franchise started as a low-budget project from a fledgling studio that was written by a novice and starred a mostly unknown cast—and no one who was

involved, even the most optimistic among them, had any idea they were about to become part of the zeitgeist.

Least of all Williamson, who was a struggling screenwriter back in 1995. He'd already sold a script, sure, but it was languishing in development hell, and he was broke.

"I had sold *Killing Mrs. Tingle* to Interscope with Joe Dante attached to direct," recalls Williamson, who took a job as a personal assistant to a director to make ends meet. "It was a very, very little option. I think it was $75,000, which sounds like a lot of money, but I was about $100,000 in debt. It was so sad because I thought I had made it—and, no, I had not made it. I was in West Hollywood in a rent-controlled apartment for $650 a month and it got hard to pay that bill, believe it or not."

Determined to make it as a writer, Williamson went back to the drawing board.

"I was trying to come up with another movie to write because *Tingle* wasn't getting made," he says. "No one was making good horror movies. So, I wrote the movie I wanted to see."

That movie was *Scream*, an unexpected and updated take on slasher flicks that simultaneously celebrated and satirized the films that came before it.

How Williamson wrote the genre-bending film has become lore over the decades.

As the story goes, he holed up in a condo in Palm Springs and hammered out the screenplay in just three days. "That's sort of an urban legend at this point but, yeah, it's true," Williamson says before clarifying, "I wrote an outline first, though."

The genesis of the story dates back even further.

A lifelong horror fan, Williamson had become hooked on storytelling as a kid thanks to his mother's Doubleday Book Club copy of Peter Benchley's *Jaws*—which was confiscated by a teacher in elementary school who thought it wasn't age appropriate. He stood in line for four hours at a small-town Texas movie theater when Steven Spielberg's movie adaptation first came out, but it was a full house and he was turned away. The next day he went back and waited even longer. "I got in, and I was in the front row," Williamson says. "I just loved the adrenaline and the way everyone reacted to that film."

After *Jaws* sparked Williamson's interest in movies, seeing John Carpenter's *Halloween* set it ablaze. "The way everyone kept screaming at the screen, the way everyone was saying, 'Don't drop the knife, don't drop the knife,' all of those things that make that film so memorable, I loved it. I went back and saw it again and again and again," Williamson says. "I knew I wanted to do that with my life. I wanted to make people feel that way."

Williamson pursued that passion at East Carolina University, where he studied theater. "In college, I had written this comedy, a one-act play, about a young girl babysitting," he recalls. "She gets this creepy call and they start discussing all the tropes of horror films. It was this forty-page mess of ideas, and I never even mounted it in college. A few people read it, and then I put it away as if I'd never written it. I totally forgot about it."

Years later, while he was living in L.A. doing odd jobs and trying to break into Hollywood, a true-crime story caught his attention. He was home alone, house-sitting for a friend in Westwood and watching a prime-time news special about

Danny Rolling, a Florida serial killer dubbed the Gainesville Ripper. "It was the most gruesome story I had ever heard. It was so horrific the way that he would break into their back doors with a screwdriver," Williamson remembers. "These unsuspecting people, he would just sit outside and listen to them on the phone. Then, when they'd get off the phone, he'd wait for them to go to sleep. It was terrifying."

It's not exactly the kind of story you want to discover while alone in a strange house—especially when you've got the imagination of a prolific screenwriter. "I remember getting so scared that night," Williamson says. "And I walked into the family room and the window was open. I was like, 'Wait, that window was closed. What is it doing open?' I was trying to call the homeowner and say, 'Did you leave your window open? Has it been open for three days and I've never noticed?'"

When he couldn't get ahold of him, he dialed his friend David before investigating further. "I was like, 'Okay, there is a window open in the house. I think someone's in the house.' He goes, 'Well, get out of the house!' I grabbed a knife and I started walking around, checking under the bed and behind the shower curtain, and he was on the phone with me to keep me company," Williamson says. "He was being a jerk and going, 'Kill kill kill kill.' He goes, 'Yeah, Michael Myers.' I'm like, 'No, that's Jason Voorhees.' And we got into this whole discussion about horror films."

Once Williamson was satisfied there was no intruder and relief set in, a lightbulb went off: "I thought, 'I'll deconstruct the horror film the way that Stephen Sondheim deconstructed [the stories in] *Into the Woods*.' That was my favorite musical. I saw it a hundred times when I was waiting tables in New York next door to the Martin Beck Theatre. I kind of used that as my inspiration. I sat down and I was like, 'Where do I start?'"

He never did find the one-act play he'd written in college, but he hadn't forgotten it either. The phone call from a stranger that he'd conceived years earlier melded with the ruthless real-life ripper that was fresh in his mind. "That's how it all came together, and then I started writing the opening scene," he says.

When it dawned on him that he needed enough story for an entire movie, he switched gears. "I realized: Forget the opening scene. This story is about someone else," Williamson says. "I created the character of Sidney Prescott and this whole big story about the death of her mother and how she's traumatized by that and how it has affected her relationships and who she is and how she navigates high school life."

This is where that fabled trip to Palm Springs comes in. Williamson's friend, the same one he was house-sitting for when Barbara Walters scared the bejesus out of him, found a condo he could have for the weekend. "I thought, 'I'm gonna go away and I'm gonna write this movie and get it out of my system,'" he says. "I wrote an outline and I took it to Palm Springs. I locked myself in a condo with no TV and for three days I wrote *Scream*. I came back with a draft. It was pretty close to what I sold."

At the time his screenplay was called *Scary Movie*—a cheeky nod to the genre he didn't realize he was about to upend. It's the story of Sidney Prescott, a teenager struggling to overcome the grief of her mother's murder as a mysterious ghost-faced killer begins terrorizing high schoolers in her small town. Unlike generations of unlucky teens before them, these kids have seen scary movies and they know the rules of slashers.

"Every horror movie has its thing. For *Scream*, I thought it could be a mystery where we have a different killer every time and that would be the gimmick," Williamson says. "I was a big Agatha Christie reader as a kid and I really enjoyed the reveals. I read that she works backwards and so I constructed *Scream* backwards. Once I latched on to two killers, I stopped everything and restructured it so that it all made sense. I already had it all planned out, but when I started taking those two characters and working them backwards, it all fell into place."

Halloween, which is still Williamson's favorite movie, was also an inspiration.

"That's the perfect coming-of-age story," he says. "You have this one character who is a straight-A student, she's a good girl, she's babysitting, she's taking care of kids, she's gonna die to protect them. She does everything right and still horror comes and knocks on her door, still violence and terror come and hunt her down. How is she going to respond to this ultimate act of life and death, and can she survive the night? I would watch that and go, 'How can I do that with Sidney Prescott? How can I turn her into the new Laurie Strode?'"

Williamson tapped into two themes that have become common in his work: betrayal and family. "I've always felt like betrayal is a big thing in my life. I write about it a lot, and lies and deceit. I always felt like Sidney had such a distrust of people around her and she is also dealing with grief. I latched on to her mother being dead and her father being absent as a result of that," he explains. "Her mother was murdered and she put the guy away, but it was the wrong guy and now she doesn't trust herself. It's all about trust. Her whole relationship with herself or with Billy was about that trust and belief in the lies. Can she trust this man she loves? Then she chooses to trust him and he, of course, is the killer."

While he was commenting on the genre, Williamson also made it a point to spotlight the current culture, something that would become a hallmark as the franchise continued. *Scary Movie* was both a love letter to and an indictment of slashers—and it was a message to people who blamed entertainment for society's problems.

"Bob Dole was going off on all the violence in cinema at the time. He was really going after Quentin Tarantino and *Natural Born Killers*," Williamson remembers.

Then U.S. Senate majority leader, Dole made criticism of Hollywood a repeated theme during his failed run for president. During a May 1995 campaign stop in L.A. he lamented that "Hollywood's dream factories turn out nightmares of depravity" and criticized the "mainstreaming of deviancy" in music and movies. He couched the comments by saying the country's problems weren't *entirely* Hollywood's fault, but in very same breath added, "But a numbing exposure to graphic violence and immorality does steal away innocence, smothering our instinct for outrage, and I think we have reached the point where our popular culture threatens to undermine our character as a nation."

Williamson channeled his frustration with the sentiment into his art. The cornerstone of *Scary Movie* was the line "Movies don't create psychos, movies make psychos more creative," which he had written on a notecard and taped to the wall. "If you look at all the reports, there's no real relationship. I watched all those violent movies growing up and I'm scared of blood. Real blood, real violence freaks me out," Williamson says. "I believe, like Quentin believes, that the movies are where you can take the darkness. Fiction is the only place you can take this darkness and live in it because you can close the book, and you can turn the TV off, and you can leave the theater. You can play in that darkness and then you step out of it and come back to the real world and you're in the light."

Ultimately, Williamson's movie was a new take on the slasher flick, one that was self-aware and infused with humor—the kind that would make an audience laugh *with* the characters instead of *at* them. It not only subverted clichés but openly defied them.

"When I had it in my hands, I was so happy," Williamson recalls. "I thought it was good, but I thought *Tingle* was good."

He sent it to a friend's manager in the Valley and the initial feedback wasn't exactly encouraging. "He read it and went, 'It's not a real horror film. Is it a comedy? Is it a horror film? What is it? I think you need to decide. This is not working,'" says Williamson. "I was devastated, and I didn't know what to do."

Williamson figured if no one bought *Scary Movie* maybe he could make it on his own—like Robert Rodriguez had done with *El Mariachi* just a few years earlier. The director had detailed how he pulled it off—including raising half of his $7,000 budget by participating in clinical drug tests—

in both DVD special features and a book. "I had read *Rebel Without a Crew* and I thought, 'Well, maybe I can get a credit card and max it out and make my own movie,'" Williamson says. "That's why the locations were minimal. I had been working in music videos, so I knew how to put little crews together. I knew how to do something for nothing. So, I thought maybe I could just make it myself."

———

WILLIAMSON WAS RIGHT TO BE CAUTIOUS IN HIS OPTIMISM. NOT BECAUSE *Scary Movie* wasn't good, but because the horror genre was all but dead. To fully appreciate why his screenplay marked a pivotal moment in Hollywood history, you have to consider where slashers stood at the time.

Despite early classic thrillers like Alfred Hitchcock's *Psycho* in 1960 and films like *Halloween* and *Friday the 13th* that reigned during the "golden era" of the '70s and '80s, the genre had stalled. Part of the problem was, effectively, too much of a good thing: Slashers did so well in the late '70s that studios and filmmakers started making too many of them. What had once been a novel evolution of horror became a source of derivative sequels and schlock. As the New York Film Academy put it: "If there's one trope that typifies the '80s, it's the slasher format—a relentless antagonist hunting down and killing a bunch of kids in ever-increasing inventive ways, one by one. . . . Some were a lot better than others as the genre descended to its most kitschy. Similar to the first horror movie, these films were not intended to scare, but to entertain. Suffering from exhaustion in the wake of a thousand formulaic slasher movies and their sequels, the genre lost steam as it moved into the '90s."

Audiences were losing interest, budgets were dropping, and the box office was struggling.

"I remember slumber parties when I was in grade school watching *Friday the 13th* and *Halloween* and *My Bloody Valentine* and all the good and terrible slasher movies," says Julie Plec, who was Wes Craven's assistant during *Scream* and went on to co-create *The Vampire Diaries* with Williamson. "They had become so ridiculous that it was embarrassing. It was not a genre that anybody was holding their head high over at the time."

Even Craven—who helmed the iconic *A Nightmare on Elm Street* franchise, *The Last House on the Left*, and *The Hills Have Eyes*—was bored of the oft-side-eyed genre.

"Horror had reached one of its sort of classical cyclical stages of ennui on the part of the audience," Craven explained in a 1998 interview with NPR's *Fresh Air*. "It kind of was in that place where it needed to be satirized, at least before you went on to something new."

The tropes were well-worn: The girl who does the dumbest thing possible in response to a threat, the clumsy victim who keeps falling down while running away, the characters so devoid of personality or development that there's no reason not to root for the killer. Then, of course, there's the sexism and gratuitous gore, neither of which Craven appreciated.

Iya Labunka was an indie filmmaker, and a Disney exec, before meeting and eventually marrying Craven in the aughts and producing *Scream 4*. In the mid-1990s, horror was nowhere near her radar. "It was not anything that I ever looked at or sought out or thought about," she says. "It was the ugly stepchild. There was no sense of the fact that actually horror has a very, very long and illustrious history in the film business. We wanted to make indie art films that were interesting and offbeat and save the world and show an ultimate point of view—but never horror, literally never horror. It just did not cross anybody's mind that this was a genre worth pursuing, looking at, validating. It just didn't register."

There were some successes, to be sure, but fans, filmmakers, and critics generally agree they were few and far between by the time Williamson penned his script.

"The '80s were like an anything-goes era for horror movies. Like, literally, if you can dream it or think about some wild, fantastical, grotesque image, someone was putting it on screen," explains Blumhouse EVP of film development and production Ryan Turek. "You had Wes Craven, John Carpenter, Stuart Gordon, George Romero, Tobe Hooper, these heavyweights of horror pushing the boundaries and limits of visual stimulation and roller coaster ride–esque thrills. The '90s came around and studios were kind of hip to it now and they were like, 'Okay, well, Freddy Krueger and Jason Voorhees and Leatherface are kinda getting long in the tooth. We need to look to other boogeymen.' You saw really bad attempts at creating the next horror icon. There were movies like *Brainscan*. There was a terrible era of films like *Ghost in the Machine* and *Man's Best Friend*. There were a lot of big studio movies taking a whack at trying to create a new franchise."

Not everyone was quite so pessimistic, though.

"Horror has been with cinema since the very beginning," says *Halloween* filmmaker and genre icon Carpenter. "Every generation renews it, and every generation comes along with an idea to add new life and new perspective to horror. That's what makes it so durable a genre. It just keeps changing and keeps growing and keeps living, and I love that about it. It's fertile ground for young filmmakers."

———

AS IT TURNS OUT, WILLIAMSON'S FEAR THAT HE'D HAVE TO MAKE *SCARY Movie* himself was far from warranted. Shortly after he sent the script to his agent, the late Justen Dardis, a bidding war began. Dardis sent it to Cathy Konrad and Cary Woods at Woods Entertainment, who had a first-look deal with Miramax, and also to the studio's senior VP of production Bobby Cohen, among others.

Around that time, Miramax-owned Dimension Films was transitioning from being an acquisition-only label to a producer. Bob and Harvey Weinstein wanted an outlet for popcorn movies that wouldn't diminish the shine of their prestige brand. Dimension's first film was *Hellraiser III: Hell on Earth*, a critically panned sequel that barely cracked $12 million at the box office. It was desperate to make a splash with something more original.

With a title like *Scary Movie*, it's no surprise Cohen didn't see it as a fit for Miramax and quickly handed the faxed screenplay off to Dimension director of production and development Richard Potter, who was working late in the Manhattan office that night.

"What attracted me to it was that it was a teen movie,

not that it was a slasher movie," Potter says. "This was a movie for an audience that was absolutely being ignored at the time. Nobody was making movies for teenagers. I liked how the teenagers spoke. No one can write Kevin Williamson dialogue like Kevin Williamson. They weren't real, but they were close to real. They had actually seen horror movies. It always killed me, and obviously Kevin also, that when you would watch a horror movie, no one in it seemed to have ever seen one. They had no awareness of the connection between what they're living through and things they had seen, even just in dialogue."

The story was so good that no one would even care it's a slasher, Potter thought, especially not the long-ignored teens it was targeting. "They'll finally have one for them. Not the fifth one in a franchise that started when they were four. It's for them," he says. "If it hadn't been a slasher movie, if it had been something else, a great exorcism movie or a haunted house movie, I would've been just as happy."

It was exactly the kind of story that might put Dimension on the map.

"Our pitch on what Dimension was going to be was: If Alfred Hitchcock was still alive, this is where he'd be making movies," Potter recalls. "We wanted to do something that was elevated. That if you saw the Dimension logo, you knew it was gonna be good."

So, he called Bob Weinstein at home and told him, "If you don't want to make this, then I don't know what you're looking for." He made copies and personally delivered one of them.

The next morning, Potter saw Weinstein at a screening of the Dolph Lundgren–starring thriller *Hidden Assassin*.

He hadn't read the script yet. "He said to me, partway through the screening, 'Is it really that good?'" Potter recalls. "And I said, 'Yeah, it really is the best spec I've ever read.' He told me to finish the screening so he could go home and read the script. On the way to the office, he called me and said, 'I'm halfway through. Is the whole thing this good or does it fall apart?' And I said, 'The whole thing is that good.'"

With that, Weinstein said, "Let's get it."

Meanwhile on the West Coast, producer Cathy Konrad read the script at home alone in a house she was renting in Nichols Canyon, a dark, hilly neighborhood of L.A. Just a few pages in she was terrified—and hooked. "I was like, 'Holy shit, what's gonna happen?!'" Konrad remembers. "And I was so surprised as the pages kept going because I really identified with the characters, with the setting, the humor. I loved what he did with the rules. I just couldn't put it down, and halfway through I was already on my BlackBerry to anybody I could get ahold of at that late hour."

Konrad also wasn't necessarily looking for a slasher. "I didn't read it as a horror movie. That's what I think is funny. I didn't go, 'Wow, this is a really good horror movie!' That's not what I picked up. Obviously, there were elements in there and I loved those kinds of movies when I was a kid. I still remember when I first saw *Friday the 13th* and *The Exorcist*—but this didn't feel that way to me, because I was laughing at various times."

At least one of Williamson's inspirations was intuitive to her: "Agatha Christie is one of my favorites. Is everybody who they say they are? It really had me and gripped me. It was suspenseful and it was thrilling. It was the power of Kevin's words. It felt like something was just jumping off the page. It was a great story, and I love stories more than I love genres."

With Potter and Konrad fully evangelized, and Bob Weinstein now a believer, they pounced. "We were on the phone with the agent and trying to take the script off the table, like we just want to preemptively buy it," says Potter. "Bob says, 'What takes it off the table? What if I say a million dollars?'" As Potter remembers it, Dardis said he had to talk to his client, and he wasn't sure if Williamson was reachable—which they thought was a stalling tactic to drum up other offers. "Bob said, 'If we hang up this call there is no million-dollar offer.'"

The aggressive push didn't work and Dimension found itself competing for the project.

"What happened was it priced itself out," Williamson recalls. "I remember Mandalay tried to buy it. Paramount made an offer and then once it went over the $300,000 mark they were like, 'We just don't pay that kind of money for a horror film. That's not gonna happen.' Then it got up to four fifty, and then it got up to six hundred or six fifty. Oliver Stone's company came in higher and Dimension came in lower—but my lawyer Patti Felker, who is my lawyer to this day, smartly said, 'Do you want the money or do you want the movie made?' She goes, 'I really think it's more important to make the movie.' I went, 'Yeah, I want the movie made.' And she goes, 'Dimension will make it. Miramax just started this division of genre filmmaking dedicated to this type of film. They will make this movie.'"

And they did, less than a year later. Despite the frenzy,

no one had any clue that it would change the trajectory of horror for decades to come.

"*Scream* comes along seemingly at a point where there is nothing left to do with the slasher genre and revitalizes it, and takes its fundamental tropes and turns them upside down," says Tony Magistrale, an author and University of Vermont professor. "It realizes its audience and it realizes what its audience expects. It blurs the line between comedy and horror, and I think that injects a certain element of playfulness that has been missing."

"It took everybody's knowledge of the genre and put this kind of lacquer over it and was funny and scary and had incredible, intense set pieces, an iconic mask," says Turek, who wrote and directed a 2011 documentary about the franchise called *Still Screaming*. "It reminded everybody that you can go into the theater and have fun watching a scary movie."

"There is not a wasted beat. There's absolutely nothing I would cut," says Jack Quaid, who stars in the franchise's revived fifth installment (also called *Scream*). "We were collectively a little tired of the slasher genre and then this thing came along that breathed so much life into it and the characters felt like real people making smart decisions, as opposed to the dumb decisions we see every horror protagonist, or even side character, make in all these movies. To audiences back then it must have just really felt like these characters lived in the actual, real world."

That was also something that struck Craven, along with returning to the idea of a realistic, human killer, which had been missing from the genre.

"*Psycho* was a great example of that. . . . It's a human

monster," Craven said to NPR. "Horror films like *Godzilla* and *King Kong* are kind of a relief in a way because they are so removed from our reality that they're a little bit more of a popular entertainment."

The Texas Chain Saw Massacre and *The Hills Have Eyes* had centered on psychotic families, Craven explained, but then there was a shift toward more mythical figures like Michael Myers, Freddy Krueger, and Jason Voorhees. "They were not really human, but some sort of almost quasi-human killing force, you know, that was completely outside morality."

What makes *Scream* so relatable is that the killer, though initially masked and anonymous, is not some monster. It is someone you know who is deeply betraying you in a very traumatic and violent way.

"There's a real culture around genre movies, and a sense of community around them, that I think Kevin tapped into in a way that hadn't been done before," says Liev Schreiber, who starred in the first three *Scream* films. "There was an awareness about the continuum of horror and where it was, and there was also an awareness about our own neuroses and our fears and our self-consciousness and how a genre played on that."

Filmmaker Eli Roth, whose hit 2023 slasher, *Thanksgiving*, was inspired by *Scream*, had a "weird experience" with the *Scary Movie* screenplay at the time. "I wrote *Cabin Fever* and took it to my agent and he read it. It was probably July of 1995, and he's like, 'This is good but *this* movie just sold for half a million dollars. You should probably read it. It's called *Scary Movie*. This is what just sold to Miramax. They're starting a new thing called Dimension. It's only gonna make horror movies, and this sold for $500,000.' I remember taking it and reading it on a bus ride home from New York City to Boston going like, 'Oh, *this* is a professional movie. This is what a real writer writes like. This is a real screenplay.' I saved that script for a long time because it was like a textbook on how to write a slasher film."

CHAPTER TWO

CONVINCING CRAVEN AND A CHARMED CAST

When Dimension suggested hiring Wes Craven to direct *Scary Movie*, Kevin Williamson thought, "Yeah, right, sure." In an already surreal moment, it was unfathomable to him that one of his heroes might translate his story to the screen. His instinct was right—at first anyway. Craven repeatedly turned down the project. Unbeknownst to the studio, the iconic filmmaker behind *The Last House on the Left*, *The Hills Have Eyes*, *A Nightmare on Elm Street*, and *People Under the Stairs* had no interest in directing another horror movie.

"Wes was really adamant about making a change in his life and not doing horror movies anymore. He wanted to flex different muscles," his longtime producer Marianne

Maddalena says. "We had just done *Wes Craven's New Nightmare*. That was really fun. People loved that movie, but we always felt that we were in a B-film world. So, we read it, it was great, but he didn't want to get caught in the horror ghetto."

Dimension wouldn't take no for an answer.

"He kept passing and we kept going back, which normally you don't do," Richard Potter explains. "Normally, a director passes on something and that's the end of the conversation."

Christopher Landon, the director of films like *Freaky* and *Happy Death Day*, who was briefly attached to *Scream 7*, was there at the inception of the film. He was an intern at Woods Entertainment, a job that kick-started his Hollywood career and introduced him to Williamson.

"They knew I was a horror fanatic. So, when a spec script came in called *Scary Movie* they gave it to me first. I read the first ten to fifteen pages, flipped out, ran into their office, and told them to buy it, even though I hadn't finished it," Landon remembers. "It was the most meta thing that I had ever read. It was very visceral on the page. A good script feels like you are literally being grabbed by the hand and pulled somewhere, and that's what Kevin did."

Even so, he understands why Craven hesitated to take it on.

"Horror still carries that stigma for a lot of people," Landon says. "Even now, in this post–elevated horror world—a term that us horror fans despise, by the way—it's a genre that has always been looked down upon. When *Scream* was in development, and when it came out, I think it really surprised people with how intelligent it was."

In the end, Craven might have never been convinced to take the job had it not been for his chatty twentysomething assistant who loved the script: Julie Plec.

Now Plec is a veteran showrunner, but back in 1995 she was just breaking into Hollywood. She'd landed the gig working for Craven thanks to Lisa Harrison, a friend of her cousin's who had the job and thought finding her own replacement might fast-track a promotion.

"I read every single submission that came across his desk," Plec remembers. "I can read really quickly, so I would just blow through them. I read one shitty horror movie after another, after another. There was one that I still remember to this day about an infestation of rats in the New York subway tunnel system, which was my favorite because it was so ridiculous."

With *Scary Movie*, she was hooked fifteen pages in. "This is a movie for someone like me, someone who has love and frustration for the genre in equal measures," Plec says.

Before Craven was finally convinced to change his mind, he and Williamson had lunch. "I remember him asking me, 'Is it funny or is it scary? What's the tone?'" Williamson says. "And I went, 'Well, it needs to be self-aware, some dark humor. I think it's more of a satire, but if it's not scary it's never gonna work. If it's not scary, it's pointless. You have to be able to have your cake and eat it too in this film.'"

Craven liked it, but he wanted to escape the genre and tell different kinds of stories. Not only was *Scary Movie* horror, but it was an especially dark and violent story.

Months later, they still hadn't landed a director, so Plec

took another shot. "I happened to be working out of Wes's house at the time and we would have lunch every day. He wasn't much of a chatter, so it was a lot of me just babbling and trying to create conversation," she says. "I said to him, 'You know, they still haven't been able to find a director for *Scary Movie*, which is a shame because that was such a good script and you were always their first choice.' And he said, kind of glibly, 'Well, they should make me an offer I can't refuse.'"

Plec relayed that to Harrison, who then made the call.

"Lo and behold, in came an offer that Wes decided he couldn't refuse and he said yes," Plec says. "I was just being a chatterbox assistant, trying to get my boss to consider a movie that I thought he should really make."

The rest is history, and it marked the beginning of a close collaboration between not only Williamson and Plec, but Williamson and Craven, too.

———

WHILE CRAVEN WAS WEIGHING WHETHER OR NOT TO SIGN ON TO *SCREAM*, the movie had already found its lead: Drew Barrymore. After her breakout roles in *E.T. the Extra-Terrestrial* and *Firestarter* as a child, Barrymore's star had continued to rise and her attachment to the project was a draw for the director.

So, imagine his shock when Barrymore had an epiphany: She shouldn't play Sidney Prescott. She wanted to be Casey Becker because it would be unforgettably jarring to audiences if she was the teen who was killed off in the opening.

Once the initial surprise subsided, Craven realized it

was a brilliant move, and it created a blank slate to look for a new lead.

The project caught the attention of a who's-who of talented young actors: Brittany Murphy and Alicia Witt were in the running for Sidney, Natasha Lyonne for Tatum, and Brooke Shields for Gale Weathers. Before Barrymore decided to switch roles, they'd been eyeing Alicia Silverstone for the opening. Jeremy London, James Marsden, and Vince Vaughn were also among the actors who auditioned.

"Back then, you'd bring people in the office and there was one every fifteen minutes," explains Sarah Katzman, who was a casting assistant on the film. "I think it was probably a hundred fifty to two hundred fifty per role."

And that's *after* they'd looked at piles of headshots and résumés and narrowed it down. Craven and the producers ultimately saw about fifty actors for each of the parts.

Neve Campbell remembers her audition and screen test for the role of Sidney Prescott vividly. She was early on in her career and starring in the Fox family drama series *Party of Five*, which hadn't quite taken off yet, and this was her chance to play the lead in a film for the first time.

"It was between myself and Alicia Witt, who's become a dear friend over the years. They had us in separate rooms to do hair and makeup and they were setting up the studio for the audition," Campbell says. "I remember Wes coming into the dressing room and giving a quick hello. He was very graceful. He walked like a gazelle. He had this energy that sort of entered [the room] and you're like, 'Who was that? What was that?'"

That energy translated into a comfortable and collaborative audition.

"I enjoyed the process of the audition, which isn't usually the case," Campbell says. "It was a creative process. We were finding the character, and we were finding the tone, and he gave great direction. He was incredibly professional and astute at what he wanted."

Craven was equally impressed.

"Wes fell in love with Neve because her screen test was so good. He was like, 'She's the one,'" Williamson recalls. "It was one of those classic cases of she won it auditioning."

Casting director Lisa Beach recalls being wowed by other cast members too. "When Matthew Lillard came in and he read the role of Stu, it was just amazing how fantastic an actor he was. So deep, but so funny. The same with Jamie Kennedy. They were head and shoulders above the rest for each of those parts."

They had a certain je ne sais quoi and it was clear they were perfect. Skeet Ulrich was harder to get in the room, but when he auditioned, he lived up to the hype that surrounded him. Beach remembers, "The buzz was, 'Oh my God, he's the next new thing.' When we got him in, there was no question."

Lillard initially auditioned for the role of Billy, but then Beach gave him the sides for Stu and asked him to come back to read for Craven a few hours later.

"Wes gave me the part in the room, which never happens. It hasn't happened since, and it hadn't happened before," Lillard says. "I'm somebody they slot in at the last minute, and my hope is that I deliver for every director that's taking that chance, but I'm never anyone's first choice. One of the great things about our relationship was that I think Wes was thrilled to have me. I hope he was, that's for sure."

Rose McGowan's experience auditioning for Tatum Riley ran the gamut of hectic to "hellish."

On her way to callbacks, she'd heard Campbell was cast as Sidney, which set off alarm bells because they're both brunettes. McGowan was new to Hollywood but she'd already picked up that "if you have one dark-haired girl in a movie, you're not going to have another, unless they're sisters."

With some quick thinking and a little inspiration from one of the producers in the room, she made an unconventional do-or-die move.

"Cathy Konrad had a great short blond cut, very sassy," McGowan recalls. "Right before I started my third and final read, I said, 'Cathy, who's your hairdresser? I'm going to turn myself blond.' And I just saw this collective group lightbulb go off. Like, 'Oh my God. We can do this!'"

It worked like a charm, and she landed the part—but her then lawyer demanded triple the $50,000 they had offered to pay her.

"All of a sudden, this man named Harvey Weinstein that I'd never heard of got involved and they rescinded the offer," she says. "Then they made me do more screen tests even though I'd already had the offer."

She'd fallen in love with Tatum. So, even though she felt like she was being punished because of her lawyer's actions, she dealt with it.

"A lot of people would have been like, 'Fuck off. I'm not gonna do this movie.' Because it was a humiliation exercise,"

McGowan says. "And it was intentional that I got paid less than everybody else to make a point. That informs what I fought through to make Tatum pure and lovable despite that. I didn't want her to be a disposable woman. I wanted people to really root for her and cheer for her so that the savage ending would be that much more horrific. I wanted people to feel like they lost a friend."

Rounding out the ensemble, W. Earl Brown, who had worked with Craven on *Vampire in Brooklyn*, became Kenny; Liev Schreiber was cast for a brief cameo as Cotton Weary; and David Arquette became Deputy Dwight "Dewey" Riley.

"As written, Dewey was a little dopey," Beach says. "David perfectly captured that, but he is such a multilayered actor. You saw the dopiness on the top, but you realize he's a lot smarter than you think. He was crazy like a fox, in a way."

Meanwhile, Courteney Cox had to convince Craven she wasn't her squeaky-clean *Friends* persona Monica Geller and was perfectly capable of playing a fiendishly ambitious TV journalist. "Cary Woods was in my manager's office and she pitched me for the part of Gale," Cox says. "Cary thought it would be a nice surprise to have me play such a calculated character after being on *Friends* and *Family Ties*, but I had to convince Wes. So, I wrote him a letter and assured him that being 'a bitch' wouldn't be a stretch at all."

They found Roger L. Jackson, the voice of Ghostface, at a casting call in San Francisco. He remembers overhearing someone else who was auditioning describe the character as a Freddy Krueger type, which he knew wasn't right based on the lines they were given from the opening scene. "He has to be interesting enough to keep her on the phone, so he's got to be a little bit sexy," Jackson says. "He had to play with her, keep her on the phone, not raise any suspicions until that line, 'I want to know who I'm looking at.' 'What did you say?' 'I said I want to know who I'm talking to. Why? What did you think I said?' Then the cat's paw starts to come down on the mouse's tail."

Originally, they'd planned to have Jackson play the scene across from Barrymore so she could have an actor on the other end of the call and then have someone else dub over it back in L.A. But they liked what he did so much that they've kept him on—for seven movies (so far).

"You're not going to get that lightning in a bottle every single role, every single time, but you're certainly going to hope for the best," Beach says. "Somebody said to me once, 'A casting director is an artist who paints with people.' That was the time I really started feeling that."

"*Scream* was just kismet," Maddalena says. "I don't know how you do better than the casting on that movie."

CHAPTER THREE

MUSIC, MAYHEM, AND THE MASK

Behind the scenes, Craven's crew was a tight-knit group that often came with him from project to project, including assistant director Nick Mastandrea and editor Patrick Lussier. It's not terribly common and speaks to how well the director treated his team.

"I would've done anything he had done," Lussier says. "It was really that simple. I would have gladly joined the circus and shoveled the elephant poop."

"He was the boss, obviously, and we all respected him greatly, but there was an atmosphere of camaraderie there that was fantastic," Mastandrea says. "It was a joy to come to work in the morning."

Composer Marco Beltrami went on to work with Craven on multiple films, but *Scream* was the first—and it was Plec who found him, in maybe the most '90s way possible.

Because Craven was self-sufficient and low-maintenance as bosses go, she had a lot of downtime and got bored during night shoots. So the Teamster captain, Derek Raser, introduced her to the Hollywood Café chat room on America Online.

"It was this group of Hollywood people in the early stages of their careers, like Bryan Singer, Brandon Boyce, Chris McCorry, Shane Salerno," Plec says. "We would stay up all night chatting in a chat room. I became kind of addicted to it, and by the way, this is back when you had to pay by the minute."

The $300 credit card bills were "a disaster" for her at the time, but it paid off in an unexpected way. They were having a hard time finding music that worked with the tone of the film, so she asked her online friends if they knew a good composer.

"I think it was Shane Salerno who was like, 'You need to meet Marco Beltrami.' I said, 'I don't know who that is.' And he said, 'You will.'"

Plec got ahold of Beltrami's demo reel and Lussier temped it into his cut. Wes loved it because it was original and Beltrami didn't seem like someone who was just trying to emulate John Williams, so they brought him in for an interview.

"I realized that this was a big break for me, that I couldn't screw it up," Beltrami says. "I was very nervous for a few reasons. The main thing was I had never seen any horror movies."

Because Beltrami was new, Craven asked him to score the opening scene of the film as a test run to convince the studio. He had a weekend and nowhere to do it, so he borrowed the home studio of his friend, composer Christophe Beck.

"To me, that scene gets almost operatic by the end," Beltrami says. "The music for me was character-driven. I think the fact that I was very naïve with horror movies actually worked to my benefit because I approached it almost like this scared person watching."

They screened the movie with his music and it went over well, which landed him the job.

"It was really a shoestring budget. It was a $30,000 package," Beltrami says. "I couldn't afford to use an orchestra on all the cues, and then even the ones that we did, I had to get a little bit creative with it. There were a few places—I think most notably you can hear it in the beginning of a track called 'Sidney's Lament'—where I had Wes and a few other people come into the room and whistle as the string players were playing. So, it was tricks like that I had to rely on to get through the scoring process. Still, I ended up spending my own money on producing the score, but to me it was an investment I had to make."

Music supervisor Ed Gerrard came on as a favor to help with the rest of the movie's sound—including a track that has become the franchise's unofficial theme. It was from an Australian group that hadn't yet broken out in the U.S., Nick Cave and the Bad Seeds. Gerrard had shared some of their music with Lussier during production of *Vampire in Brooklyn* and suggested they consider it for *Scream*.

"There was a cinematic thing about his music, and a soulfulness. Even though it was dark, there was something cool about it," Gerrard says. "'Red Right Hand' had this sort of mysterious tongue-in-cheek vibe to it. Patrick immediately goes, 'Oh man, I think I've got an idea for this.'"

"We put in the intro for the first scene where it appears, and then the actual lyric part for closing down the town," Lussier says. "I put those in the initial edit of those scenes. So, the first time Wes saw those scenes it was with that music, and that music never changed. It was the one thing that the Dimension guys were like, 'We need to pay for that. We need to have that song.'"

Gerrard talked to the record company and took care of the licenses.

"You need a master license, which is for the physical recording, and you need a synchronization license," he explains. "It was $2,500 a side, if I'm not mistaken. It could have been less. It was not more than five grand total."

In retrospect, that's a hell of a deal, though it was worth much more than that in terms of exposure for Cave and his band. Even though it wasn't written for the film, it feels like it was: "He's a ghost, he's a god, he's a man, he's a guru / You're one microscopic cog in his catastrophic plan / Designed and directed by his red right hand."

"The thing about *Scream* is that the killers are smarter than everybody else," Lussier says. "If they hadn't let their arrogance take them away at the end, they would have gotten away with it. Their plan was really good. That song really captures that vibe, the idea of something that is bigger and more sinister than the average Joe will figure out because you can't imagine something that awful."

"I don't think that phenomenon will ever happen again," Gerrard says. "Not in my wildest imagination did I think it would become a cultural icon. I brought the song in because

I was a Nick Cave fanatic, but Patrick did the work and deserves a lot of that credit. His instinct for creating a vibe around something, it was just the perfect storm."

———

AS IF THE DIRECTOR REPEATEDLY REFUSING THE JOB AND THE LEAD DEciding to step into a different role weren't challenging enough, the dream location had its share of nightmarish moments too. Craven had set his sights on wine country, and the first hurdle was getting Dimension to approve it.

"We had a budget of something like $13 million and Bob wanted it down to $12 million," producer Marianne Maddalena recalls. "We were up in Bob's office with Cary Granat, and Wes said, 'I want to shoot in Northern California.' Bob said, 'No, you need to shoot in L.A.,'" Maddalena recalls. "Wes said, 'Well, I don't want your movie,' and walked out. We went downstairs to Tribeca Grill, and we were like, 'Oh my God, we lost a movie.' Five minutes later, Cary Granat came running down saying, 'He's giving you the million.' Wes was tough. He was quiet but he was tough."

That tenacity was tested when their permission to film at Santa Rosa High School was pulled by the district school board, launching a heated public debate about violence in movies.

The local paper, *The Press Democrat*, covered the dustup extensively before and after the April 16, 1996, meeting during which the school board voted 4–1 to ban filming. A March 28 article titled "School Board in Quandary over Gory Film" said that a board member was "appalled at a script featuring disemboweled teen-agers and four-letter words." Community members argued over whether the boost to the local economy and the financial benefit to the school itself—which started at $10,000 but was upped to $30,000—was worth seeming like they were endorsing "gratuitous gore."

Much of the conversation centered on the content of the movie, though the district's lawyer cautioned that it might run afoul of the First Amendment if that was its reason for saying no. The day of the meeting Craven was quoted as saying he'd "sue their asses." It was clear he felt backed into a corner. "We're nice people, dammit," he said. "Normally, we wouldn't be making these kinds of threats. But what kind of choice do we have?"

A local lawyer hired by the production attended the meeting and said they'd decided not to sue. During a three-hour meeting before a packed house, with nearly fifty speakers, the board ultimately decided filming would be disruptive to school operations. In an April 18 article, columnist Pete Golis made clear he wasn't buying the excuse: "There will be no Oscar for this obvious staging."

Further proving the point, just weeks later Ron Howard's *Inventing the Abbotts* was given approval for an eight-day shoot at the school. Craven went back to the district with a revised production schedule and requested just four days. This time it was rejected "because of a scheduling conflict with a local theater group."

"You know when you were a little kid and there's something you know you're supposed to be allowed to do and, for some reason, an adult says you can't? The feeling of being powerless and it's just not fair," Richard Potter says. "I remember having that feeling in my stomach. Like, 'How is this happening? You already told us we could shoot here.'"

It was disheartening, but they still had a movie to make. They'd already measured the principal's office, a classroom, and a few other rooms. So, they built them as a set on an old car dealership lot. The rest was filmed at the Sonoma Community Center for a fee of $27,000.

Not passing up the opportunity to have the last word, the film's end credits read: "No thanks whatsoever to The Santa Rosa City School District Governing Board."

"That's Wes for you. The same guy who walked out of Bob's office put that in there," Maddalena says. "He was being pilloried for being in horror, defending it yet feeling like a second-class citizen, like we were doing something bad and dirty. He was mad. It was like being tarred and feathered and kicked out of town. So, he didn't forget it."

When it came to the characters' homes, they needed houses that not only fit the scene but felt relatable to the audience. They scouted places like Vancouver and Wilmington, North Carolina, and couldn't find what they were looking for. Northern California not only had the right kind of homes but also had an attractive town square in Healdsburg. Production designer Bruce Alan Miller remembers director George A. Romero telling him on *Day of the Dead* that viewers have to believe they could be the person on screen to go along for the ride.

"Our characters were supposed to be middle-class American kids," he says. "Drew Barrymore had to be in a house that you thought you could be in. You thought you were safe behind all those glass doors, but you're really not."

Stu Macher's house was quirky, but it worked. "Rarely

do you find a house that is so perfectly suited to the particularly weird things that were in this script," Miller says.

They put in a new driveway, made the existing one look like a street, built a front porch, added fencing, and created a cul-de-sac. The biggest challenge, though, was that the house was on top of a hill in Tomales and it would have taken the actors five to ten minutes to get to the set from the base camp they'd set up.

"I built this fake two-sided barn and they put the makeup trailers behind that," Miller explains. "So, the actors could just walk across the driveway to get to the house."

A routine scouting trip for Tatum and Dewey's house gave them more than just a shooting site: That's where Maddalena found the now-iconic Ghostface mask. "I remember wandering upstairs, it was a very small bedroom, and there was this mask hanging on the bedpost, but it had a white shroud," she says. "I ran downstairs and I showed it to Wes and Bruce, and I said, 'Oh my God, you guys. This is it. This is perfect.'"

They shot it down because they wanted to create something original, so Maddalena reluctantly put the mask back where she'd found it. Later, when they still hadn't come up with anything they liked, she suggested going back to get it.

What most of the world now knows as Ghostface then was a readily available Halloween costume sold by Fun World as part of its Fantastic Faces line, though there's some debate about the origin of the underlying image. *Fangoria* did a deep dive into the history in 2023 and featured an artist named Loren Gitthens who said he'd created the mask, dubbed "the Wailer," for the Alterian Ghost Factory in 1991. Another artist named Brigitte Sleiertin-Liden said she was tasked with creating masks for Fun World based on a picture she was given, and those were released in 1992. Of course, the ghastly image is often likened to Edvard Munch's 1893 painting *The Scream*, and Roger L. Jackson pointed out that it's shown up in famed cartoonist Marie Severin's work over the years as well. At any rate, at the time Dimension needed it, Fun World was the owner of the particular mask they licensed and it has become the company's claim to fame. (Fun World's media contact responded to my request to interview its president, Alan Geller, with a list of interrogatories that puts even the most fastidious Hollywood publicists to shame and then ghosted me. Pun obviously intended.)

"I had contacted someone who was the distributor of those masks in the U.S., just to cover ourselves," co-executive producer Stuart Besser says. "The lawyer wanted me to get ahold of them and see if we could get some sort of letter. I think I offered him $2,000 or something and he accepted that. People could say wow, what a great deal on our part, but when you look at it in the long run, the sales of the masks went through the roof. So, I think it worked out for everybody."

"Here's the funniest thing," Potter adds. "Kevin had written a line in the script that 'they sell these things in every five-and-dime in the county.' Ironically, by picking the costume that Marianne had found, they really did sell that mask in every five-and-dime."

From there, they set out to design the rest of the killer's look because Williamson hadn't described it in his script. The white gown that came with the mask was too much like a bedsheet ghost, so they went with black, which created more of a Grim Reaper vibe.

"I remember always being like, 'That's it? That black muumuu?'" Plec says. "It's like a death cloak. There is nothing fancy about it. There is nothing remotely individually scary about any of the elements that put Ghostface together. So, I give the credit to Kevin, obviously, and Roger L. Jackson. We heard his voice before we saw Ghostface. We were scared already and then when you have that face popping into the glass in extreme close-up, you're like, 'Fuck!' The scare is so primal. It could have been a chipmunk. You're programmed to now be afraid of this image."

CHAPTER FOUR

THIS ISN'T SCARY

The phone rings. A pretty blond teen answers to find a charming stranger chatting her up on the other end of the line while she's home alone and making popcorn in her kitchen. What starts as a flirty exchange quickly becomes a living nightmare for Casey Becker. It's a breathless thirteen-minute scene that ends with our teenage heroine's bloody corpse hanging from a tree while her devastated parents scream in anguish.

The opening of *Scream* is an entire three-act story, and Drew Barrymore's shoot felt, in many ways, like a separate movie all its own. It was filmed in just one week, before much of the other cast had even arrived on location in Santa Rosa.

The scene feels real because a lot of it *was*. Barrymore would run around until she hyperventilated before takes, and she absolutely refused to fake tears for the camera.

"I remember not knowing what Wes was saying to her, but watching as the cameras were rolling, as she would

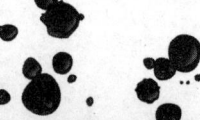

shriek and cry and break down and sob," says Julie Plec, who was Craven's assistant at the time. "I was like, 'My God, what is going on in there?'"

What was going on, it turns out, is that before shooting, Barrymore and Craven were enacting a plan they'd come up with to make sure she could cry on cue: He'd remind her of a horrible story she'd read in the newspaper about a boy who had set a dog on fire to torture it.

"Every time on the set, if I wanted her to cry, I'd say, 'The boy has the lighter,' or something like that, and she'd burst into tears and be just frantic," Craven recalled in a DVD special feature.

Even though he used such a graphic, emotional tool to pull the best performance out of Barrymore, the actress found him to be "a sweetheart" and said that he made her feel "incredibly safe." The ability to challenge actors while also protecting them, and the empathy that requires, is one of the reasons that Craven is so admired both as a director and as a person.

He was also patient. *Scream* was Kevin Williamson's first time on a movie set. He was thrilled to be there, excited by the process, and asking Craven a million questions.

"I remember the first day of shooting, standing there in the cold, freezing outside of the house where Drew Barrymore was picking up the phone," Williamson says. "I remember Wes taking the time to sit down and explain to me not just his shot list but why he was shooting these shots this way and what his plan was for shooting the entire opening scene. That was when I realized, 'Oh, I put it on the page and he turns it into a real, breathing thing."

Scream's first director of photography, Mark Irwin, says

they slowly transitioned from a light, nonthreatening palette—blond girl, pastel clothing, mostly white house—to something darker and more dangerous.

"I had to start neutral so everyone buys into this girl with the Jiffy Pop and the flirty stuff," Irwin says. "The plan in my mind was to change the character of this white, comfortable place. You think you're safe inside if you lock the doors, and then somebody is pounding on the windows and you realize, 'I'm not safe in here.'"

As the scene progresses, things slowly get darker. They created shadows and moonlight, so the visual mood changes along with Casey's as she realizes there's no way to win the game that she's been unexpectedly and unwillingly pulled into.

"She sneaks outside, there's shadows everywhere, and we really started cooking," Irwin says. "There is a frame for lighting called a cucoloris, which is a floral pattern that will create shadows. We had a special one for Drew. She could stop and lean and look over, and all this dapple would heighten the tension, the sense of danger.

"Then she starts running in her bare feet, and she runs around this corner and Ghostface comes out of nowhere and stabs her in the chest. You want to build to that, so the audience is now on her journey and they're inside her trauma, her vulnerability."

It all ends with Casey unmasking her killer before she's dragged away, still grasping the phone and weakly saying "Mom" as her distraught parents listen from inside the smoke-filled house. You can feel their hearts break as they discover what happened to their daughter.

"Wes was keen on the deaths being as emotional as possible," says *Scream* special effects artist Greg Nicotero. "The audience will identify with the person who is cowering in fear or screaming, and if you relate to them in the last moment of their life, then it's going to have an impact on you."

Casey Becker's death was also visually stunning, which made it immensely disturbing.

Nicotero says it took about five weeks to create her corpse for the "aftermath" shot, from having Barrymore come in to make a cast of her head to sculpting and painting and adding details. It's a lot of buildup for just a few seconds of screen time, but the work pays off.

"That is classic genre storytelling where you want to unsettle the audience members so that, from that point on, they don't trust you," Nicotero says. "You're on edge because you don't know what to expect, and the buildup to it is almost as unbearable as actually seeing it in person. Wes crafted that perfectly when he did the opening of all the movies. They had that same visceral gut punch that disarmed the audience."

One of Craven's most ingenious moves was making sure Roger L. Jackson, the voice of Ghostface, remained a mystery to the rest of the cast. Having an actor play the lines instead of a crewmember reading them off-camera was Barrymore's idea.

"They kept me away from [the rest of the actors] so they would not have a face to associate with the voice. The scariest monsters are the ones you make in your own mind," Jackson says. "That started the then-tradition of having me live, on the set, playing the scene with the actors instead of just dubbing later. I could interact with them, so it became my job to scare actors—a job I enjoy very much." (Jackson went into the voice on those last few words, and despite being able to see on Zoom that it was him and not Ghostface, it was chilling. So, for the record, I think he'd still be able to scare the actors even if they'd already met him.)

"That voice is remarkable," Neve Campbell says. "It's set in our minds now. If any of us hear that voice, we know what it is and what movie it's from—and it gets me every time I hear it. The resonance of it, and he's so vicious. It's wonderful. It's a lot of fun."

The first night, Jackson was under a canopy outside looking in through the window. The second night, they moved him into the garage and set up a camera feed. Later in the shoot, at Sidney's house, they hid him in a walk-in closet.

"I felt bad for him, ya know, because we had to keep waiting 'til everyone was on set and then sneak him somewhere," assistant director Nick Mastandrea says. "But he was good-natured about it all."

"Drew was phenomenal in that sequence," Williamson says. "She memorized it to a T. She got every scream, 'No, no, no, aah!' She had it all down pat. She was such a professional. She was so prepared and she just committed. Her performance set the stage for what was to come."

There's a reason *Scream*'s opening is iconic. It's at once clever, chilling, and heartbreaking, the kind of unforgettable storytelling that can make something as routine as turning on patio lights at night give you pause decades after watching it. Sure, it's unlikely that there's a disemboweled high school football player strapped to a chair just steps outside your back door, but you may still find yourself nervous as you're flipping that switch. Because when a movie catches you by surprise the way the opening sequence of *Scream* does, it leaves a mark.

It's also the scene that almost got Wes Craven fired just a week into filming.

The cast and crew on the ground in wine country that first week saw Craven's vision come to life and knew they were making something special. Dimension Films head Bob Weinstein, however, was utterly unimpressed based on what he was seeing in the dailies, raw footage shot during any given day of filming that helps the studio keep tabs on a project from afar.

One day while sitting in the parking lot of the grocery store where they filmed the shopping scene with Sidney and Tatum and the news footage clip of Cotton Weary getting into a police car, Craven got a scary call himself.

"I just watched his shoulders slump in his director's chair when he got the phone call from Bob saying he hated the dailies," Williamson remembers. "It was devastating that day. It just broke all of our spirits."

Cathy Konrad had made several movies with the Weinsteins and she braced herself for the worst. "I was the only one that knew to the depth of my soul what could happen when the train comes off the track," Konrad says.

Executive producer Marianne Maddalena remembers that Weinstein told Craven his shooting was "workmanlike at best" and complained that it was "just a girl running around with a telephone in her hand."

Dimension executive Richard Potter says there was a disconnect between what Weinstein was seeing in the raw footage and what he had been expecting. "When Wes shoots, he is shooting for Patrick to edit. Patrick knows in a forty-second shot that there's twelve seconds three-quarters of the way through that Wes wanted. That's what he was going for," Potter says. "When Bob watched the dailies, he thought it looked boring. It didn't look like anything was happening, and he was kinda freaking out that the movie wasn't going to be good."

"Wes built it in his brain as he was shooting it," Konrad says. "He knew the building blocks he needed to create the tension and to give the audience what they want. That's a gift. A lot of people have a hard time looking at rough material and imagining it to be something."

Craven and his team knew they were on the right track, but hearing someone say he was phoning it in was hurtful. "Wes was a very sensitive man, a very sensitive artist," says Julie Plec. "And that was really, really, really heartbreaking for him to hear."

Much of the issue came down to the now-iconic Ghost-face mask, which Weinstein hated.

In retrospect, it's hard to believe there was ever a doubt.

As actor Jamie Kennedy puts it: "Ghostface is like Mickey Mouse. That sounds weird, but they're that recognizable."

President of the studio Cary Granat flew out to Santa Rosa from New York to deal with the situation—which he says has "grown into its own mythos" over the years—and to talk to Craven about the mask and the direction of the movie.

"The first meeting was very tough because Marianne and Cathy were, rightfully so, protecting Wes and being very ardent that everything is fine," Granat says. "That first meeting was very heated and didn't really go anywhere."

That's one way to put it.

Plec's description is a little more colorful: "Cathy said, 'If you don't like it, then shut us down or fuck off.' Something to that effect."

"Yeah, I did. I said that to Cary Granat," Konrad recalls. "He wanted me to help him talk to Wes and have the cast shoot the same scenes, multiple versions, with different masks to show Bob and have him pick. It was so audacious, the request."

There was pent-up frustration simmering because of her experience on past movies with Miramax when during the *Scream* shoot she got a late-night call from a man asking, "Do you like scary movies?" At first she thought it was a prank, and she wasn't in the mood.

"It was Wes inviting me to the room to hash this out with Cary," Konrad says about the tense meeting with Granat. "I was so mad. Yeah, I said, 'Shut us down or fuck off,' basically."

He did neither. Instead, Craven and crew came up with a plan: Lussier would cut the entire opening scene so Weinstein could see that everything was going exactly as it should.

"I don't remember whose idea it was, but I'm sure nine people will take credit for it," Plec laughs.

Lussier had edited *Wes Craven's New Nightmare* and *Vampire in Brooklyn*, so Craven knew he'd be able to turn it around quickly. "I had a reputation for being able to cut fast, but I would also cut things with music and sound effects so they looked like a finished movie," Lussier says. "I would send tapes to set, back when you sent VHS tapes of the cut scenes, and Wes wouldn't even watch them first. He would just show them to the crew."

So, even though it was out of the ordinary, it was a pretty safe move. Craven's only note when he saw Lussier's cut was to make a bigger orchestral crescendo for the very last moment when you see Casey Becker disemboweled and hanging from a tree.

"He was confident that he could win them if they saw it cut together, and he was right," Lussier says. "It very clearly worked. It was an empirical thing. It wasn't a subjective thing. It wasn't like a fan blowing across the desert and it depends on what your mood is when you watch it. It was a really visceral, gut-wrenching thirteen-minute experience and it was a complete story."

Potter arranged for Dimension trio Bob Weinstein, Cary Granat, and Andrew Rona to fly to Santa Rosa and watch the cut-together scene. He hadn't seen it himself at this point, so he was a little worried that it would be a disaster and Weinstein would tell him to "fuck off," fire him, and shut the whole thing down. To everyone's relief, it went the other way. "They saw the scene cut together and it was exactly what everyone was hoping it would be," Potter says. "And it is a hundred percent true that Bob went up to Wes and said, 'What do I know about dailies?'"

"They backed way off and let him just make the movie," Lussier says. "Suddenly, there was money for everything. There was money for an orchestra. All that changed because of that thirteen and a half minutes. My whole career has changed because of that sequence."

"It was brilliantly done by Wes, and from that moment on there was tremendous trust with Wes in terms of what he needed moving forward," says Granat. "As difficult and painful as it was, it was the right thing to do at that moment. If that summit, so to speak, didn't happen, there would have been a lot more frustration and pain throughout the entire shooting process. I think it would have affected the outcome of the film. The fact that it was nipped in the bud so early enabled the shoot to just move forward and let them push the envelope as strongly as they could."

"It was a fraught relationship," Plec says, "as is the case with most movies that were made by those guys. A lot of drama, a lot of emotion, a lot of anger, a lot of chaos, but at the end of it all also a lot of support. They paid for the movies, they marketed the shit out of the movies, and they made them hits."

Years later, Craven used the experience as a cautionary tale when asked what advice he had for young filmmakers. "Don't trust anybody and persevere, really, really persevere. Don't trust anybody's judgment about what will work except your own," Craven said. "If you don't have that knowledge inside of yourself of what's going to work for you when you're making a film, you probably shouldn't be doing it. But if you have the drive and you have the talent, then don't let somebody talk you out of it."

Without naming Weinstein, he recounted how a studio exec told him his camerawork was boring and suggested he watch another filmmaker's work. He didn't watch it, by the way.

"The Drew Barrymore sequence became kind of a classic," Craven said. "You have to be very, very careful about guarding yourself against being influenced by other people who will act like they know exactly what they're talking about and more than you do. So, just follow your inner vision and really stick to it."

CHAPTER FIVE

WHAT'S THE MOTIVE?

To say the early days of *Scream* were tumultuous is a massive understatement, but the one thing that remained untroubled was the story itself. Very little of what happens on screen deviated from Kevin Williamson's original screenplay.

The studio only made two major notes, and one of them was that there was a lull in the middle where no one dies.

Principal Himbry, played by national treasure Henry Winkler, became the unfortunate casualty. Hearing he'd been killed also created a reason for most of the teen partiers to leave Stu Macher's house before Ghostface arrived, as they scattered with morbid excitement to get to the football field and see his body before it was removed.

"When you make a horror movie it takes way more cuts than normal because you've got to build the tension," Winkler says. His office was across the hall from Woods Entertainment, and his cameo came together after he got to know Craven over sushi lunches.

Winkler remembers Craven being very specific and knowing exactly what he wanted.

"I had a costume where there were slits on the clothing and they had blood pipes, a blood delivery system," he says. "When I was stabbed the first time, he came over and he said, 'Do you think it would be a little more excruciating?' And I said, 'Probably.' He said, 'Could you scream louder?' I changed, I washed, I retubed the clothing, and then I was on the floor for about two hours so he could get the shot of Ghostface in my eyeball."

The other issue Dimension had with the script was more existential: The killers had no motive.

That was Williamson's intent. He was inspired by Leopold and Loeb, notorious teen killers who in 1924 kidnapped and murdered a fourteen-year-old boy for no reason other than wanting to commit the perfect crime. Williamson explained that to Bob Weinstein, to no avail.

Thankfully, it was a relatively easy adjustment.

The backstory with Cotton Weary being set up for the murder of Sidney's mom, Maureen Prescott, was already baked into the story. So, Williamson added a couple of lines about her having an affair with Billy's dad, which gave him a new motive, and Stu went along for the ride folie à deux style.

Scream editor Patrick Lussier prefers the original concept because, as Billy says in the movie, "It's a lot scarier when there is no motive."

"'Because your mom fucked my dad' was not in the original script. Their speech before that was, 'We did it because we could,'" Lussier says. "That holds true. Terrible shit happens every single day to so many people, and so much of it behind closed doors that never even gets reported. I think part of the film's success is it gives you a way to vanquish that.

"Wes used to always talk about horror movies being a way to cathartically survive the challenges of your life. The people who dismiss them, I don't think they understand the primal need we have to be scared in the dark and then wake up. That's why art exists. It's a way to make sense of insanity. Because, if not, we'd all be just fuckin' mad."

———

THE QUESTION OF MOTIVE WAS ALSO RAISED WITH REGARD TO SOME major on-set drama—and, to this day, the people who were there still have some starkly different perspectives on what exactly happened.

One day the cast showed up to set and, without warning, saw a bunch of new faces in the crew.

Mark Irwin, who was the director of photography for most of the *Scream* shoot, had been fired, along with his team, ostensibly because there were issues with shots being out of focus.

People who worked on the movie before, during, and after it happened are divided on whether that was the reason or an excuse. Some people say certain takes would be out of focus, entirely or in part, and it limited choices for Craven in the editing room. Others say the production was behind schedule and they needed a scapegoat to get more time and money from Dimension—and replacing the camera team was a way to fix a problem that didn't exist in order to convince the studio. There are also people who say the truth is somewhere in the middle: Focus was part of the issue, but producers wanted to make an impression with Craven and thought a new DP and Panavision equipment would upgrade the look of the film.

Before we get to that, let's back up a bit, because it may be hard to imagine that out-of-focus footage would even be an issue on a studio movie—especially now, when everyone is used to iPhones doing all the work for them on their TikToks, or whatever.

Scream was shot on thirty-five-millimeter film.

Here's how Scott Ressler, who took over as the focus puller on the new camera team, explains why that matters: "The camera operator, the person who was looking through the lens, could see the image, but it had a heavy flicker because the shutter was turning twenty-four times a second. Judging if something was in focus or not was an imprecise science at best. So, a day or two later, when you saw the dailies of that day's footage it could be an extremely intense or angst-filled experience, not knowing for certain if you got everything in focus. These days with digital cameras, you see immediately on a large monitor what you've done and you can play it back to check. In those days, you didn't have that luxury."

That's why actors hitting their marks—the spots where they'll be in focus—is so important.

Scream was also filmed using anamorphic lenses, which allow for a wider shot and have a shallow depth of field that creates less room for error. Dark scenes—like the ones abundant in horror films—add another layer of difficulty.

Okay, so back to the dueling accounts of what happened and why—starting with the simpler version of events: There was out-of-focus footage and that's the beginning and end of it.

"There were repeated focus issues during the first few weeks of production on *Scream*, with the bedroom scene between Neve and Skeet at Stu's house being the most egregious. So much so that Wes, Marianne, and Cathy called me to cut it right away to see if the scene could even work," Lussier recalls. "There was a version that could work, the version that's in the film, but other performances Wes wanted to consider in that scene were not available. What you see cut together is pretty much the only way that scene could work given the focus issues."

Lussier says there had been issues working with the same team on *Vampire in Brooklyn* as well. He remembers tension between Craven and Irwin because Irwin thought the footage was fine. "To Mark, that seemed to mean that we had enough of the various takes to cut something together. It did not mean, in reality, that we had each of Wes's preferred moments in focus. This wasn't just a thing that happened on *Scream*. It came to a head on *Scream* and should've sooner."

Williamson wasn't privy to the behind-the-scenes decisions, but he does remember watching dailies and studying the footage to understand what they were discussing.

"I'd be like, 'Huh, it's not in focus. I see what they're talking about. That part's usable but that part is not usable.' I remember all those conversations happening, and people were trying to explain it to me because I was such a newbie. Then one day [Mark] was gone," Williamson says. "Wes was a real human being, and the reason he was a great director is because he could balance his assertiveness with his kindness and his compassion. You'd never feel like he's yelling at you, but if he's unhappy with you, you'd know it. If he's unhappy with a situation or he's chasing daylight or he's not making his shot list, you'd know it and you'd have to work harder and you'd have to move faster. I'm sure Mark got a lot of that and he saw the side of Wes that was a professional who had to fight for his film a little bit. So, he may not have all the pleasantries to say about Wes."

Irwin does have a lot of nice things to say about Craven, including that he invited him to stay at his house after the massive Northridge earthquake of 1994 while they were working on *Wes Craven's New Nightmare*. He doesn't love how their working relationship ended, though.

"Most of the time when I have these interviews, someone will say, 'I want to talk about *Scream*,' and I go, 'Just google "Mark Irwin fired by Wes Craven,"'" Irwin says. "The party line is that I was fired because everything was out of focus."

Irwin says what actually happened is that the shoot was behind schedule because of physical logistics with the location and they knew they needed to give Dimension a better reason than "Sorry, we went over" because time is money.

Gary Ushino was Irwin's first assistant camera operator, and the one responsible for making sure footage was in focus.

"Doing horror movies is extremely difficult because it's usually very dark, which means there is very little exposure and very little depth of field to maintain focus," Ushino says. "That takes a lot of skill and talent, and it's the one job on set that nobody wants to do because the only time people notice your work is when you screw up."

That scene Lussier mentioned as being egregiously out of focus, the one with Sidney and Billy in Stu's parents' bedroom—Ushino didn't shoot that.

"One night I was out sick, so my assistant had to bump up and cover me, and they developed a problem that I wasn't aware of until the next day when I got in," he says. "One of the lenses they had shot with had developed a slack in the focus mechanism. My assistant didn't notice that when he put the lens on the camera. There was one scene that was shot almost entirely with that lens, which was then out of focus."

They both vividly remember Craven putting on his bifocals to watch those dailies, and then complaining that everything was out of focus—not only in that scene, but in the weeks leading up to it.

"I'm just the idiot saying, 'Okay, so what do you suggest?'" Irwin recalls. "That's when Marianne steps in front of him and says, 'I think you should fire your camera crew, the grip crew, and the electric crew, and get a different camera package.' And I said, 'Are you sure you don't want a new DP as well?' This is me jumping in front of the train, lying on the tracks, thinking they won't run me down. And her only response was, 'Good idea.'"

And that was that.

"Information spread about me getting fired. Does that help your career? No, it doesn't," Irwin says. "When Wes passed away, *Hollywood Reporter*, *Variety*, they asked, 'Any last impressions, fond memories?' Nobody ever quoted me, but I said, 'I knew Wes was my friend because he stabbed me in the front as opposed to the back.' And that's what he did. With a straight face, to point to a screen and say, 'That's out of focus.' First of all, it's not out of focus, and second of all, it ended up in the goddamn movie."

"They threw me to the wolves, saying that two weeks of my work was bad, which was an absolute fallacy," Ushino says. "They got two weeks' worth of reshoot money, and I know that they didn't reshoot anything because the guys that took over the show are friends of mine. They just needed the money to finish the movie. Wes needed that lifeline to save his career and it did."

It's hard to reconcile that with the way everyone else talks about Craven.

"Wes wasn't all into making a change. He was talked into it," says co-executive producer Stuart Besser, who was tasked with making sure the new director of photography, camera department, and equipment were in place almost immediately.

"I got a call from my representative saying that they were shooting the first *Scream* movie up in Northern California and that there were some technical issues and they were going to change out the camera team," says Peter Deming, who took over as DP on the film with just a couple of days' notice. "It was sort of trial by fire."

Deming brought along Ressler, who now teaches cinematography at the University of North Carolina School of the Arts, as his first assistant camera.

"When we arrived, probably eight people walked up to me and said, 'You know, the last crew was fired because of bad focus.' That was a little bit of added pressure. I'm the person responsible for focus, so it was a little intimidating," Ressler says. "It became apparent very quickly that really wasn't the reason the original crew was fired, that it was political. I didn't know Gary Ushino at the time, but I talked to a friend who knew him and said he's one of the, if not *the*, top first assistant camerapersons there are in the industry. Now, I've worked with Gary and it's absolutely true. Definitely, there were other factors involved."

Even though Ressler wasn't to blame for the change, he felt the fallout for the rest of his time working on the franchise.

"Gary is a really likable person, very warm and friendly and outgoing. To some people, I represented his demise, I guess," Ressler says. "There were people who I never connected with because of that. That was a little awkward, doing two and a half movies with people I barely talked to."

CHAPTER SIX

WINE COUNTRY

When you talk to the *Scream* cast and crew about the shoot, you hear the words "summer camp" a lot. It's easy to write it off as a sound bite people give on autopilot because they've been talking about it for nearly thirty years, but it's more than that.

Making this movie was unlike anything they'd done before or since. They were living together, working together, and creating something they could feel in their bones was special.

It was the time of their lives and they knew it wouldn't last forever, just like summer camp.

Some of their stories are really relatable, typical twentysomethings-hanging-out anecdotes.

Then there's what Skeet Ulrich did to his hotel room.

The budding '90s heartthrob was just coming off of filming Paul Schrader's *Touch*, in which he essentially played the second coming of Jesus Christ in modern-day Los Angeles. Going from playing that character to a serial killer was a leap, to say the least, so he created a physical space that would help him get into Billy's mind.

"I had a suite, a bedroom, and then this massive living room space," Ulrich remembers. "I immediately went to the mall, bought all these things, and I made his bedroom in my suite.

"I had all these tapes from *Faces of Death*, anything that I felt like he was consuming that twisted his brain, books and posters and black lights. I created his space and that really helped put me into his mindset. It really informed a lot of the angst of Billy and the decisions that I made in terms of what was he hiding and what was really going on. I was trying to recapture my high school years, which were very angsty—not to Billy's level, but they were very angsty. I was literally one of three punks in my school, and we didn't fit in anywhere. I was twenty-six when we shot *Scream* and I was playing an eighteen-year-old. So, I was trying to go back to that time and really bring all that forward, and it definitely helped."

The cast and crew all stayed in that same hotel, a DoubleTree in Santa Rosa that burned down in a devastating 2017 wildfire. It was rare, and still is, for everyone to stay in the same place. It helped to forge bonds—many of them are still close friends—and that showed on screen.

"It was springtime into early summer in wine country and I have never had more fun in my life," says Julie Plec, who was dubbed "Julie McCoy cruise director" because she'd organize their social activities during downtime. "We'd have these dinners that would go on and on for hours and end up with us singing around the table. There was a chemistry to the cast that was really meaningful. You were in the middle of nowhere, you had nothing to do but eat, drink, and chill, and that is basically what we did for eight weeks."

"I don't think I ever had wine 'til that movie," Jamie Kennedy says. "Wes always had the best bottle of wine. He would set up dinners. We'd be done [filming] by seven, and we'd be eating dinner by eight."

"Cast and crew hung out a lot more on Wes's films than almost any other movie I've done," assistant director Nick Mastandrea says.

There were dinners at Ca' Bianca, drinks in the Teamsters' makeshift lounge, days by the pool, and endless hours listening to music by bands like the Fugees, Oasis, Wu-Tang Clan, and Nirvana.

"We all hung out in my room at the DoubleTree with the black light posters and lava lamps," says David Arquette. "The whole experience was very '90s, fun and care-free, the whole world ahead of us."

"We'd get home at five or six in the morning, once the sun's gone up, still covered in blood, shower quickly, go to David's room, and have a drink because we need to unwind," says Neve Campbell. "Then rinse and repeat."

They got kicked out of the hotel—a few times.

"We were so loud and rowdy. They made the mistake of spreading us throughout the entire hotel, instead of putting us all in one wing," actor W. Earl Brown remembers. "David's room was kind of party central and that's usually where we would congregate. It got to the point where the security guy would just come and be like, 'All right, guys, it's time to go.'

"Somebody, on a walk, found this barn that was a half mile, maybe a mile away. We would get the boom box, the cooler of beer, and the weed, and we would head out to the barn at around midnight or one o'clock in the morning and stay there and watch the sun come up. That happened at least half a dozen times. Those were special moments of being young and excited, just a great group of people that success had not spoiled yet."

Like much of the cast and crew, Kevin Williamson and Julie Plec bonded for life on set. There were times when there wasn't much to do, so they'd sit in a rental car to keep warm and listen to music.

"I don't know what I'd do without her," Williamson says. "She is that person that will always be in my life who I worship. We were the two people at video village who were just sort of sitting there and we bonded and became great friends."

"We'd just talk and get to know each other in the middle of the night," Plec says. "I remember the day he told me he wanted to write a show about Fannie, his best girlfriend growing up." (That show would become *Dawson's Creek*.)

Craven created a sense of family, and when you ask the people who worked on *Scream* what memories come back to them most often, they always start with talking about their friendships and off-set experiences.

"It's so long ago, and it's in some ways a blip in a career," Ulrich says. "I don't mean that tritely. It's just the way you're always moving on. So, when I think back about it, I think about the fun of being in Napa Valley with some of the coolest people you could ever be around and all these little moments off set. People really bonded and connected. It was a special time in all of our lives."

"The memories really are all about the life around the

movie rather than the movie," Matthew Lillard says. "We were young. We were super excited to be there. We were all over the age of twenty-one, and so we'd go to somebody's room and drink and hang out. There was this real family, collegiate experience built around the movie. I've never experienced that in another film."

Lillard says it felt more like being with friends than going to work, and that fed into the project.

"You are working together as a band of merry actors and you're like, 'I want to be fucking great for these people, for this fellowship, for this ensemble. I have to bring my A-game,'" he says. "I look back on it now and it's a little embarrassing because it's such a shitshow of energy, and it was *a lot*, but it was out of this need to try to be brilliant."

The fact that no one was really expecting much from a low-budget slasher movie worked to their advantage and created a sense of freedom, which was enhanced by the director's style.

Ulrich says Craven created an environment where he felt safe to try things and fail, and he always felt seen. "One of the most important things as an actor is that you feel like your director is truly watching," he says. "If they're not, you start doing it a little bigger—'Did you see that moment?' And a little bigger—'Did you see *that* moment?' You always knew Wes was really, really watching and that was a godsend creatively."

———

THE CLIMAX OF THE MOVIE, A MONSTER FORTY-TWO-MINUTE SEQUENCE that starts with a house party and becomes a kitchen killer reveal, was mostly filmed during night shoots. Hours of darkness are scarce in the summer, so sometimes they'd tent the house to hide the light and shoot interior scenes during the day.

"It was tiring, man," Campbell says with a sigh. "That scene took a long time. I was covered in blood. They wouldn't even wash the clothes because there was no point. They needed continuity on the blood. So they were just spraying water on these costumes that were like cardboard at that point. They were so hard from the blood. They'd wet them down and I had to get myself in them. Oh my God. I was so over those costumes. It was disgusting."

Night shoots are never easy, but it's hard to deny the results.

Tatum's crushing demise is a fan-favorite scene, especially the line "Don't kill me, Mr. Ghostface. I want to be in the sequel." Rose McGowan says fans will still come up to her and ask why on earth Tatum would try to escape through a dog door.

"I'm like, 'Imagine you're in this garage. You've got a buzz on from your beers and you're going back for more. All of a sudden, there's some scary dude in a cloak and a mask, and it dawns on you that this person is trying to kill you. What are you going to do?'" she says. "They always act as if everyone would have a hundred percent control of their faculties in that moment. 'Well, *I* would do this.' And I'm like, 'Well, Tatum didn't.' I thought it was genius—absurd genius, which is my favorite kind." (Also, McGowan actually tested it with her own dog door and got through with no issue. So, let's give Tatum some grace, shall we?)

While filming the scene Craven learned something surprising about McGowan: She can't scream.

"I can yell, but I can't scream. The sound won't come," McGowan explains. "I felt like I'd hidden this secret from them the entire time."

So instead of unleashing "a Jamie Lee Curtis scream-queen scream" like they may have been expecting, she improvised. "I yelled the word 'Mom' right as my neck gets crunched," McGowan says.

McGowan did her own stunt because she thought it would be too obvious if they used her double, but beneath the mask was stunt performer Dane Farwell, who remembers the scene well.

"Ghostface does a little bit of silent acting," Farwell says. "She opens the top of the freezer door, hits me, knocks me back. It was minimal stunts, but it was still fun."

Meanwhile, W. Earl Brown also did his own stunt work and was almost thrown off the top of the news van while filming Kenny's death scene. He was supposed to slide down the windshield, but the stunt driver went at full speed. Thankfully, the stunt coordinator had him by the belt buckle. "I remember grabbing on to the windshield wiper like, 'Oh fuck, I'm going off this thing,'" Brown says. "That left a definite impression."

During the weeks of shooting the scene—dubbed "People live, people die"—Ulrich and Lillard were fully dialed in to the unmasked and unleashed versions of Billy and Stu.

"There was a point where we were deep into what we were playing and finally getting to release the psychotic-ness of these characters," Ulrich says. "It was time for Courteney to enter the scene, and we were pacing the set like serial killers. She walked in and was instantly terrified of the look in my eyes. You could see it and Wes saw it. He was like, 'Skeet, just save it for the take.'"

As we saw in the opening sequence with Drew Barrymore, Craven had a natural talent for being able to understand what his stars needed to hear to bring out their best performance. The rest of the film proved no different.

"During the final sequence, it was very challenging to get the levels of fear right and keep it interesting," Campbell says. "Wes came up to me and he whispered in my ear, 'Just imagine,' I think he said, 'either a thousand or a million bullets ricocheting through your body right now' and he walked away and that was it. It gave me what I needed for that moment."

"Living at that level of energy for so long is indelible in my memory," Lillard says. "If you did that sequence today, I don't think that it would be the same. I think directors and actors would play it down, temper it a little, and it would be more manicured. There was something about that time in filmmaking, and Wes, and us, that ended up equaling that result."

Campbell was impressed by how her castmates took a disturbing and odd idea—voluntarily stabbing each other to appear as lucky-to-be-alive victims of the murder spree—and created an unforgettable on-screen moment.

"Getting to see Skeet and Matt play off one another in that scene and capture the sadistic mentality and create a playfulness amongst these characters was a lot of fun," she says, adding that Lillard's improvising brought it to another level.

"There are a lot of directors now who would never let me improv funny lines," Lillard says. "You watch Skeet and I in the last sequence and we are chewing scenery. We're like small little hamsters just gnawing at every corner of that frame. Most directors would be like, 'You guys are doing way too much. Be cooler, be simpler.' I think that's part of the je ne sais quoi of that last sequence."

He may feel like he was a bit over-the-top, but so many people quote his ad-libs as some of their favorite lines in the movie—"You hit me with the phone, dick" and "My mom and dad are gonna be so mad at me" among them—including the guy who wrote the movie.

"I loved all Matt Lillard's ad-libs, and I think we used every single one of them," Williamson says. "Him crying on the phone, none of that was in the script. He did it all himself."

"The Stu character is very good in the script, but the pairing definitely belongs to Billy in the script. In the movie, Matt's performance turns that into a real two-hander," Richard Potter says. "How has no one ever said, 'We've got to do a TV show with these two'?"

Craven came up with his fair share of quotable moments too.

Brown now signs autographs "Kenny, not Jesus." It's a nod to the bit where Gale says, "Jesus, get the camera," and Kenny quips under his breath, "My name's not Jesus."

That moment didn't originally have dialogue, but Craven suggested it.

"I remember the way he worked with actors," Brown says. "Wes would pull you aside and just kind of whisper in your ear. 'Now, in this scene, when she says that, do you remember what she said to you in that scene we shot out at the school? Remember that? Okay, think about that when you're in this moment.' That's the way he would work. Instead of giving broad notes to everyone, he would give you individualized notes."

David Arquette remembers Craven helping dial in the romance between Dewey and Gale too.

"He would come up with little things like when Dewey says, 'Do you know what that constellation is?' Gale says, 'No, what is it?' And he says, 'I don't know. That's why I asked you.' That was a direct Wes joke and that's a sign of his sense of humor. I think where me and him and Dewey meet is we're alike in our sense of humor, and we're romantics."

Another moment is after they narrowly dodge being hit by a teenager speeding off to see Principal Himbry's body and roll into the woods. Dewey is looking at Gale, while she spots Neil Prescott's car. "She says, 'Is that what you're looking for?' And I say, 'My whole life.' That was a really sweet Wes moment."

Meanwhile, there were a couple of lines Williamson wrote that he was a little worried about. He and Craven reminisced about them in the film commentary. One involved a Hollywood urban legend dating back to the '80s about Richard Gere and a gerbil.

"I was like, 'Wow, are you even allowed to say that about Richard Gere?'" *Cabin Fever* filmmaker Eli Roth says. "Is this breaking the code of movie ethics that you're not allowed to make fun of an actor?"

McGowan, who delivered the line, remembers kids in school whispering about the bizarre rumor not long after she'd moved to the U.S. from Italy. She didn't know who Gere was at the time and wasn't sure she even knew what a gerbil was, but that moment in American pop culture stuck. "The whole thing was just so strange," she says. "Then, later, I'm the one who winds up saying that in the movie, and I always felt bad."

An agent did make an impassioned plea to take the line out, but they liked it, so they refused.

"We just said, 'No, we can't. Sorry, we're going to leave it in,'" Maddalena says.

The other line they thought might create a stir was when Tatum is talking about renting *All the Right Moves* starring Tom Cruise and says, "You know, if you pause it just right, you can see his penis." There has been gossip over the years that Cruise had the scene edited after that, but at least when it comes to the widescreen DVD from 2001 and the Apple TV+ rental in December 2023, it's still there. (Yes, I checked. My mother-in-law, who was visiting for Christmas, can attest.)

There were more than a few jokes that didn't make the cut. Craven enjoyed dad humor, but some ideas were a little much. Like toward the end of the shoot when they realized Sidney's father was still tied up in the closet and improvised a scene of her letting him out.

"We were trying to figure out a line, basically spitballing on the spot," Peter Deming says. "Nick [Mastandrea] really wanted him to say 'I've been tied up at the office before, but this is ridiculous,' or something like that. There was a whole list of bad lines like that, and I think we actually tried a couple. Ultimately, it was a dialogue-less moment, probably rightly so."

"I feel lucky to be a part of such an original franchise combining humor and horror the way Wes and Kevin

Williamson did so beautifully," Courteney Cox says. "It's always fun when Gale has a zinger, like when she says to Sidney, 'I'll send you a copy,' right before getting punched in the face. And 'I guess I remembered the safety that time, you bastard!'"

Cox's last scene, the final shot of the film, was totally impromptu.

"I remember how we were chasing the sun in that last shot of Courteney Cox giving the news report. We didn't have it written and I remember I was writing it on her sides, and she was trying to memorize it in the moment," Williamson says. "We did a take and she nailed it, and the birds flew at the right time. I remember that moment, and I realized the magic of cinema and how you really can just accidentally make art."

"It was a solid movie from beginning to end," co-executive producer Stuart Besser says. "A good movie holds. Time won't kill it. I think *Scream* will hold for a long, long time."

"What always happens, as time marches on, is everyone likes to say they found it. 'I was the one, I'm the reason,'" Cathy Konrad says. "This thing was really a sum of many moving parts. What was so beautiful about this movie, on a lot of levels, was it was a real collaboration, and everybody brought their A game to the table. Nobody on their own could have ever survived that environment. It took everybody working behind the scenes. It was like we were all super spies trading secrets and knowledge to get across a very hard finish line."

CHAPTER SEVEN

SELLING A HOLIDAY HORROR SHOW

B efore the movie was released, two things happened that just about everyone thought were absolutely horrible ideas: The title changed and it was set for a December 20 opening. As it turns out, both were ultimately the right call.

"The script was called *Scary Movie* when it first came in. I hated the title. I almost didn't read it that night because it sounded like a stupid spoof," Richard Potter remembers. "Of course, by the time the movie is getting made, everyone has fallen in love with the title because they've fallen in love with the movie."

It was Harvey Weinstein who came up with the now-iconic title, inspired by the duet Michael and Janet Jackson had just released. "We are on the jet flying to L.A. for some meeting, everyone's doing their own thing, and then Harvey just goes, 'Wes Craven's *Scream*.' That was it," Potter

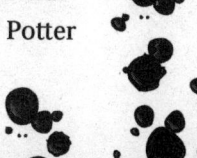

says. "Everyone on the production hated it. Now it's hard to believe that it was ever not called *Scream*."

"I was outraged," Kevin Williamson remembers. "Drew Barrymore was upset. She signed on to a movie called *Scary Movie* and when she heard it was *Scream* she said, 'How could they do this? How could they just change it?' I was upset because I thought *Scary Movie* was sort of irreverent and cool and quirky. The film needed to be cool. If the kids didn't think it was cool, they wouldn't go see it. So yeah, I was upset—and then I shut up when it became a huge hit."

Bob Weinstein was the one who insisted on releasing the movie right before Christmas. He considered it counterprogramming to typical holiday movies, thinking it would attract high schoolers and college kids who were on winter break.

Cary Granat thought it was "risky, but a genius move."

Pretty much everyone else thought it was batshit, which is obviously a technical term.

"No one thought it was a good idea," says Potter. "The conventional wisdom at the time was that family films were the way to go during the holiday break."

Dimension's marketing team was the pioneer of what they called Rushmores, chest-up shots of stars on posters that look a little bit like, you guessed it, Mount Rushmore. *Scream*'s featured Campbell, Cox, Arquette, Ulrich, and Barrymore—who was the center of the pre-release marketing campaign.

"You're ahead of the movie thinking, 'Drew Barrymore is not going to die, she is obviously the star of the movie,'" Potter says. "Then she is dead and suddenly anyone could live, anyone could die, you have no idea."

While they maximized Barrymore's presence in the marketing, they intentionally hid Henry Winkler's.

"I distanced myself a little bit because an executive from the movie company said, 'We're not gonna put your name on the movie. You were the Fonz and that's gonna knock the balance of the horror off. We can't put your name on the one-sheet,'" Winkler recalls.

It quickly became clear that hiding his presence was a mistake.

"Apparently, they showed the movie to the audience for tests and I got applause when I walked on the screen," Winkler says. "The same executive came to me and said, 'Would you do press for the movie?' I said, 'You didn't even put my name on the movie and now you want me to do press?' Ah, show business. It all works out in the end. Here I am, twenty-seven years later, signing posters of *Scream* everywhere I go. So, I finally got my name on the one-sheet."

ANOTHER KEY TO THE MARKETING, AND AN UPHILL BATTLE, WAS MAKING sure *Scream* was rated R.

"We went back to the MPAA several times because they gave it an NC-17 rating," Williamson says. "They did not want that opening scene with Drew running in slow motion when he stabs her. There were five people in the MPAA at the time, and I guess three of them were mothers, and they were really struggling with that sequence."

Patrick Lussier, the film's editor, was on the front lines of that fight. Not only did they balk at the slow-mo stabbing, they also didn't like the shot of Casey Becker hanging from a tree, Tatum getting crushed in the garage door, some of the slashing between Billy and Stu in the final scene, and one particular line of dialogue.

"They hated 'Movies don't create psychos, movies make psychos more creative,'" Lussier says. "It was saying a truth that they did not want out there voiced so clearly."

To show the minutiae of the process, on the fifth pass, which Craven sent to the MPAA (now known as the Motion Picture Association) on September 30, 1996, here's what they changed: They deleted four frames from the shot of Steve's guts and swapped in fifteen frames of "static" guts to replace moving guts; deleted one frame of Kenny's throat slash; and deleted six frames from a wide shot of Stu stabbing Billy, eleven frames of Billy slashing Stu the first time and Stu's reaction, two frames from Billy slashing Stu a second time and his reaction, and three frames of Stu's bloody hand, plus they swapped that shot for a "less bloody take."

In the letter that accompanied the submission, Craven explained that they made changes that "lessen the impact of what are pivotal scenes for this movie," which he said was "extremely painful and unfortunate" for them to do. He also said they had self-censored by keeping some of the more gruesome injuries distant and brief: "There was, in fact, far more material shot on Tatum's death in the garage, which included copious blood, given to us with great enthusiasm by our special effects team. We chose not to use a single frame of that footage."

Focus puller Gary Ushino remembers them also shooting a gorier version of Steve's death. "They had a bunch of special effects, pig guts from the butcher and chemical smoke that would act as steam," he says. "We shot this version where he dies and his hand falls away and all these pig guts and intestines come falling out onto the ground in front of him. It was disgusting. It was amazing. We shot it knowing it would never make the movie. It was just too graphic."

Craven also told the MPAA that none of the violence in the kitchen scene is glorified in any way. "I would respectfully point out that in the turning point of the entire film, none of this challenging and powerful scene is ever shown to be slick, clever, funny, without human consequence or attractive," Craven wrote. "In fact, the two young murderers, who have until this time callously inflicted hurt on others, are shocked to find the amount of pain, and indeed peril such acts involved, no matter how carefully planned. It is the beginning of their downfall, and in fact it is the whole point of the movie that these two have had to learn the hard way just how devastating their past acts have been. I know this scene is disturbing, but the script was about a disturbing, real and important subject. I respectfully implore you to honor our intentions of framing these acts as responsibly as the material allows."

"I think it went back nine times," remembers Lussier. "Bob Weinstein got the R rating by telling them it was a comedy. This was a satire on the violence, and nothing was real, and it was all social commentary. That certainly was not what it was, but that's how he eventually won them over."

———

BEFORE THE RELEASE, DAVID ARQUETTE WORKED AT A NEWSSTAND ON Melrose and came across a flyer for a test screening for

Scream. They were hesitant to let him in, since he was in the movie, but eventually said he could watch from the back of the theater. He sat next to Craven. "I got to watch him watch the audience's reaction and it was so funny," Arquette says. "He'd get this little sly look on his face. He got such a kick out of it."

"The *Scream* screening was such a relief for all of us, but especially Wes," Lussier says. "The Dimentoids had been such dicks to him during the first part of production; to come back with scores in the eighties and a film that hooked the audience with such a relentless grip from the two-minute mark was astounding. It was a pretty big high for all of us."

Even though test crowds seemed happy, no one expected what was about to happen at the box office.

"You have to understand, nobody knew what this was. I mean *nobody*," Cathy Konrad says. "It's so hard to talk about it now as if nobody knew, but they didn't know that anybody would like it and we had terrible reviews. *Variety* said it's DOA, dead on arrival. I'll never forget that headline."

They were opening up against Mike Judge's *Beavis and Butt-Head Do America* and *One Fine Day*, starring George Clooney and Michelle Pfeiffer, plus *Jerry Maguire* and *101 Dalmatians* were still going strong in theaters, which didn't bode well.

Scream opened to just over $6 million, and Craven and crew left for their holiday vacations thinking it was a bomb.

"Normally a movie drops fifty percent each week," Potter explains. "That would mean around $3 million week two, $1.5 for week three, and then done. A theatrical movie generally has to make double its budget to break even."

But, thanks to word of mouth, something remarkable happened: The second weekend *Scream* brought in more than $9 million at the domestic box office, and the week after that $10 million. It didn't dip back below its opening $6 million until week six.

"Today, horror films open up and everything is front-loaded into Friday and Saturday," Granat says. "At the time, we were reintroducing horror. So, we didn't have that massive up-front opening. It was very unique that the film increased in numbers. That is very rare for a wide release."

"We were just this little movie that could," Jamie Kennedy says. "It's definitely something that no one could predict. I knew it was great, but it's a phenomenon. It is a straight-up phenomenon. It's only going to get bigger."

Audiences loved it, which Julie Plec attributes, at least in part, to the Barrymore bait and switch. "I think Drew's presence in the movie gave it the right credibility, and then the surprise that she died in the opening scene, I don't think anybody saw coming," she says. "People were so gobsmacked by it that it created a level of chatter and awareness that is rare in movies. It's hard to surprise an audience."

Filmmaker Edgar Wright was one of those audience members.

"I'll never forget the first time I saw *Scream*. It didn't come out in the UK until May of 1997, but the hype was through the roof after the American release," Wright says. "I remember being both inspired and green with envy. The fact that it had this metatextuality and self-awareness about the genre and yet completely worked as a sincere slasher film too was very exciting to me. It was a groundbreaking entry in the '90s horror scene."

Wright says *Scream* left a lasting impression on him, and its blend of humor and horror paved the way for films like his *Shaun of the Dead*.

"Obviously, the opening sequence is a superb set piece and brilliantly updates Hitchcock's *Psycho* by bumping off the most famous actor in the film," Wright says. "The film works hard to match up to the brutal surprises of the opening, and I think it manages to do so in the gloriously twisty finale. The final twist that there are two killers is a great nod to the giallo genre that inspired the first wave of '70s slashers. I'll also never forget Rose McGowan stuck in the garage door and the audience losing their mind."

Meanwhile, Michael Kennedy, who wrote *Freaky* and *It's a Wonderful Knife* and cowrote horromcom *Heart Eyes*, had no idea what he was walking into. He wasn't a horror fan back then, so his friends lied and somehow convinced him that a movie called *Scream* wasn't scary.

"Within about five minutes of the movie starting—I remember it was the moment Ghostface says, 'I want to know who I'm looking at'—I was scared out of my mind but realized I was loving it," Kennedy says. "By the end of the opening scene, I was completely transfixed, and I could feel a chemical change in me. I actually walked out of that movie and said to one of my friends, 'I'm going to make one of those one day.' My love of horror and my desire to be a writer started the same day with the same movie."

Even though *Hostel* director Eli Roth had read the

screenplay, he still had a visceral experience seeing the movie for the first time.

"There are the jump scares and the shocking scares and then there are the resonating, deep scares," Roth says. "Sidney is such a vulnerable character. She trusts Billy and when she realizes she can't trust him, it's like she has no faith in anyone, no faith in herself. You question your own ability. You're like, 'I thought I was such a good judge of character.' If you're a good person, you would never think to do that to someone, so why would someone else do that to you? It's disturbing. It's scary."

He says *Scream* reset expectations of what's possible in a slasher film and redefined horror in general.

"Everyone told me, 'Horror is dead,'" Roth says, "I'm like, horror is not dead. Shitty movies are dead. Make a great movie. If you build it, they will come."

The film was deeply influential for the people who'd go on to make future *Scream* movies too.

James Vanderbilt, who cowrote *5* and *6* and produces the new wave films, became hooked on horror with *Scream*. "That movie hit like a freight train," he says. "Everybody was talking about *Scream* when it came out. As someone who wanted to be a writer, it is such a great, show-off script. They fuckin' had it on the page. Wes deserves all the credit in the world, but Kevin should be right there with him. That script was stone-cold great."

Vanderbilt's cowriter Guy Busick, who penned *Scream 7* solo, had a similar experience. "By the time the credits rolled my whole view of horror had changed," he says. "You can draw a straight line from the original *Scream* to *Ready or Not* in terms of tone and vibe and trying to create characters that are memorable, that you actually care about and don't want to get killed by the bad guy."

It's no surprise—you may be noticing a pattern here—that seeing *Scream* was also a seminal moment for Matt Bettinelli-Olpin and Tyler Gillett, the directing duo known as Radio Silence who helmed *5* and *6*.

"My experience with it was feeling like it was a wildly unsafe situation, especially the opening," Gillett says. "This movie that I thought was going to be kind of a dumb horror movie is so much smarter than everybody who sits down to watch it. It's so manipulative. And the particular nature of the terror of that movie is that somebody you know is doing something terrible and it could be anyone. For as smart as that movie is, it's also very basic in the fear premise of it, which is why it is so effective and so lasting."

"The original *Scream* is the gold standard for all movies," says Bettinelli-Olpin. "It's this underdog that becomes a cultural phenomenon."

It was a hit, and now it's a classic. For the young actors working on the film it was a formative experience, but not necessarily in the ways you might assume.

"People are like, '*Scream* changed your life,'" Matt Lillard says. "*Scream* didn't change my life. When *Scream* came out, a lot of credit, duly, went to Courteney and to Neve and to Skeet. I think that really changed their careers. It did not change my career. Now, I'll walk down the street and they're like, 'You're the guy from *Scream*.' So, that has changed people's perception of me, but the idea that the movie all of a sudden opened up all of these doors is not the case in any way, shape, or form. So, the movie didn't change my life."

It also didn't help him much financially, especially when you factor in taxes and commission fees.

"At the end of the day, I probably cleared $11,000 to $12,000 for a month of work," he says. "I don't think that people really understand that it was a little tiny independent horror film."

Even though not much changed in the short term, he remembers the experience fondly and says it's like looking back on a first love.

"It's not just a normal transaction, doing a *Scream* movie, because it's so intimate to all of our lives. It's a pivotal memory. There is a level of love that is different than other films," says Lillard. "All those people, in that moment, were the most important people in my life. You don't remember any of the drama. You just remember all the beautiful parts of it. There is this sweet place in all of our hearts for that film. I think it's because of Wes. I think it's because of who we were in that moment. To have something that you're proud of working on and that still matters is super rewarding in an emotional way."

CHAPTER EIGHT

TAKING A STAB AT A SEQUEL

Hollywood always chases a hit, and *Scream 2* shot out of a cannon—one that was now loaded with expectations. The original *Scream* certainly wasn't without challenges, but at least they started with a near-perfect script that barely changed during the course of production. *Scream 2* was the polar opposite.

"When *Scream* became this massive hit, which was in January of '97, Bob decided that *Scream 2* needed to happen in Neve and Courteney's next hiatus window, which was in May," says Julie Plec, who was still Wes Craven's assistant at the time but earned an associate producer credit on the sequel. "The entire experience of the spring of '97 was trying to get the script for *Scream 2* ready to shoot in time before we would lose Neve and Courteney to their shows. There was nothing easy about it. There was nothing fun about it, but it was an adventure."

"We were green-lighting a movie that we were budgeting without having a firm script," former Dimension Films president Cary Granat says. "At least in my career, at this level of budget, that had never been done before."

Scream 2 follows Sidney Prescott to Windsor College, where a killing spree starts at the premiere of *Stab*, the movie-within-the-movie inspired by the Woodsboro murders. The four stars—Campbell, Cox, Arquette, and Kennedy—returned, and Liev Schreiber got significantly more screen time as Cotton Weary in the sequel.

Sidney's circle includes her boyfriend Derek, played by Jerry O'Connell; best friend Hallie, played by Elise Neal; and eccentric film student Mickey, played by Timothy Olyphant. When things go awry, of course, Dewey is there to help and Gale Weathers shows up with a new cameraman, played by Duane Martin. She's plagued by a local journalist, Debbie Salt, a.k.a. Mrs. Loomis, played by fan favorite Laurie Metcalf.

Scream was so buzzy that even cameos landed major actors, like *Dawson's Creek* star Joshua Jackson and Buffy the Vampire Slayer herself, Sarah Michelle Gellar. "*Scream* was the start of a new trend," says Gellar. "Before, horror had the reputation of hot people who couldn't always act, but *Scream* had great acting and true humor to bookend all the horror. It was filled with wit and heart. After *Scream* we began to ask more of the genre. I truly believe Wes was an innovator."

Even Tori Spelling, who was the butt of a joke in the first movie, was game to play Sidney in *Stab* and bring that extra-meta moment to life. "As I recall, she jumped at the chance to do it," casting director Lisa Beach says. "Everybody wanted to be part of it."

Scream's success was a double-edged sword. With the upside came heightened expectations from the studio—and, of course, there's always inherent pressure with a sequel.

"The second one has to be better than the first to be seen as equal to it," former Dimension exec Richard Potter says. "Then people will want to see a third one. For *Scream* to become a franchise, versus just a movie with a sequel, *2* had to be better. The only reason you can have a *Godfather III* is because *Godfather II* is better than *The Godfather.* You get a *Scream* franchise because *Scream 2* is better than *Scream*. Wes hit it out of the park, but Kevin's writing on that is next-level."

The movie opens with a couple going to see *Stab*. They're in a crowded theater, so they should be safe. Of course, they aren't, and Jada Pinkett Smith and Omar Epps joined the ranks of actors killed off in an iconic *Scream* opening—one that forever made movie theater bathrooms feel extra creepy.

"Based on the success of *Scream* and the hype around it, it was pretty clear that the audience was going to see this in a theater. So, we put you in the same situation as the characters in the movie," Potter says. "They're going to see *Stab*, you're at *Scream 2*, and you're going to experience what they experience.

"Part of the fun of that was opening the movie with two Black characters talking about how there are no Black people in *Stab*," he says. "We had spoken about that between *Scream* and *Scream 2*. In *Friday the 13th*, the camp, in the *Halloween* movies, Haddonfield, they are always populated by the same type of people. So, *Scream* has those people in it."

"Those people" being attractive white teenagers who look like they should be on TV.

"*Scream* is a commentary on horror movies," Potter continues. "People always talk about how *Scream* breaks all the rules, but it doesn't break any rules of a horror movie. They tell you what they are, and then they happen. So, you make the first movie following the tropes, and then in the next movie the first two characters you meet are talking about this ridiculous world that the movie takes place in."

That bit of social commentary continues throughout the story, taking on the trope that the Black characters who do exist in these movies are usually the first ones killed—which is exactly what happens in *Scream 2*. They flipped it later in the film when Gale's cameraman Joel does the sensible thing that no one ever seems to do in these situations: He leaves.

"Duane Martin, who is amazing, and has the line where he says, 'Given what you guys have already been through, why would you stay?' And he even says, 'Black folks don't do well in these situations.' He survives and at the moment that Gale needs to be Gale he is back, camera on his shoulder, ready to do his thing. *Scream 2* starts out with throwing that trope in your face, living up to the trope, and breaking it later."

Director of photography Peter Deming has a cameo in the scene, which Craven loved to do with his crew. "I decided I wanted to be at the concession stand. In the script, it was way in the background. I thought that I'd get a kick out of that," he says. "When I got to set, Wes, being the trickster that he can be, had moved the scene to the concession stand and had Jada actually come up and order popcorn. I'm proud to say I made it through without embarrassing myself, I think."

They shot the *Stab* opening with Heather Graham first so they could actually play it on the screen in the theater. The on-screen audience was really watching the movie based on the movie the real audience had fallen in love with, which added another layer to the meta feel.

"The *Scream* opening is probably the best thirteen minutes of the franchise, but the *Scream 2* opening that literally does the exact opposite—no phone call, killed in public—it shouldn't work at all, and it works beautifully," says Michael Kennedy, cowriter of horromcom *Heart Eyes*. "It is so daring and smart. God, what a risk. I don't think I'd have the balls to write something like that the way Kevin did."

Horror filmmaker Eli Roth says sequels usually suck because you probably won't top the original, and you certainly can't copy and paste what worked about it to increase your odds. "It's the conundrum of the sequel," he says. "People are there to get more of what they liked in the first one, but you can't do exactly what you did in the first one because then you're just repeating yourself. You gotta give them what they're there for, but not in the way they think they're gonna get it. You have to have very high standards and go, 'That's not good enough, that's not good enough.' You knew *Scream 2* was going to be a great sequel because in the opening they nailed it. They came up with another iconic opening. It's really hard to do."

WILLIAMSON HAD THE IDEA FOR THE OPENING OF *SCREAM 2* WHILE HE was writing the original. It's a riff on *He Knows You're Alone*, a Tom Hanks film in which brides-to-be are being killed and one is stabbed while watching a movie in a theater. He couldn't figure out how to make it fit in *Scream* and, because he has a "television brain" that thinks about serialized storytelling, he thought it would be great for a sequel. The opening, and a synopsis of the full movie, was attached to the *Scary Movie* screenplay when they sent it around.

By the time the sequel was in the works, that story Kevin Williamson had told Plec about wanting to create a fictionalized version of his teenage years as an aspiring filmmaker had become a reality. So, he was juggling writing the *Scream* sequel with launching his first television series.

"I was down in Wilmington shooting *Dawson's Creek* and I remember they sent Richard Potter and Andrew Rona as the two sort of mafia who came down and made sure I wrote," Williamson says. "They were super nice, and they were like, 'We're here because we have to be here or we're going to be fired.'

"I wrote super fast. I was writing it, handing it to Julie, read this, read this, read this, and she would be noting it up. We were trying to put it together as fast as we could, and she was helping me shape it. That was a write-as-you-go situation. I would come to the set, and they'd be like, 'Why aren't you in the hotel room writing?'"

Plec describes *Scream 2* as "a constantly evolving organism born from chaos and time pressure."

And, because *Scream* had generated so much interest, they also had to worry about people trying to spoil the sequel.

This is where memories begin to deviate a bit. Some people remember real leaks, some insist only dummy versions got out and it was intentional, and some don't remember anything about the leaks themselves but do remember the preventive measures they took to protect the story that made it to screen.

"Kevin and I finished what was essentially an outline, or maybe an early draft of the script, that then leaked on the internet," Plec says. "We were like, 'Well, that's good because that was bad anyway.' We rebroke the whole story, new killers, and we were writing all the way through shooting."

Williamson isn't so sure, but as a general rule he always trusts Plec's recollection of things. "I remember rebreaking the story many times, but I don't remember that being the reason," he says. "That's not to say it isn't true."

Whether part of the real story leaked before they created a labyrinth of protocols doesn't necessarily matter in hindsight.

"The issue was not the content that got out, because it was not significant," Potter says. "The issue was that content *could* get out."

"I had settled on Mrs. Loomis being the killer, but the person who was her accomplice we changed a few times," Williamson says.

"There was discussion of Derek as the killer, but that was too close to *Scream*," Potter says. "There was talk of Hallie as the killer, but Mickey was the best idea and, as far as I remember, was the only version of the ending ever actually written."

The only *real* ending that was written, anyway.

"David, my assistant, wrote a decoy script where Dewey was the killer," Williamson says. "I sent it to a friend of mine who had a *Halloween* blog, or something, and he leaked it in some other state. So, it looked legit. We thought if that one leaks first, then if the real one does leak no one's gonna care. So, that one got leaked by design and it has created this folklore that Dewey was the killer. Well, in one version he was, but not in the version we were filming."

They went to great lengths to prevent the final story from getting out—or, worst-case scenario, be able to catch the leaker if it did—including printing scripts on this special paper that had a maroon-ish brown stripe down the center of the page so it couldn't be photocopied. Potter also unbound the pages and wrote code numbers inside the margins.

"Everyone's script had a different number on it. I knew who got what number. So, if a script was copied and I was able to get the copy, I would take the brads out and look in the margin of a certain page and I would see a number there and I would know whose script was copied," Potter says. "I also wrote letters, abbreviations, and numbers in the margin on a few other pages in case anyone ever saw it, but only I knew which page had the real security number. By not sharing that information no one would know what to fake or where to fake it."

Williamson had a sneaky trick too: "On a certain page, I would spell a word wrong and I knew what draft. I had it all listed. So, I would know what date it leaked and who I gave it to that day," he says.

The actors only saw the first seventy pages during their auditions. During production, only a handful of people had the real ending—even most of the crew didn't get to see the full script. They got a version where toward the end of the movie every name and pronoun had been replaced with the word "character."

"Everyone can see exactly what's happening, but no one reading it will know who is talking or what they're talking about," Potter says. "If Mickey lifts the knife and menaces Sidney, it just says, 'Character lifts the knife and menaces character.'"

"It was pretty intense and a very arduous process to get the script out to the people that needed to read it. I remember the maroon paper, and the numbers, and the driving, having various people from Dimension hand-deliver or sit outside people's places," says producer Cathy Konrad. "I remember saying, 'I can't read a fucking thing. How is anybody going to read this?' It was like black on black. We needed a little special light to read the print. Nothing could get faxed and it had to be hand carried. It was just so silly."

Because the top secret script wasn't locked, they also had to guess the budget.

"It truly was the perfect storm, organizationally and operationally," Granat says. "We had to reconstruct how we worked with a film at the studio level. Think about this: Before the film was even green-lit, we were spending money on it to get it ready to be green-lit."

That included new pacts with their writer and director.

Dimension had made Williamson's deal for *Scream 2* early on, but he remembers they gave Craven a hard time.

"They tore Wes to pieces over his deal with *Scream 2*," Williamson says. "They said, 'We've got Robert Rodriguez waiting. We don't need you.' That's the kind of shit that Bob Weinstein pulled with *Scream 2*. They never had Robert Rodriguez. I was already talking to him about *The Faculty*, so I knew it was bullshit."

Ultimately, they made a multipicture deal with Craven that included two more *Scream*s and his passion project *Music of the Heart*. The prospect of finally making a film outside of the horror genre was too appealing to pass up.

Craven's team returned with him. Among them were executive producer Marianne Maddalena, cinematographer Peter Deming, assistant director Nick Mastandrea, editor Patrick Lussier, composer Marco Beltrami, production assistant John Embry, post-production coordinator Tina Anderson, and Plec.

"The movies got increasingly less interesting to work on because the studio got more and more involved when they realized they had a hit," Beltrami says. While it was nice to have a bigger budget, especially when it meant Beltrami didn't have to pay anything out of his own pocket this time, that's where the positives stopped. They were testing the movie more and asking him to emulate music they'd used in those test versions. "They started controlling things that they really shouldn't have been. They were like, 'All right, we want you to do something like this music here,' which became a pain. I don't want to copy music."

Dewey's theme is a Hans Zimmer piece that had previously been in *Broken Arrow*. They paid about $35,000 to license it because Beltrami refused to mimic it, which was more than his entire budget for the first movie.

It pales in comparison to what they paid for Danny Elfman to guest compose the score for the Greek play within the movie, which was Craven's idea. He wanted that scene to have a different feel and asked music supervisor Ed Gerrard to find out if Elfman would be up for the task. So, Gerrard set up a meeting, and they talked about the scene.

"The manager calls me, and she says, 'He really wants to do it, but here is the deal. He wants one million dollars and he wants two tickets to the premiere for him and his daughter,'" Gerrard recalls. "I'm like, 'No problem.' I had all this money. I controlled the budget. Nobody was telling me no. So, we paid Danny a million bucks just for that piece of music."

"That scoring session was very strange, having Danny Elfman come in as this guest composer," editor Patrick Lussier recalls. "Wes was thrilled with it, but it's such a strange interlude and it stands out from all the other films. It is incredibly powerful and effective and has the whole Cassandra story, being cursed to see the future and have no one believe you. That's all Wes, his English professor background and his intellectual passions mixed in with the chaos of these crazy slasher movies. That scene, more than I think anything else in the whole franchise, is a reflection of who he is."

CHAPTER NINE

BUCKETS OF BLOOD

Scream 2 may have felt like it was teetering on the edge of disaster during the process of making it, but its action-packed set pieces, compelling villains, and Randy's shocking and emotional death made the sequel one of the best films in the franchise.

"Depending on the day, I would actually say sometimes that *2* is better than *1*," says Blumhouse film exec Ryan Turek. "The high-water mark for me is when Sidney and her friend and the bodyguards are leaving campus and Ghostface attacks in the car."

That scene ratchets up the tension as Sidney and Hallie are stuck in the back of a crashed squad car that Ghostface hijacked. There's only one way out—and it means crawling over the seemingly unconscious killer and out the driver's-side window.

Williamson originally wrote a version of the scene for Sarah Michelle Gellar's character in *I Know What You Did Last Summer*, but the director, Jim Gillespie, balked.

"The director goes, 'I don't know how to shoot this. How am I gonna film it without showing the fisherman?' I go, 'Well he's wearing the hood. You won't see his face.' He's like, 'I don't think it's scary,'" says Kevin Williamson.

So, he reluctantly cut it out of the script and put it in his graveyard file, a folder on his computer with spare parts that he wants to keep.

"When I was writing *Scream 2*, I gave that script to Wes. I handed him the dog-eared section and I go, 'Please read this scene, and tell me if you think it's scary. What if we did that in *Scream 2*?'" Williamson remembers. "He goes, 'Let's do it. I know exactly what to do with that.' The very first time I saw it, I went, 'Yep, that's why he's Wes Craven.' He just really made it sing."

Elise Neal plays Hallie, who escapes the car only to be stabbed by Ghostface just down the street. She decided to lean into the fact that Hallie hadn't been through the Woodsboro massacre and didn't expect any of this to happen.

"This is all foreign to her. I thought it would be a disservice to not act like what a person would act like in this situation," Neal says. "I'm gonna go for it. I'm gonna scream, I'm going to kick the door, I'm going to do anything that I would naturally do in this situation, which I think heightened it a lot."

That continued with the moment Hallie was murdered—or, rather, stabbed. Neal points out that Ghostface "ran after Neve's character and you never saw what happened" and not so subtly hints that she thinks Hallie survived and could reappear in the franchise. (There are characters who are much, much more dead—extremely, unequivocally dead—so, you never know.)

Still, Neal really sold it in the moment. "With Ghostface, I was like, 'Okay, if you're supposed to stab me, do it as hard as you can. Make it look believable.' I'm that type of person. I told him not to hold back. Grab me for real. Scare me for real. Make it as real and as believable as possible."

The pole that impales the officer in that scene was supposed to go through the dummy's chest, but it wound up going through his head. "When you do real stunts, you get surprises like that," Lussier says. Craven decided to keep it, but they were worried it wouldn't sit well with the MPAA, which surprisingly didn't seem to mind. "We were prepared for a fight. There's nothing worse than being prepared for a fight and discovering there's no fight to be prepared for. You're like, 'What?! I'm ready!'"

Earlier in the movie, the sorority house scene where Gellar's Cici Cooper is chased, stabbed, and thrown out a window offered a classic Wes Craven "more blood" moment.

"The shot is looking down and it's a fairly wide shot," Deming recalls. "They piped her up and this little trickle of blood would come out. He's like, 'No, no, no, no. This has to be like a flood. She just cracked her head open.' We'd do it again and it never got to what he wanted. So, Wes said, 'Wait here and when I say "roll," roll.' He went downstairs and he took a bucket of blood and he asked Sarah to raise her head. He poured the blood right where her head went and ran out of the shot as she put her head back. All this blood just gushed out from her head. That's the shot in the film. He was like, 'Okay, we got it, let's move on.'"

"Not only did he do that, but once it was done he poured all the blood on himself and took a pic with me," Gellar remembers. "He knew how uncomfortable that process was, and it was important to him that his actors knew he wouldn't ask anything of us that he wouldn't be willing to do himself."

And, of course, who could forget the cafeteria serenade when Derek belts out "I Think I Love You" in an effort to win back Sidney's trust after she's started to suspect he might be the killer.

"Listening to Jerry O'Connell sing in *2* was probably the most painful moment," assistant director Nick Mastandrea says with a laugh. "Jerry is lovely. He is the sweetest man on earth, but the singing was painful and he'll admit that."

The movie also has one of Dewey's best lines: "How do you know my dimwitted inexperience isn't merely a subtle form of manipulation used to lower people's expectations, thereby enhancing my ability to effectively maneuver within any given situation?"

David Arquette says it was a mouthful, and a challenge to film, but when he thinks back about working on the movie what he remembers most is life-changing advice he got from Craven.

"*Scream 2* was really hard for me," Arquette says. "My mom was really sick and about to die. When we had gotten back to L.A., he just sat me down and gave me this really sweet man-to-man, fatherly conversation that had a huge impact on my life. It was just about 'I know you're going through a hard time, but I really want to see you do great things and get your life together.' At the time, I was dating Courteney, we were on-and-off. And he said, 'I think she really likes you, but she's scared like a lot of people are that you're gonna hurt yourself.' It was something that not a lot of people do in Hollywood."

Craven, of course, was not most people. And Arquette and Cox were in the unusual position of having the relationship of their characters evolve on a similar timeline to their own.

"It kind of was like life imitating art. The meta elements went even beyond the story," Arquette says. "We ended up having our daughter and that was in large part because of the advice Wes had given me to get my life together."

The franchise's antihero, Cotton Weary, was an integral part of the *Scream* story despite only having a blink-and-you'll-miss-it cameo in the first movie. Schreiber was thrilled to have a much more substantial part in the sequel.

"Acting, it's a con game, right? Your backstory is like your shell, and Cotton's backstory was all set up. It was all there," Schreiber says. "One of the great tricks for characters is you don't just read your lines. You look for all the references. Who talks about you? What's the story?"

"I fucking love Cotton Weary in *2* and what they did with this tiny little character. They were so lucky to cast Liev Schreiber," says James Vanderbilt, who cowrote *Scream 5** and *6*. "I love that he turns out to be a decent dude. People don't talk about him enough when they talk about *Scream*. His flavor is so different than everyone else's and it's delightful."

Not only did Schreiber get more screen time in the sequel, but his dog, Rudy, made an appearance outside the

---

* Obviously, I'm aware the title is *Scream* not *Scream 5*. For the sake of your sanity, and mine, I'm calling it *5* throughout. Fans do it, the people who made the movie do it, and the one that came after it is called *Scream 6*. I briefly considered calling it *5cream* but, let's be real, that's only funny when Jack Quaid says it.

frat house. "I was joking, and I said, 'Can my dog be in the movie?'" he remembers. "Wes said, 'Absolutely.' And that was it. He put him in the movie. I didn't expect him to do that."

They realized in post that in the scene where Cotton Weary is being interrogated by the campus police chief, played by David Arquette's father, Lewis Arquette, no one acknowledged in any way that Randy had just been brutally murdered. They needed to change some of the dialogue in ADR—but Schreiber was out of the country filming *Jakob the Liar*, so they went with the next best thing.

"I was never supposed to tell this story, but I'll tell it anyway," Lussier says. "Jerry O'Connell could do a great imitation of Liev. So, he did the temp ADR. He is not in the final. We got Liev back to do the final, but we previewed with Jerry's imitation of Liev to make those lines work because it was like, 'Oh my God, this scene totally ignores this murder that just happened.'"

That murder is one of the most emotional deaths in the franchise, the moment when Randy Meeks is ambushed in broad daylight while on the phone with Ghostface.

When Jamie Kennedy saw in the script that Randy gets killed, he initially thought he might get a last-minute save like Dewey did at the end of *Scream*—but his character wasn't so lucky. Williamson has said if he realized there would be so many more movies, he might have kept Randy around a little while longer. Kennedy is on the same page: "Had I known it was gonna be this Marvel-intricate universe I would've been like, 'Damn, where's my thumbs-up?'"

Kennedy's parents were on set at Agnes Scott College the day they shot the scene.

"I'm like, 'I'm gonna get killed today!'" Kennedy remembers. "And my mom was like, 'Oh boy.'"

As usual, Roger L. Jackson was hidden away from the cast but doing the Ghostface calls live. He started improvising more on the sequel and really enjoyed it. "It started with the scene with Jamie Kennedy," he remembers. "We got a few takes in the can of the script and then we did a take where I dropped in something I thought of. I said, 'Have you ever felt a knife slice through human flesh and scrape the bone beneath?' Of course, I'm watching the camera feed and I could see his face. Wes called cut and Jamie said, 'That was great! Do that again!'"

At one point, he ad-libbed something a little more personal.

"Roger is like, 'I'm sitting here with your mother,'" Kennedy recalls.

Keep in mind that Jackson doesn't break character. So, this is Ghostface talking.

"After we got a bunch of takes in the can, I just started playing and saying stuff like, 'Your mother should get ready. I'm gonna cut her a new smile from ear to ear,'" Jackson recalls.

"I didn't know where Roger was, I didn't know where Wes was, and I didn't know where my mother was," Kennedy says. "And then he tells me he's got my mother. I was like, 'Fuck, really?'"

Embracing the morbid motivation, Kennedy asked to do it again, but bloodier. "Wes goes, 'All right, you wanna go bloody? You don't have to tell me twice.' In hindsight, I wonder if I did too much blood because now people are like, 'You're definitely dead.'"

After they wrapped the scene, the actor was reunited with his parents. "I'm like, 'Did you know about this? Why didn't you tell me?' She said, 'It made the scene better.' That kind of makes me cry. My mom was a part of that scene. It was really beautiful. It was a beautiful day to be murdered. Hot summer Georgia day."

Because of the narrowly averted NC-17 rating on *Scream*, they submitted a much more violent version of the sequel than they actually wanted. That way, if the MPAA told them to dial it back they wouldn't have to cut anything that mattered.

"Wes shot a lot of extra violence," Lussier recalls. "Omar Epps got stabbed in the ear three times. Jamie Kennedy's death was so much gorier. We had more violence everywhere throughout and that version got an R because they thought the opening sequence was socially relevant and responsible, holding the audience to account for their behavior. So, we rigged the version that we sent to them and they surprised us and said yes. We didn't keep all that extra violence. We toned it back down to what it was supposed to be."

"That's where I learned to do it in TV," Williamson says. "Every time I deliver a cut I make it as bloody as I can so that when they give me the cut notes I get it to where I wanted it to begin with. I learned it from *Scream*. We went overboard with the blood and they were like, 'Yeah, that's fine,' because it was a hit. It was a franchise."

———

AS FAR AS MOTIVES GO IN THE *SCREAM* UNIVERSE, THE SEQUEL HAS ARguably the most relatable.

Billy's mother, Nancy Loomis, is determined to avenge her son's death. It's unbridled maternal rage paired with an apparently hereditary streak of lunacy. It's simple, really.

"That was what was so brilliant about it," says Laurie Metcalf. "It made total sense once you figured out that it's a mother. It didn't really need much more explanation after that. It was pure revenge."

If she'd been up front about her identity from the start, it would have been extremely obvious that she was the killer. But she hid in plain sight as an annoying small-town journalist, which only worked because she deftly avoided the Woodsboro residents who would have recognized her.

"I loved the way that they built Debbie Salt into the storyline because it makes sense that there could be a reporter hanging around," says Metcalf. "That left the reveal even more surprising because not only are you wondering why is this reporter getting so much screen time but you're also wondering, 'Okay, well if she does have a significant role to play other than being a reporter, what could it possibly be?'"

To the audience, Debbie Salt and Nancy Loomis feel like two distinct characters, but Metcalf didn't see it that way.

"Debbie Salt is not trying to hide behind a different persona, per se. She is just going by a different name. She's trying to hide her motive of course, and her anger, but I wasn't trying to impersonate two different people," Metcalf says. "It's the same person, but their motivations were entirely different. So, all I had to do basically was play what was on the page for each of the characters."

And what was on the page for Mrs. Loomis was the aftermath of a grief-stricken psychotic break.

"You know it's going to be really intense and emotional and loud and scary," Metcalf says. "All you can do as an actor is go a hundred percent with your character's motivation, and that was to destroy somebody and get revenge. It sort of brings out the monster in you."

Her accomplice Mickey Altieri, meanwhile, was driven by narcissism. He was a killer for hire who aspired to be infamous and thought it would be fun to get caught and blame violent movies during his trial.

Filming the reveal was especially memorable for Metcalf because, even though she'd been acting for longer than most of the cast, she hadn't done many movies.

"I remember the long hours that we spent on the big, climactic scene that took place in the deserted theater and how difficult it was logistically to block it and figure out how Neve and I were going to get around that giant space but still make it tense," Metcalf says. "And I remember having a whole prosthetic made of my forehead. Special effects then weren't the way they are now, so we actually had to rig up this thing that exploded out from my forehead.

She adds, "How many people it takes, and the amount of planning that goes into creating five minutes' worth of a climax of a movie, it's amazing."

AFTER ALL THE SECRECY WITH THE SCRIPT, WHEN IT CAME TIME TO SCREEN the movie for an audience, they didn't want to take any risks that would make all their hard work a waste—so they didn't even tell some of the crew where it was happening.

"They didn't want anything to leak, so there was this

whole mystery," post-production coordinator Tina Anderson says. "The guy at Miramax was like, 'Okay, we're going to send a car to pick you up and it'll bring you to LAX. You'll meet me and then I'll tell you where we're going.'"

It was Tucson, Arizona—and they misled the audience about the film, too.

"Whoever introduced it came out and said something like, 'Okay, we know we told you that you were going to see movie X, but you're going to be the first audience in the world to see *Scream 2*,'" Anderson says. "They went bananas."

But, once the movie started rolling, things got eerily quiet.

"The movie is playing and we're noticing that no one is screaming, no one is laughing, no one is reacting," Richard Potter says. "We're looking at each other like, 'Could we really have missed it that badly? Did we really get it wrong?' After the screening, people fill out their cards and then you have the focus group. Every comment that they're giving is how much they loved it. They loved the main characters, they loved the plot twists, they thought it was scary. Meanwhile, in another room, they're tabulating the cards. The scores come back as we're coming out and it's one of the highest-rated test screenings we have ever had. We're like, 'So how come nobody was reacting?'"

A theater employee stopped them on the way out and solved the puzzle.

"Someone comes up to the group and asks what we thought of the theater because it's state-of-the-art and it even has sound baffles in it so that you don't hear all the people around you, so you can just enjoy your experience," he says. "We were like, 'Oh my, God. Thank God!' That's why we didn't hear anything."

Those test scores were a good omen. Like its predecessor, the sequel also premiered just before the holidays. It brought in nearly $33 million its first weekend and $172 million globally during its theatrical run. *Scream 2* managed the impossible: living up to the original. Many fans think it's actually better than the first, even though it's a bit taboo to admit—which explains why it went on to become a franchise that's still alive and well decades later.

"I think my favorite line of the entire series is when Sidney says to Mickey, 'Well, you're forgetting one thing about Billy Loomis.' And he's like, 'What's that?' She's like, 'I fucking killed him,'" Michael Kennedy says. "I love that so much because it's such a definitive moment in her arc that really says she's done with this shit. She has become this strong woman. I love the way she says it, she leans in and hits him over the face with her Greek letters, which is such a great touch."

"We went deep into *Scream 2* on *History of Horror* and had Kevin Williamson talking about trauma and the effects of trauma. I love that Sidney gets the phone call and she's got caller ID set up and knows exactly who the person is," says Eli Roth, whose slasher *Thanksgiving* will soon have a sequel. "That's something that I want to continue with *Thanksgiving*. What are the lingering effects of this? Let's really game this out. If you really went through this, what would that do? How would that change things? Would it make you bitter, would you be hardened, does it ruin your life? All of those things."

"*Scream 2* is my favorite *Scream*, and I know you're

not supposed to say that," horror filmmaker Christopher Landon says. "*Scream 2* is the movie where everyone involved, from Kevin to Wes to the cast, was firing on all the cylinders. Sidney's story became more interesting and more defined. The set pieces were insane. The sound booth sequence with Gale is still in my top five set pieces. There was so much momentum and it had everything I think a *Scream* movie should have: the wit, the commentary, the great villains. There is a Greek tragedy element to it because of the betrayal—because it is always someone you know."

CHAPTER TEN

META

Scream 3 tells the story of *Stab 3*, a franchise film plagued with production issues and rewrites and made by a studio whose leader has been exploiting and abusing women for decades. Things really go south when a killer in the now famous Ghostface garb murders talk show host Cotton Weary and then starts targeting the cast of the film.

Except for the whole murder bit, it felt very much like art imitating life. In fact, there's a line in the movie that they'd quote to each other on set. Fictional actress Sarah Darling, played by Jenny McCarthy-Wahlberg, says, "Has there been another goddamn rewrite? How the fuck are we supposed to learn our lines when there's a new script every fifteen minutes?"

Like *Scream 2*, the third installment started without a completed script—but this time they didn't have Kevin Williamson.

He wanted to write *Scream 3*—and had penned an outline and thirty-page treatment—but Dimension was in a

rush to churn out another movie after the sequel's critical and box office success. The studio got cocky and thought it didn't need to wait for an opening in Williamson's schedule—which Dimension had filled with its other projects.

"I was doing *Wasteland*, I was finishing up *Tingle*, I was doing *Halloween H2O*," Williamson says. "I was like, 'Guys, it's not like I'm off working with someone else. I'm working for you. There are only twenty-four hours in a day.'"

"When we were doing *2*, Bob already saw this as a trilogy," former Dimension Films president Cary Granat says. "There was no question."

"We really wanted it to be Wes and Kevin," former Dimension exec Richard Potter says. But, even so, time was of the essence. "It was kind of like, 'Wes is hot again, he's super-hot. We don't want to lose him, and who knows what the actors' availability will be.' You strike when the iron is hot."

The treatment Williamson had written was mostly tossed aside because of the Columbine High School massacre in 1999. No one wanted to make a movie about kids being murdered by their classmates, and who could blame them.

"We had a really cool idea of what the third movie should be, and we were really excited about the concept. Then Columbine happened. That basically threw out the general idea of what *Scream 3* was going to be," says Julie Plec, who's credited on the movie but was already working with Williamson by this point. "Bob was again saying it has to shoot in this window with Courteney and Neve, and Kevin said, 'I can't write a whole new script in this time. I am not personally, emotionally, or creatively available to do that.' They decided to proceed anyway, which I think was the heartbreak."

"It happened a lot, the 'We can do it without you,'" producer Cathy Konrad says. "There was this sense that now that there was a formula for this movie, and certain things were in place, that it was something that you could duplicate. Somebody else could do it."

Dimension brought in Ehren Kruger. Now he's an established screenwriter with films like *The Ring* and *Top Gun: Maverick* on his résumé, but back then he was beginning his rise and had impressed Dimension execs with his script for *Reindeer Games.*

"Kevin wasn't available, and Bob gave Ehren the job to write it in two weeks—and he did," executive producer Marianne Maddalena says. "Of course, we assumed we would then have Ehren around to do rewrites, but Bob immediately stole him away and put him on *Reindeer Games* and a hundred million other movies. Bob would take a writer and just work them to death, like he did with Kevin. He left us with no one. So, we hired Laeta Kalogridis, and we had to write as we prepped."

It wasn't exactly the best timing for Wes Craven to make the movie either.

"*Music of the Heart* and *Scream 3* completely overlapped," recalls post-production coordinator Tina Anderson. "Still to this day I have this schedule that I did for August 1999. I color-coded it. We were shooting these days, and then on Thursdays and Fridays we had post on *Music of the Heart.*"

Co–executive producer Stuart Besser puts it bluntly: "Nobody wanted to do *Scream 3* at the time. It wasn't a labor of love. Everybody was bought, and I don't mean that in a derogatory manner toward any of the actors or Wes or any of us. There wasn't a script that people gravitated toward, so giving them the money was a way to get them there. We all worked hard because that's what we were paid to do. The actors didn't phone it in by any stretch of the imagination."

Still, the endless changes made it near impossible to plan ahead.

"There were rewrites happening the morning of," Besser says. "We almost were given a concept of what the script would be, and we built sets and prepared based on that conceptual idea. Then pages would come in and the actors would get them before coming to set. The budget was less restrained because everybody knew we didn't know what we were doing. Are we gonna build this whole neighborhood on the stage? Are we just building a piece of it? What are we doing? Are we running down Hollywood Boulevard?"

Besser continues, "I can't think of one moment on *Scream 1* when there was a rewrite. There were some pages, but it was minimal and it was embraced. *Scream 3* was not that. It was a payday. It's not as intense, it's not as different. The original one brought back that genre. Now you're competing with other films that have picked up on that. If it isn't on the paper, you're in trouble—and the paper kept coming the night before and the day of."

"We had a trailer for Laeta near our offices and we would fill it full of food and she would just stay in there to write," Maddalena says. "Before shooting we'd be on a conference call with Bob about the pages and he would scream at us for two hours and then we had to go on the set. He didn't like this in the script, and he didn't like that. So, it was really hard. I wouldn't say it was a disaster, because we still had fun, but it was harder. We didn't have Kevin, so we missed him a lot, and then Bob stole Ehren after two weeks. Who does that to a director?"

"Mostly Ehren kind of ran wild with it," Williamson says. "Wes did a lot of development. All that stuff with Sidney's mother and the dream sequence, none of that was me. I don't know anything about that movie. I couldn't tell you who the killer was or what the motive was."

Maybe that's lucky for him, because the motive is one of the more criticized aspects of *Scream 3*—for several reasons. Starting with the most straightforward: It retconned a new character into the canon and essentially rewrote the motive of the first killers, Billy and Stu.

Laeta Kalogridis, who is technically uncredited on *Scream 3*, explained to filmmakers of the *Still Screaming* documentary how the "secret half brother out for revenge" plot was born.

"Ehren did a partial script. It wasn't finished when I came on. The ending was missing, which was an issue," Kalogridis said, laughing. "I started trying to shape, I think more than anything else, the latter half of it with Wes."

She said Craven wanted the story to return to the beginning, looping back around to how it all started. "The best way to get there, to how everything began, was to literally make it about that same story, about her mother and about her mother's behavior, who she was and what she'd done," Kalogridis said.

It does fit into the meta mood of the franchise. As Randy Meeks explains in a posthumous video message to his friends, "If you find yourself dealing with an unexpected backstory and a preponderance of exposition, then the sequel rules do not apply because you are not dealing with a sequel. You are dealing with the concluding chapter of a trilogy. That's right. It's a rarity in the horror field, but it does exist, and it's a force to be reckoned with—because true trilogies are all about going back to the beginning and discovering something that wasn't true from the get-go."

Potter quit working for Dimension during development of *Scream 3*. He was around long enough to see where the story was heading, and he wasn't a fan—especially since he knew what Williamson's original plans were.

"I think they made a good movie. I think Scott Foley, in particular, really does a great job with that role. The cameos in it are amazing. There is nothing about the movie *as a movie* that I can say I don't like, but it's not where the *Scream* movies were headed.

"My other issue with *Scream 3* is that it makes *Scream 1* not make sense. I just don't buy that Roman convinced some kid he'd never met that he needs to kill Sidney's mother."

Potter explains, "Billy is a psycho, and a psychiatrist could tell you about a thing called the folie à deux, which is a shared psychosis. In a real folie à deux, what would happen is you separate the two of them and the weaker one recovers. Billy is a psycho. Stu shares the psychosis with Billy. So, he will do the things that Billy wants done when they're together. If you were to separate them, over time Stu would have recovered and Billy would still have been a psycho. Kevin wrote a brilliant folie à deux movie. I like *Scream 3*. I can watch it and enjoy it, but it doesn't make sense."

In case you were wondering, Skeet Ulrich hasn't seen *Scream 3* and had no idea that the story involved retroactively giving his character a new motive. (I asked him what he thinks about it, assuming people have brought it up to him over the years. And, well, you know what they say about making assumptions.)

"Wow, okay," Ulrich says. "That's new to me. I don't know. My creation of Billy was drawn from one script; obviously the other one didn't exist. I guess I don't think much about it, to be honest. I haven't had more than ten seconds yet to consider it, but it's intriguing."

NEVE CAMPBELL, COURTENEY COX, DAVID ARQUETTE, AND, OF COURSE, Roger L. Jackson all reprised their roles for *Scream 3*—and even Jamie Kennedy had a cameo as the dearly departed Randy courtesy of that video message delivered by his younger sister Martha Meeks, played by Heather Matarazzo.

"I got a call from my manager that Wes Craven had asked if I would be open to playing Jamie Kennedy's sister in *Scream*," Matarazzo says. Other than that, she knew next to nothing about her character. "Everything was very secretive, as it still is, but I remember that they said, 'You're going to be working with Courteney and David and Neve,' and I was obviously to the moon about that. Rising tides raise all ships, and I feel that working with Wes and those three individuals definitely raised my ship just by being in their presence. My biggest memory is not necessarily a visual or a physical memory but more of an energetic one. I remember that they made me feel at home."

She continues, "And I remember thinking, 'Oh my God, am I gonna get killed? What's this gonna be?' It didn't end up being any of what I thought it might be. I just remember being very happy and excited to be a part of a story and a franchise that was as terrifying as it was comedic."

Except for the cameos, casting pros Lisa Beach and Sarah Katzman remember everyone else auditioning. "There was no such thing as self-tape back then, really," Beach says. "I remember on *Scream 3* there were late nights with the double-videotape-machine transfer in real time with twenty-five people on a tape who each did a five-minute thing. Those were long days."

This time around they had to cast not only the movie itself, but also the movie within the movie.

"In one way it was easier, because we could give the Courteney Cox material to the actors to read for Gale," Katzman remembers. "When we got down to the final callbacks, we actually used the real material and they had to come into the office and the whole works."

"Wes was simply lovely," remembers Parker Posey, who plays actress Jennifer Jolie, who plays the *Stab* equivalent of Gale Weathers. "I was trepidatious about the role because I didn't want to be scared all the time. I'm a sensitive one. Wes assured me I'd be fine. The thing I remember most is talking about why horror movies were so popular, how much fun it was to see the first *Scream* in Chelsea when it came out, the cultural splash, or group awareness, of the fun of screaming together in a movie theater with other people. And, of course, the sense of humor in the film, how they rode comedy and horror at the same time."

Emily Mortimer was in L.A. to visit her then-boyfriend, now husband, whom she'd met in London on Kenneth Branagh's musical *Love's Labour's Lost*. Her agent set up some meetings while she was in town, and one of them was *Scream 3*.

"I was completely certain I wasn't going to get the part because it was this fiendishly ambitious actress from Bakersfield. I had never even heard of Bakersfield. I didn't know what that was or where that was or what that meant," Mortimer says. "I remember sitting in the corridor waiting to go in, and there were all these girls that were very much Californian beauties. I was this kind of skinny, very pale English girl with yellow teeth. I was sure that this was never gonna happen. I've found there's a kind of freedom to having zero expectations and just thinking, 'I'm so not right for this and I'll never get it.' You throw caution to the wind a little bit."

Whatever she did worked, and she was cast as Angelina Tyler, the actress who replaced Tori Spelling as Sidney in the *Stab* universe. She remembers everyone thinking their character was the killer because no one had the full script.

"They didn't give us the end. It was cleverly written, I think, so that all of us were performing as if we were the murderer," Mortimer says. "I was really upset when I realized I was going to get killed. I was like, 'Oh shit. I thought it was me.' Then I thought, 'Oh my God, I would've performed that completely differently if I thought I wasn't the person that did the killing.'"

Ironically, Scott Foley had a similar reaction when he found out he *was* Ghostface, which didn't happen until about two weeks into filming.

Foley had been on set rehearsing and stopped to chat with Maddalena and Craven before heading back to base camp.

"We talked about who knows what for a few minutes and, as I was about to leave, something was mentioned that seemed like insider information," Foley remembers. "I kind of smiled and nodded along and I think she caught my reaction. She then looked at me with a wry smile and said, 'You don't know, do you?' I responded that I wasn't sure what she was talking about, and it was then that both she and Wes let on that I was the killer."

It was a shock, but it didn't change how he approached his character.

"I remember thinking of all of the ways that I might be able to play with that information, to lean in a bit to what I now knew," Foley says. "I ultimately decided that if it wasn't important enough for them to let me know from the beginning, then it probably wasn't important to any choices I either had made or might make going forward."

———

EVEN WITH ALL ITS CAMP, THE PLOT OF *SCREAM 3* IS DARK. ITS META-commentary on the treatment of women in Hollywood isn't limited to Maureen Prescott's newly revealed backstory. It's also reflected in ambitious young actress Angelina Tyler.

"Only in Hollywood do we try to make it that the highest thing that a woman could ever aspire to is being an actress," Potter laments. "What was Sidney's mother's dream? To be an actress. Hollywood is always patting itself on the back and saying it's so great. That always stuck in my craw."

For Mortimer, playing an actress who's playing the fictional version of another character in the same movie was surreal, as was being killed by Ghostface in a literal haunted mansion.

"I can remember just running, running, running, and being chased down this corridor. It felt almost like therapy or something because you never get chased in life, hopefully, other than when you're a child," Mortimer remembers. "It was such a hugely weird and wonderful experience. I just remember laughing and laughing and screaming and screaming and being totally out of breath and feeling like a child again. My God, that felt so good. I can remember saying you should be able to do this for therapy. You should be chased around the house and then got. It gets things out, somehow."

There was one thing that made all that running more difficult. Well, two, technically.

"I had these huge fake boobs," Mortimer says. "They gave me chicken fillets. I was like, 'Oh God, as I'm running along one of them is going to slip up.' It was a constant stress, trying to manage fake boobs, because they didn't have the best technology. It was the beginning of those chicken fillet days and they were always popping out of your bra."

Mortimer also vividly remembers her line "I did not fuck that pig Milton to get a leading role just to die here with second-rate celebrities like you two!"

"I'm never shy of doing weird stuff, but that was quite shocking that I had to say that," she remembers. "It felt quite like, 'Whoa,' you know? There was something fantastically shameless about that line."

It's a line that resonates differently in hindsight—as does Milton's gross monologue in his lakeview high-rise office after Gale, Dewey, and Jennifer Jolie confronted him about hiding that he knew Sidney's mother when she was an aspiring actress going by the name of Rina Reynolds.

It was in the '70s, everything was different. I was well-known for my parties. Rina knew what they were. It was for girls like her to meet men, men who could get them parts, if they made the right impression. Nothing happened to her that she didn't invite, in one way or another, no matter what she said afterwards.

After a brief interruption by Gale, he continues:

I'm saying things got out of hand. Maybe they did take advantage of her. Maybe the sad truth is, this is not the city for innocents. No charges were brought. And the bottom line is, Rina Reynolds wouldn't play by the rules. You wanna get ahead in Hollywood, you gotta play the game, or go home.

If you think about the events of the *Scream* franchise chronologically it's even more fucked up: Sixty people and counting have died because of what happened to Maureen Prescott in Hollywood. She brought her trauma back to Woodsboro, she had an affair with Billy Loomis's father, and—regardless of whether you believe Roman Bridger tipped him off or not—it led to her murder and a spiral of death and destruction that has now marked four decades.

"*Scream 3* hits harder now more than ever," Blumhouse film exec Ryan Turek says. "I was like, 'Lance Henriksen is playing Harvey Weinstein, straight up.' That's what this movie is about. What had happened to Sid's mom, all of that stuff pre–Me Too, is definitely prescient. It's super wild and it had this predictive quality to it that we were like, 'Oh my God.' Tangentially speaking, Wes always had a nature for doing that in his movies. He's not a cinematic Nostradamus, but he was just tapped into the world."

"People comment on that like, 'Oh, the irony of Harvey Weinstein producing that movie.' Harvey had really no interest in this," Potter says. "His name went on everything that Bob's name went on and Bob's name went on everything Harvey did—but I don't even know if Harvey read the script. I mean, Harvey really didn't like Dimension. It stole focus from Miramax, and every time Bob was successful it stole focus from him personally.

"Let's be clear about one thing: What Harvey did was not the casting couch. The casting couch is a shitty, immoral transaction. The woman knows what she's going there for, and the guy knows what's expected of him to deliver afterward. Harvey is a convicted rapist. You can argue the morality of the casting couch, you could argue the power dynamics of it. It's all wrong, but in the casting couch situation the woman knows why she is going there, and she has the right at any point to say no."

LIKE THE FIRST TWO FILMS, *SCREAM 3* HAS A DRAMATIC OPENING KILL—BUT this time the victim is a returning character: accused murderer turned vindicated talk show host Cotton Weary.

"In the third one, I kind of didn't want to do it anymore. I felt like I was a big enough character that it might be meaningful to take me out early on as a surprise open kill," actor Liev Schreiber says. "I wouldn't say it was my idea, but I think I suggested it. I wanted to have an opportunity to be the first killed, so I thought that was kind of fun."

That wasn't the original plan, or even the second— *Scream 3* editor Patrick Lussier says Kevin Williamson's version played like *Alien* and had motion trackers, and another discarded story involved an actor named Ben Damon. Ultimately, they landed on Schreiber's suggestion.

"The Cotton Weary sequence at the beginning was shot over and over. We kept bringing Liev back. The first version did not have the girlfriend in it at all," Lussier says. "It was all from Cotton's point of view, which was a note from Kevin: Don't make this story about rescuing a girl and then just have her be a body coming out of a closet."

They reshot the scene with Kelly Rutherford playing his girlfriend Christine.

"I love the way the sequence ended up," Lussier says. "I think it's great. The whole *100% Cotton* thing was a joke we had during *Scream 2*, that he was going to get his own show called *100% Cotton*."

Script supervisor Sheila Waldron learned some unforgettable wisdom from director Wes Craven while filming that scene. It's the moment when Christine has just gotten out of the shower and is walking down the hall, and the camera shows her point of view as it pushes in.

"Wes said, 'There is nothing as scary as a dolly into a closed door,'" Waldron remembers. "Whatever is on the other side is way scarier in your brain than anything you would see. The approach to the door is the fear. As soon as the door opens, you're either afraid or not afraid—but the approach, the tension leading up to it, that dolly in, is what grabs you. It's the thing that makes you catch your breath in your throat, like 'What's behind the door? Is it the thing that that singular viewer fears the most?' I always thought that was so fucking brilliant. You'll never be able to capture everybody's fear once that door opens, but the approach, the dolly in, is what will get you. He was just smart. He was innately aware of what is scary. There is nothing scarier than a dolly into a closed door. I'll never forget it."

The endless script revisions were also scary for Waldron, who was tasked with making sure there weren't any continuity errors in the film.

"Sometimes they'd want to put somebody across town, and I was like, 'We just saw them in the next room. They're not across town.' It's a big deal when you throw some pages in there you think might be a fun little run and it throws everything off, because it has to make sense at the end. Hopefully it did. You have to keep track of all the logic of it, and that was always challenging. That and blood levels."

"More blood" was a common refrain on all Craven's shoots—not because he wanted to lean into the gore but because it doesn't look as dramatic on camera as you'd think.

"We would go take to take, he'd throw in more blood, and he'd just tell me not to worry about it. I still worry about everything, but he taught me how to figure out what's really important in a scene," Waldron says. "People think we're exaggerating but it was gallon jugs of blood. It just made him happy. We used to do it in stages so he would have choices in the edit room."

"Wes always loved when I was on set because he knew that if he said 'a lot of blood,' I would put even more than I thought he would want," says special effects makeup artist Greg Nicotero. "The thing about the blood, if you really think about it from a filmmaking standpoint, is it's like the barrel in *Jaws*. You see the barrel on the ocean and you know that the shark is nearby. When you have these people that are covered in blood, it's implying the significance of the wounds and the devastation. The more blood there is, the more the audience reacts."

CHAPTER ELEVEN

THE END OF THE TRILOGY

Because *Scream 3* was set in Hollywood, shooting it there made perfect sense—and it added to the campy, extra-self-referential mood.

"The shoot was fun and loose," Parker Posey says. "Scary at times—one of the locations was said to be haunted—but the team of *Scream* was fantastic."

The location she's referring to is John Milton's mansion from the third act of the film, the one with all the secret passages and creepy two-way mirrors. It's a monstrous 1923 Mediterranean-style estate on Micheltorena Street in Silver Lake that's now a hotel dubbed the Paramour Estate. It was built as the home of oil heiress Daisy Canfield and silent film star Antonio Moreno, and has since been a convent, the fictional Hillcrest Academy in *Halloween H20*, and the set of a Britney Spears music video.

"It was a great house," recalls set designer Bruce Alan

Miller. "There had to be the secret door in the library and that house happened to have a door that went outside; it might have been the library or a little room off of the main hallway. So I could cover that door and that's the bookshelf that they escape behind.

"We had to build the bedroom that had the mirrors that you could watch someone in bed on stage, and it had to be made to look like it was all in the same house. That's a set designer's dream. The final scene that happens in the bar slash movie theater in the house, that was all built on a set too."

Of course, shooting in L.A. also had the advantage of being near home base for most of the cast and crew. Wes Craven—who lived in a Hollywood Hills home that had been owned by actor Steve McQueen—could walk to work on days they filmed the scene at Jennifer Jolie's house. You know, the one that explodes after they get a fax from the killer—after the power goes out.

"As much as *Scream 3* was a big mess, there was something really fun about shooting it all at home, and being in a really good place and not in some dramatic moment in my life," David Arquette says. "It took this turn because of the state of world, and there was a lot of humor involved. There are moments in it where we were like, 'Oh, this is like *Scooby-Doo* or something.' Wes also had fun with that. *Scream 3* was fun because it was just silly."

As was typical with Craven's projects, the fun extended off set too.

"We were pals," *Scream 3* script supervisor Sheila Waldron says of the director. "We were shooting at this mansion, and we were on three weeks of nights or something. The lighting took forever, no offense to Peter Deming, so Wes and I got bored. We would run around and chase each other with a video camera through this elaborate foresty backyard and do our own little *Blair Witch Project*. After the movie was over, Wes had quadruple bypass surgery. So, I always think I could have killed Wes Craven chasing him like a killer in the woods while we filmed each other doing scary bits."

Waldron joined the crew on *Music of the Heart*—where she was nicknamed "Stella" thanks to Meryl Streep pretending not to know her name and assistant director Nick Mastandrea running with it. It wasn't their only inside joke—far from it, actually.

"We ended up making a whole language for ourselves," she remembers. "Nick has a whole set of Nickisms, phrases that he would say that nobody else on the planet says. Wes typed up a glossary of all the words, every Nickism he could think of, with the meanings attached to them."

Craven started the glossary off with a note: "This is a final compilation of Nickisms as jotted down by Yours Truly on the sets of SCREAM and SCREAM the SEQUEL. It is offered as a language guide. No responsibility is assumed for accuracy or completeness, as the vernacular described herein is highly organic, and the process of collection ongoing," Craven wrote on September 1, 1997. He ends his preface with, "Nick is a treasure that this is one small attempt to preserve."

Some of them were references to specific people: line producer Daniel Lupi was "El Cheapo," Marianne Maddalena and Cathy Konrad were "the Hollywood Sisters," and to take "Dan Pills" was to be extra enthusiastic like Dan Arredondo, a beloved crew member who died in 2003.

Then there were phrases like "couldn't throw a meatball past a hungry dog," which more or less means the same thing as "as dumb as a pigeon with a nail through its head."

They were all entertaining, and some of them proved to be extremely helpful in practice.

"We developed a word for when you're talking shit about someone and the person you are talking about is coming up behind you," says Waldron. "So, if somebody is coming up and you go 'posy,' you stop talking or you switch the subject immediately. That has saved us on many occasions."

There is a backstory to this one, but don't worry, it wasn't in reference to Parker Posey. They wouldn't have dared. After all, if there's one unifying factor among all the polarized opinions of *Scream 3*, it's that everyone loves Jennifer Jolie.

"It's actually aged better than I thought it would," says *It's a Wonderful Knife* writer Michael Kennedy. "It's still so goofy and it's not scary, but Parker Posey is reason enough to watch that movie."

"I absolutely adore the movie," says Blumhouse film exec Ryan Turek. "I will fight anybody over *Scream 3*. Parker Posey is an MVP of that movie. She is so good. My favorite line reading is when she's like, 'My lawyer liked that.'"

That's the part where Gale Weathers is fed up with her copycat and punches her in the face. She says Courteney Cox actually hit her too, accidentally.

"I laughed so hard because I had a premonition it would happen," Posey says. "She didn't really sock me, though. It was a brush, but it did hit me. It was late!"

Everyone has a favorite Jennifer Jolie line—but Posey's is more of a vibe.

"I remember Wes let me mouth Courteney's line 'Dewey' when she said it, as if I was so in character that I *was* her."

Director of photography Peter Deming remembers shooting the scene where Gale Weathers and Jennifer Jolie realize that Angelina Tyler has been killed and look down and scream as they see her body being pulled away.

"We were doing the shot looking up and they had to appear over the banister. The first four or five takes Parker just cracked up laughing," Deming says. "We were like, 'What's going on, Parker? Why are you laughing?' She goes, 'This is like the most fun I've ever had making a movie in my entire life.' She was just having a blast."

"There's a lot of energy in making a performance intense in that genre," Posey says. "One of the things that made me laugh was that I could be a *Scooby-Doo* character come to life—and also break the fourth wall a bit with the audience by doing really ridiculous things you'd see in a cartoon, like when I jump into the bodyguard's arms. But when I died, Wes was very serious with me and said, 'This is not funny at all and to be taken seriously.' I assured him I was scared and only wanted to do two takes, please."

———

LATE *STAR WARS* ICON CARRIE FISHER HAS A META CAMEO AS HER own doppelgänger. She plays studio employee and former actress Bianca Burnette, who lost out on the role of Princess Leia in the *Scream* universe.

"I went to Carrie Fisher's trailer first thing to introduce myself," Parker Posey remembers. "I was a fan of her, and her books especially, and was thrilled to meet her. She had a carton of Marlboro Lights, or was it Camel Lights—but what stood out was a few boxes of Froot Loops and a case of Diet Coke. I started laughing and she did too. She said, 'You know when they ask you if you want anything in your trailer? This is what I asked for.'

"We laughed so hard in our scene—but my favorite was being with her in the makeup trailer and then getting invited to her parties and watching old movies on her bed smoking cigarettes. I loved how she engaged with her surroundings and others. She was very funny—her mind was quick and she had funny observations. She had a continual story going; she talked about her mother and Hollywood. She was entertaining. A big storyteller, vibrant and creative."

Fisher wrote her own dialogue for the movie—and it created an awkward situation for Craven, who handled it brilliantly on the spot.

In the film, when Gale and Jennifer approach Bianca, they seem to recognize her and it's implied that they think she's famous actress Carrie Fisher. "I've been hearing it all my life," Fisher's character says. "I was up for Princess Leia. I was this close. So, who gets it? The one who sleeps with George Lucas."

It cuts to a reaction shot and Gale says she didn't mean to bring up a sore subject.

"Sure you didn't," Fisher says dryly. "None of them did."

Sheila Waldron remembers it vividly, and cites it as another example of Craven's cleverness. *Scream 3* filmed a couple of years after Fisher split from CAA partner and mega-agent Bryan Lourd, the father of their daughter, Billie Lourd, and she infused a little bit too much of her personal life into the on-screen story.

"Carrie Fisher wrote her own dialogue. She went on and on about, 'I'm not that actress. She's got a great life. She has a husband,' and in the middle of the weird bit of dialogue she pulled a cigarette out and lit it.

"Wes knew he was going to cut the middle out and he didn't want that cigarette to suddenly appear in her hand. Instead of saying, 'I'm gonna cut that part out,' he just said, 'Oh, it'd be great if you could light that cigarette right away.' So, he wouldn't have a jump cut with the cigarette. He was so smart. I learned so much from him—not only about where you're going to cut and what happens in a cut, but how to deal with actors when they really want to dig into things and you've got to dig around whatever they're doing."

Lussier says the reveal on *Scream 3* was also difficult to cut, mostly because of where it deviated from the first two films. "You only had one killer. You didn't have a reveal upon a reveal, which the other movies have," he says. "Its trick was it was trying to say that Roman was part of the whole story, which I think works to some degree."

Who Roman truly is, his connection to Sidney, and his motivation for going on a killing spree took quite a bit of explanation.

James A. Janisse and Chelsea Rebecca, the husband-wife duo behind the popular *Dead Meat* YouTube channel and podcast, point out that Sidney and Roman never shared a scene before the reveal. In *Scream 2*, as soon as she saw Mrs. Loomis she knew exactly who it was. In *Scream 3*, not so much.

"Roman's motivation is cool, but the out of nowhere existence of him is like, okay, sure," says Janisse.

"I love *3*, it's silly," Rebecca says. "It is so funny that there is a Ghostface reveal where Sidney is like, 'I don't know who this guy is.' They have never met. It is just a random guy until he explains who he is."

Foley couldn't just stand there and monologue as his confused half-sister stares in bewilderment, so he worked with Craven on how to incorporate action into the reveal.

"I remember that scene being a beast! The dialogue was mostly exposition, but it was important," Foley says. "Once the set was ready, Wes, our first AD, the DP, and I spent a lot of time in there while the crew was lighting other scenes. Wes had ideas about how I might use the room, how I would tear it apart looking for Sidney. I remember wanting it to be as organic as possible and not wanting to time out certain lines of dialogue with specific actions or locations."

The hours of prepping paid off.

"It was definitely a challenge, but by the time Wes called 'action,' we'd figured out how to do it all in mostly one take," Foley says. "Of course, there were multiple cameras, but for the most part, until Sidney pops up from behind the bar, it was a 'one-er!'"

SCREAM IS A SEND-UP OF SLASHERS LIKE THE FICTIONAL IN-WORLD *Stab* franchise, so another way the third film leans into the meta nature of the franchise is by making fun of itself.

"You're trying to give it a different feel for the movie within the movie, because you didn't want them to run together. The title lent itself to mid-'80s schlocky horror films," Deming explains. "In the third one, that really got ramped up because we were making fun of the actresses who are in it and the executives who are on set. You can't hit too close to home, but you can certainly pull from experience."

"We love the third film. In some respects, we put ourselves on trial," Cary Granat says. "The movie is about the studio making the film of the events. Obviously it's meta. We were like, 'Without going overboard and becoming a Fellini movie, how do we step into that with the *Stab* franchise and own that process?' I've never been part of a franchise that so quickly responded to the times and the reaction to it, put it in the film and then made the film about it. *Scream 1*, *2*, and *3* are very unique in that sense."

With so many references to moviemaking, Patrick Dempsey's Detective Mark Kincaid creates some balance and brings the story back to reality a bit.

"Any time you get movies that become too 'Hollywood inside baseball,' they run the risk of being too in love with themselves. The second you get too in-joke, you betray a good chunk of the audience. His character is a great way to step outside that," editor Patrick Lussier says.

"I think one of the first scenes shot was the scene with Patrick and Neve in his office, and he didn't know whether he was the killer. He didn't know anything that happened before that scene or after that scene, and he plays it in such a 'you don't know what to think of him' way. Is he the leading man, is he a psycho, is he this, is he that? That is my favorite performance in the whole film. I think he brought so much more gravity to it."

He also gave Sidney a glimpse of a future on the other side of all this tragedy.

"I'm glad he survived in the end. There were two versions of that last scene, one where he is in it and one where he isn't," Lussier says. "We used the one where he was in it because that's a hopeful thing. The idea that Sidney gets a happy ending—because, at the time, that was the end of the three movies and that was that."

NOTHING IS ABSOLUTE, BUT JUST ABOUT EVERYONE WHO'D WORKED IN the franchise up to that point was sure *Scream 3* was the end.

An interesting thing happens in the *Scream 2* director's commentary as the credits roll: Craven, Lussier, and Maddalena predict the future. They recorded it right after *Scream 3* had wrapped and were lamenting the end of the run.

MADDALENA: I'm sorry it's over.

LUSSIER: Until *Scream 4*, perhaps.

MADDALENA: Maybe in ten years, right.

CRAVEN: Ten years. *Scream Redux.*

MADDALENA: It's a shame that we killed Cotton, though, because it would be fun to see what his show would be like then.

"There's always a way," jokes Craven, after suggesting that he could come back in a prequel or as a ghost, or maybe Cotton faked his death.

LUSSIER: I'm sure many a script will be crossing the desks at the Miramax offices.

MADDALENA: Even though we all say we're not going to do another one, you never know.

CRAVEN: Oh really? Is this an announcement?

MADDALENA: I'm just saying, you never know. Certainly not in the next five years, but you never know.

They're kidding around, but on some level they must have thought it wasn't beyond the realm of possibility because they made sure to time-stamp it. They finished *Scream 2* just before Christmas in 1997 but didn't record the commentary until St. Patrick's Day 2000. *Scream 4* was filmed in the summer of 2010, almost exactly ten years later.

CHAPTER TWELVE

A NEW NIGHTMARE

Kevin Williamson thought *Scream* was over when the trilogy ended, but roughly a decade later a new story idea came to him. He was still under an overall deal with Dimension Films, so he thought it through and sketched out a vision for the future of the franchise.

"I pitched *Scream 4* and Bob Weinstein said, 'Well, you need to pitch it to Wes.' So, Wes and I went to dinner, and I started pitching the opening scene. Because I was nervous, he stopped me and he goes, 'Okay, we're making this movie. Now keep going.'"

The movie picks up just before the fifteenth anniversary of the first Ghostface killing spree. It's become something of a morbid holiday in Woodsboro, and the next generation views their town's bloody tragedy as more of a novelty than anything else. That is, until Sidney's cousin Jill, played by Emma Roberts, and her social circle become the new targets.

Time had passed and Hollywood had resumed killing

off hot teenagers. Just about every slasher franchise was being revived, including *Halloween*, *The Texas Chain Saw Massacre*, *Prom Night*, and profitable but critically panned crossover *Freddy vs. Jason*. The horror genre as a whole had gotten bloodier and darker with the massive success of films like *Hostel* and *Saw*. So, any zeitgeist momentum against Ghostface returning to terrorize the students of Woodsboro High School was long gone, and Williamson was able to use some of his *Scream 3* ideas that were scrapped when Ehren Kruger took over.

"I pitched *4*, *5*, and *6* together as a trilogy, loosely," Williamson says. "The motive in my original *Scream 3*, and the theme of the celebrity victim, I was able to put into *Scream 4*."

The opening of *Scream 4*—the movie within the movie within the movie—was written by Williamson, but it's not what he first had in mind. In an earlier version Sidney takes on Ghostface in a big chase scene in her house.

"She gets stabbed several times and you think she's dead, and then she rises up and she kills Ghostface," Williamson says, recalling his original idea. "Then it went dark, and it said, 'Two years later,' and then you come back in. That killer was connected to *Scream 4*."

Before *Scream 3* moved forward without Williamson, he had talked with Neve Campbell about who Sidney was and where she would be in her life at that time. "She was like, 'Well, she's a survivor. So, I think I'd see her working with other survivors and dealing with trauma.' You know how Sidney was trapped away in the cabin being a crisis counselor? That was all Neve's doing."

Williamson remembered that conversation when it

came time to write *Scream 4* and decided Sidney should be an author, a parallel of sorts to Gale Weathers writing her series of books following the Woodsboro murders. Gale and Dewey's relationship struggles were meant to be a larger part of the story, but that was scaled back.

"There's an original draft of *Scream 4* where their relationship is more front and center, their dynamic and who they are to each other and how unhappy she is in Woodsboro. She's kind of given up her career to be with Dewey, and that frustration leaks into their marriage and creates all sorts of problems. That got subplotted too much," Williamson says. "At the end of the day, you can't ignore Ghostface. It's not a domestic drama. So, I had to backseat that a little bit."

In his initial idea for *Scream 5*, Jill survived and went on to college as a celebrity victim, just like she wanted. Or so she thought.

"Everyone wants to be her friend, and then someone has figured her out," Williamson says. "Someone knows she killed all those people in Woodsboro and that she got away with it. So, in a weird way it's killer against killer and Ghostface starts killing all of her new friends."

Scream 6 would have ended the trilogy and focused on Sidney and her love story.

"*Scream 6* was just about Sidney Prescott truly finding happiness and rising out of her trauma and putting Ghostface behind her, once and for all. I had *5* much more in my head than *6*. Bob made me go pitch that to investors at a film market. I'll never forget that. I was like, 'What am I doing? These are all businesspeople. They're not gonna want to hear it.' That's when it was all ending."

It wasn't long before Williamson was experiencing "we don't need you" déjà vu. He was no longer a fledgling writer trying to break into the business. His new series *The Vampire Diaries* had premiered the year before and was a bona fide hit—and he couldn't be at Weinstein's beck and call.

"Kevin had other responsibilities. He could not be as present as Bob required in terms of the rewrites," *Scream 4* producer Iya Labunka says. "Wes had the utmost respect for Kevin. Frankly, if it had just been the two of them, it would have been a completely different experience. But Kevin was not available—and he made it very, very clear he would not be available—because of the way the schedule was going, because Bob kept asking for different things and rewrites. It was untenable."

Williamson understands the studio was trying to protect its increasingly valuable asset, but still, he was facing a veritable Sophie's choice. "It was no longer this little script that I conjured up in a Westwood house-sitting situation. It was now this huge financial investment, and they were throwing everything they could at the wall," Williamson says. "I understand we were behind. They were in preproduction and they needed a script and I was torn between worlds, between *Vampire Diaries* and *Scream*. *Vampire Diaries* was so massively important to me. That show brought me back to life in so many ways, and I loved it with all my heart. I loved *Scream*, but it seemed like my past. I was in this horrible conundrum. I was working as fast as I could. I was dancing as fast as I could."

It wasn't fast enough, and he never could have anticipated what came next.

"I had just turned in a draft and they gave me notes for a rewrite of *Scream 4*," Williamson says. "I was in Atlanta with *The Vampire Diaries* at the W hotel the morning when Wes called. I remember this phone call very clearly.

"He said, 'Kevin, I just have to tell you this. We have been through too much together.' And I go, 'What? What is it? I'll have the pages for you by the weekend, I promise. I just need the weekend. I can get them to you by Sunday.' And he was like, 'No, no, no. That's not why I'm calling. I need to tell you this: I just got pages from another writer. It seems like Bob has had other people writing *Scream 4* as well.' I went, 'What?! Are you kidding me? *I'm* writing *Scream 4*.'

"I got really panicked and I got scared. I got upset. After all of this, they had another writer? Was it like a bake-off? Like, the best scenes get to be in the movie?"

Williamson continues, "Wes was like, 'Iya made me call you. I was hesitant because I didn't want to upset you.' He was such a fatherly figure in a lot of ways—and he was also the director of a movie that had to be made. He's like, 'I'm in a hard place. I have a movie to make, Kevin. I have to film something and you're not here.'"

Labunka says Craven would have made the call even if she hadn't nudged him because he knew it was the right thing to do. "Wes loved Kevin and felt so horrible about the way that this was developing and how Kevin was being treated by Bob. It was very, very toxic."

"That was the moment that changed everything for my relationship with Dimension, and that story has never been told. I was never going to tell that story ever, but that's the truth. That's what happened," Williamson says. "It's legendary that I had a big fight with the studio. That's where it all started. I said, 'I need to get out. Let me just walk away.' That's when I negotiated my way out of my overall deal with Dimension. I gave up all my rights to *Scream*. I gave up any sort of first refusal, or any other rights that typically a writer has. I gave them up so that I could walk free out the door."

Bob Weinstein hadn't just brought in one other writer to cover his bases, by the way. When all was said and done, Williamson and at least seven other people had put pen to paper on *Scream 4*, which created a headache for WGA writing credits.

"Written by," "story by," and "screenplay by" may seem like interchangeable euphemisms, but they each come with specific writers guild requirements—and the distinction is important for both building a writing career and calculating residual payments. If there's a dispute about who deserves credit for a project, a Writers Guild of America arbitration committee will decide the matter.

"When I got the arbitration papers, there were eight writers and they brought in stacks of scripts. I just couldn't even read them," Williamson remembers. "Usually, you get your lawyer to write a letter and say 'Here's why I deserve credit' because these residuals are everything to writers. All those writers were writing letters, and I just said, 'No, you guys decide. I'm letting this go. This has hurt me. I don't care anymore.' I just washed my hands of it. Then it turned out that I got sole credit."

Craven likely had something to do with that.

"The WGA wanted to give Wes writing credit because of the amount of writing that he had contributed," Labunka recalls. "He was actually the one that said no, which I thought was quite generous of him. He was writing every night. I saw a lot of grace under pressure."

That's one of the things that sticks in Ghostface stunt performer Dane Farwell's memory: "A lot of times I would ask him what he'd been up to, and he'd say, 'Writing.' I don't know if somebody was having him change certain things or what, but it seemed like he was writing a lot."

As with *Scream 2* and *3*, not having a completed script before filming created issues for everyone on the production.

"It was insane," Labunka says. "That script was being written until the day it locked, until the last day that we shot."

"For me, it was a little frustrating. If you have ten years, you should really nail a script down before you get back in the saddle," director of photography Peter Deming says. "It's like, is the movie coming together for the right reasons? I mean, sure it's monetary, but also let's make the story great because you're asking people to come back after ten years. I think it's a good film. I think it could have been better. It certainly proved that there was another generation that could take over, which now they are doing."

"The thing about all the *Scream*s, and the thing about working with Wes, is we never panicked and tempers never flared," assistant director Nick Mastandrea says. "We laughed a lot and had a terrific time, but the problem was we just didn't have the script. I was already there on location, trying to do a schedule. I don't think I ever really did a whole board or a schedule for that movie, because I never had a whole script to do it on. It was almost like a week at a time.

"Wes could've gotten really ugly. I mean, it's one thing for me as an AD. I don't have anything to schedule, what am I gonna do? It's another thing as a director to say, 'I'm supposed to be directing a movie for a script that doesn't exist.' I don't think most directors would know how to handle that. We got through it, and that's mainly because of him. I know guys that walk off sets because their coffee is cold, and here's this guy directing a movie where we would get pages and just try and make it as good as possible."

Wes Craven's assistant Carly Feingold was involved with everything from location scouting and casting to costumes and crew staffing. She also helped Frankenstein the script together when locations required changes or shooting schedules meant things needed to be pared down.

"When things had to be rewritten on set that was usually me, because there wasn't a writer there," she says. "We would need dialogue for something, and I would take from Kevin's old drafts because I had everything. I was moving things around to make it work and trying to be respectful of keeping it true to his voice and his tone. I do remember writing a lot for the Stab-a-thon party because whatever was originally there didn't make sense for where we were shooting."

One late night at the house Craven and Labunka were staying in stands out. "At one in the morning, or two in the morning, it started thunderstorming," Feingold remembers. "It was so scary, every huge boom. It would shake the house, and all the lighting, as we're reworking a kill scene."

Labunka remembers it too. "It's one of the great examples of the stamina of Wes Craven," she says. "He was seventy at that point. He shot a full day, which was fourteen hours; he wrote all night with not a moment of sleep; he shot a second day; wrote all night without a moment of sleep; shot a third day; and then collapsed for two days on the weekend. Literally shot, stayed up, shot, stayed up, shot, collapsed."

Even after the blowup with the studio, Williamson did come back to take a pass at the hospital sequence at the end of the film. Originally, because of his idea for the fifth movie, the story ended at the house where Sidney and Jill both survived.

"I did that with Wes because we wanted just one more scary sequence," Williamson says. "Whenever Wes called me, I would say, 'What do you need?' I would do anything for Wes. So, I stayed part of the process through Wes, but not through the studio."

———

PRODUCER CATHY KONRAD ALSO HAD A FALLING–OUT WITH WEINSTEIN between *Scream 3* and *Scream 4*. She learned from press reports that the film was in development without her involvement.

"I sued them," Konrad recalls. She didn't go into details, but it was widely covered at the time. Her suit argued that she had a first opportunity to produce under her contract, and it settled pretty quickly, but it didn't become public until just days before the movie was released. "That was a pretty controversial time for myself and my career. I was really pushing back quite hard with the brothers. I had a lot of other things going on, and they always liked to make things difficult. My experience with *4*, it wasn't a shining time for me.

"There's this picture of me, it's black and white and I'm sitting on the steps of a trailer in a parking lot in the middle of nowhere. I think it was the wardrobe trailer. I'm clearly in a tense conversation, but I'm a dot. I'm this little dot and it just sort of very much summed up how things began to feel. You're getting calls left, right, and center. You're not able to satisfy anybody, it seems. It was a lot of pressure. Those were not fun times. I mean, the cast was always lovely and Wes and his crossword puzzles, all of that was always nice and level, but all the politics just became a bit much to bear."

"I remember when that went down," Williamson says. "Cathy Konrad had called me and was like, 'You know, I'm supposed to be producing *Scream 4*.' And I go, 'Well, me too, but I'm not.' I was the person who didn't get into any drama. I wanted to be so far away from the Weinsteins. The further I was away from them, the better my life was. It was tough because I had this relationship with Wes. I don't want to make this movie with the Weinsteins, but I don't want to let Wes down. I felt like I was made a little bit of a yo-yo, but I navigated it as best I could."

Music supervisor Ed Gerrard was surprised to not be brought on for *Scream 4* too. Dimension wanted to use someone internal as the music supervisor on the film, but because of the relationship he'd built with "Red Right Hand" crooner Nick Cave over more than a decade, he still played an integral role—just not the one he was expecting.

"Nick comes to me and says, 'What's the story with *Scream 4*? Are they going to use you?'" Gerrard recalls. "I'm like, 'Nick, I don't know what to tell you because I don't think I'm going to be involved, but don't let them fuck with you. Don't let your record company or your publishing company take stupid-ass money. This is a character in this film. It should be paid like a character in this film, okay? My opinion is they can't do the movie without it, and I would hold out.' He goes, 'Okay.'"

Gerrard, who became Cave's adviser and intermediary on the proposed deal, suggested a price and it wasn't long before the new music supervisor called him saying it was too steep. Even Bob Weinstein picked up the phone, but Gerrard didn't budge.

It felt like the only person he hadn't spoken with was Craven himself.

Eventually, they made an "okay" offer, which Gerrard says was as if they were licensing a song from "a pretty big rock star for the end title of some stupid movie."

They reached an impasse and Gerrard called Cave to break the news. "I thought there was no way in hell that they could refuse it," Gerrard says. "At that point, Nick was okay with not approving it for the movie. We just felt like they weren't treating him right. Forget the money, because Nick did not give a shit about money. It was the principle of the fact that his song became iconic in a billion-dollar franchise."

That's how *Scream 4* became the only film in the franchise that doesn't feature "Red Right Hand."

"I think if it was up to Wes in *4*, he would've paid whatever we asked him, but the Weinsteins were tough to work with when it came to money and budgets," Gerrard says. "They weren't pleasant guys, and you just didn't want to deal with them."

"Dimension wouldn't pay. That's the long and short of it,"

Labunka says. "We really, really tried to make it work. The budget was absolutely minuscule. There were so many other battles being fought and it was just a hard, hard, hard no."

The score for the movie wasn't treated much differently, and working on the film wasn't a high point for composer Marco Beltrami, who hadn't done a Dimension film in years.

"They were super controlling on *Scream 4*. Plus, they went back to having no budget—after all the money they made," Beltrami says. "I did it because Wes asked me to, but it was definitely not one of my more fun projects. I didn't actually have that much contact with him on it. It was more like 'Here's the film, write the music.' The only people that would call me about music were some stooges for the Weinsteins."

———

BY THE TIME OF THE EVENTS IN *SCREAM 4*, WOODSBORO HIGH IS HOME to a new generation of students. They were too young to understand the Ghostface massacre when it was happening, and the fictional *Stab* franchise has desensitized them to their town's bloody past. Once they had Neve Campbell, Courteney Cox, and David Arquette locked in to return, finding the newcomers proved easy.

"It had a fan base at this point," Feingold remembers. "People wanted to be part of it. People were contacting Dimension being like, 'Hey, what roles are there? I want a role.'"

The good news? *Scream 4* has more speaking characters than any of the other films so far.

Lucy Hale, Shenae Grimes-Beech, Kristen Bell, Anna Paquin, Aimée Teegarden, and Britt Robertson all make an appearance in the cold open, a multitiered sequence that includes clips from two *Stab* films. Emma Roberts and Mary McDonnell play Sidney's cousin and aunt, respectively. Anthony Anderson and Adam Brody are Woodsboro sheriff's deputies, along with Marley Shelton. Alison Brie plays Sidney's insufferable publicist, while Hayden Panettiere, Rory Culkin, Nico Tortorella, Erik Knudsen, and Marielle Jaffe round out Jill's friend group.

"I think Jill was definitely the hardest to cast because we wouldn't tell anyone who the killer was," Feingold says. "I remember it being hard to decide between Emma and Hayden because they were both strong. It was like, 'Who's going to be which part?' One of the decisions to keep Hayden as Kirby was to bring her back because we let her live."

Marley Shelton had gone out for the role of Tatum in *Scream* and, despite not getting it, was a huge fan of the franchise. When the opportunity to audition for *Scream 4* came around, on her birthday no less, she was thrilled.

"I remember telling Wes I had all these different takes on Judy," she says. "I was like, 'I could do it this way, this way, this way, or this way.' And he's like, 'Okay, well, how about just doing it?' He was really funny and really warm. I took a big swing and I didn't hear back until months later."

Shelton was in Budapest on set with her husband, producer Beau Flynn, and her nine-month-old daughter when she got the call that she needed to be in Ann Arbor in just four days.

"I was so jet-lagged and upside down with my brand new baby, but it was all worth it," Shelton remembers. "I'd strap her into the BabyBjörn and we would hang out. There's all this blood and gore and I remember that juxtaposition being really funny, having this cute little baby in the middle of this wacky world with Ghostface and all kinds of carnage."

Rory Culkin missed his audition for *Scream 4* and was going to just forget about the movie until his manager called and talked him into taking it seriously. "She was like, 'Don't let the *4* fool you, don't let the *4* put you off,'" he remembers. "Because the fourth installment of something usually isn't the most appealing thing to do. She was like, 'This one should be really interesting. You should go in on this.'"

Culkin went in and read for it and then got a call asking him to come into Bob Weinstein's office and read the script. He remembers it was missing the opening sequence and the end of the film.

"Bob Weinstein came in, sat down, and he introduced himself. He was like, 'So, I should probably tell you. I gotta tell you. Should I tell him? I should probably tell him.' He went quiet and I started leaning in, staring at him kind of intensely. And he was like, 'Oooh. I love that. Bring that to set. You're the killer.' Then he shook my hand, he left, and another producer came in and was like, 'Welcome aboard.'"

Culkin shook his hand, thinking to himself that he hadn't actually said yes yet.

"They sort of acted like it was a given that I was going to accept this, and I remember going back to my studio apartment in the East Village and really thinking about it," he remembers. "I grew up acting, since I was nine, and I was always playing the pushover. I was playing a kid that would get bullied all the time, and now they want me to fuckin' bully some people. Cool.

"I remember having a dream that night that I was in my apartment, but the ceiling was black and there was a little Ghostface on the ceiling. I remember waking up being like, 'Yeah, okay, I'm supposed to do this.'"

For Erik Knudsen, who plays high school cinema club president Robbie, there was never a doubt. He was a long-time fan of the franchise, growing up watching *Scream* at sleepovers. "The *Scream* movies were made for fans of horror. Ghostface toys with victims like a horror fan that already knows the ending of a scary movie," Knudsen says. "I remember it being like nothing I saw before. It seemed to be a brand-new genre for me, horror mixed with self-aware comedy—and I wanted more, but nothing came close to matching those movies. The Ghostface mask also became a tool for my grandmother to scare us out of the basement when it was time to come upstairs for dinner."

The same basement where he'd film his audition, using a blue thrift store curtain as a backdrop and wearing a sweatband in place of Robbie's livestreaming headset.

"As a huge fan it took me almost three hours to finally get a take done that I felt was actually submittable," Knudsen remembers. "Thank God it wasn't an in-person audition because my nerves of possibly working on something I love would have had the better of me. I felt like I was dreaming, or this was all a hoax. I was some Canadian kid that was about to work on a movie I adored with the people I grew up watching."

Since the movie centers on a friend group that includes multiple cinephiles who love horror, the *Stab* franchise is a big part of the story.

Feingold created a *Scream* bible so they could make sure any references to the previous films were accurate, as well as the mentions of the movies within the movies.

"I went back and studied the first three films, and I wanted to be sure to only study what was on screen and not anything in the scripts because that would muddle what was true and what wasn't," Feingold says. "I studied every character, every interaction people had, and kept track of all of it in a binder that I carried around. When we needed to reference something, we were like, 'Oh yeah, that was in *Scream 2*.'

"One thing that was hard to track, because they weren't always said, was the name of every *Stab* film. I had to figure out what preexisted and then we named more in *Scream 4*."

She still has the prop *Stab* box set from Kirby's house. There's *Stab: The Woodsboro Murders*; *Stab 2: The Murders Continue*; *Stab 3: Hollywood Horror*; *Stab 4: Knife of Doom*; *Stab 5: Clock of Doom*; *Stab 6: Ghostface Returns*; and *Stab 7: Knife of the Hunter*.

It's truly a monument to the schlockiest of slasher schlock—but in a movie where teens get drunk from red plastic cups, in a barn, at an annual party dubbed Stab-o-thon, it fits right in.

Marianne Maddalena, Drew Barrymore, and Kevin Williamson during filming of *Scream*'s opening sequence.

Courtesy of Marianne Maddalena

It took the special effects team from KNB EFX over a month to create Casey Becker's disemboweled body for the "aftermath" shot in the film.

Courtesy of Greg Nicotero / KNB EFX Group

Wes Craven and Julie Plec on the set of *Scream*.

Courtesy of Julie Plec

Part of the *Scream* team having dinner at Ca'Bianca in Santa Rosa.

Marianne Maddalena, Wes Craven, and Courteney Cox.

The final sequence of *Scream*, dubbed "people live, people die," was a massive undertaking—as shown here by the number of cast and crew who took a moment to commemorate their work.

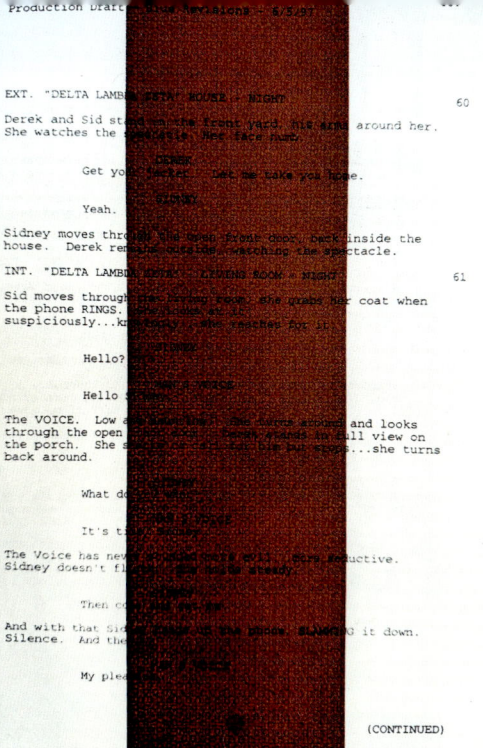

EXT. "DELTA LAMB___ ZETA" HOUSE - NIGHT   60

Derek and Sid sta__ __ the front yard, his arms around her.
She watches the _____. Her face numb.

                    DEREK
      Get yo__ _____.   Let me take you home.

                    SIDNEY
      Yeah.

Sidney moves thr____ the open front door, back inside the
house. Derek rem_____ outside, watching the spectacle.

INT. "DELTA LAMB__ ZETA" - LIVING ROOM - NIGHT   61

Sid moves through ___ living room, she grabs her coat when
the phone RINGS. ___ _____ at it
suspiciously...kn_____. She reaches for it.

                    SIDNEY
      Hello? __

                    MAN'S VOICE
      Hello _____

The VOICE. Low a__ ____ her_. She turns around and looks
through the open _____. Derek stands in full view on
the porch. She s_____ ___ ___ ___ ___ _____...she turns
back around.

                    SIDNEY
      What do__ _____

                    MAN'S VOICE
      It's ti__ ___ ___

The Voice has nev__ _____ __ll _ __re seductive.
Sidney doesn't fl____. Her voice steady.

                    SIDNEY
      Then co__ ___ ___ me

And with that Sid__ _____ up the phone, SLAMMING it down.
Silence. And the___ _____ _____

                    SIDNEY
      My plea____ _____

                                        (CONTINUED)

A page from the *Scream 2* script showing the specialty paper they used to deter attempts at unauthorized photocopying.

Richard Potter, Jamie Kennedy, and Jerry O'Connell during filming of *Scream 2*.

A candid shot of Courteney Cox as Gale Weathers in *Scream 2*.

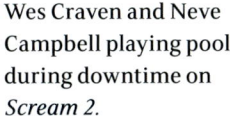

All images on this page are courtesy of Richard Potter.

Wes Craven and Neve Campbell playing pool during downtime on *Scream 2*.

The cast and crew of *Scream 3* gathers on set for a photo, documenting what they thought was the final film in the franchise.

Courtesy of Tina Anderson

Marielle Jaffe getting bloodied up on the set of *Scream 4*.

Courtesy of Carly Feingold

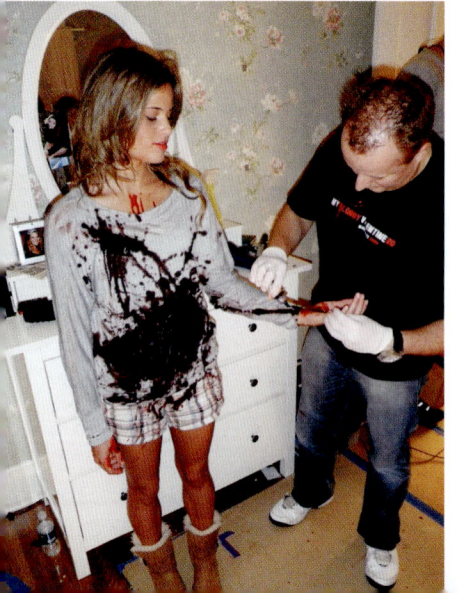

A close-up of the bedroom door that was splattered with fake blood in a real house in Ann Arbor, Michigan.

Courtesy of Carly Feingold

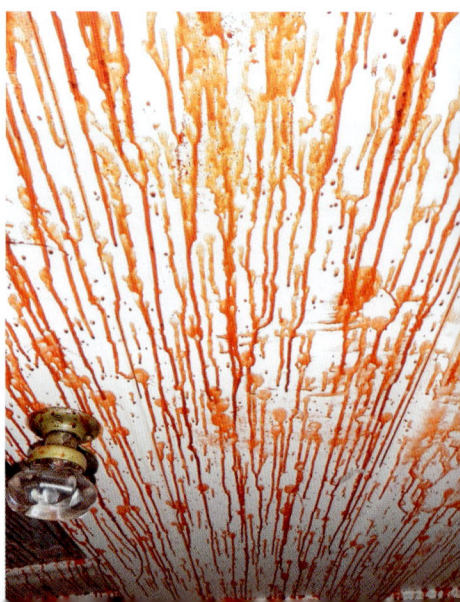

Iya Labunka and Wes Craven balanced their husband-wife and producer-director relationships on *Scream 4*.

Courtesy of Carly Feingold / photographed by Gemma La Mana

Wes Craven and crew toast as they wrap *Scream 4*, his final film.

Courtesy of Carly Feingold / photographed by Gemma La Mana

Neve Campbell, Courteney Cox, and Kevin Williamson take a selfie on the set of *Scream 5*.

Courtesy of Paramount Pictures

Jack Quaid and Mikey Madison on the set of *Scream 5*.

Courtesy of Radio Silence

Group photo outside the re-created Macher house on *Scream 5*.

Courtesy of Radio Silence

Melissa Barrera, Dylan Minnette, and Jenna Ortega testing the gravitational resistance of Dairy Queen's Blizzards in Wilmington, NC.

Courtesy of Mason Gooding

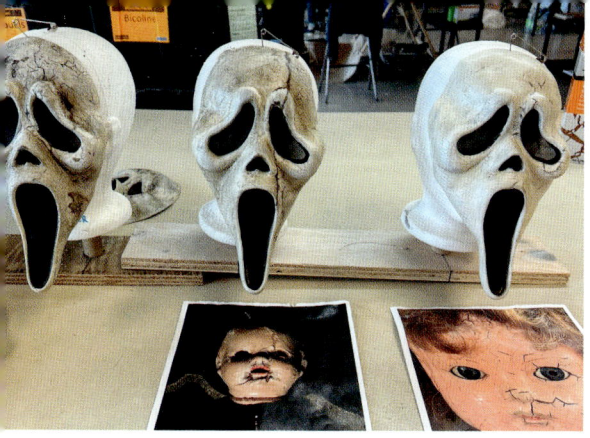

A behind-the-scenes look at the creepy dolls the costume designers used as inspiration for the *Scream 6* Ghostface masks.

Courtesy of Avery Plewes

Mason Gooding and Tony Revolori take a selfie on the set of *Scream 6.*

Courtesy of Mason Gooding

Matt Bettinelli-Olpin, Devyn Nekoda, and Tyler Gillet during *Scream 6.*

Courtesy of Radio Silence

Group photo while filming the final sequence of *Scream 6.*

Courtesy of Radio Silence

Scream 7 director Kevin Williamson talks with his first assistant director Rudy
Persico and cinematographer Ramsey Nickell.

Courtesy of the author

The cast and crew filming *Scream 7* during a night shoot in Atlanta.

Courtesy of the author

CHAPTER THIRTEEN

CRAVEN'S FINAL *SCREAM*

The passing of time not only allowed *Scream 4* to revisit Woodsboro on screen but also led to things changing behind the scenes, too. Much of Craven's crew returned, and found themselves working alongside their longtime helmer and a new voice in the room: his wife.

Iya Labunka had been a successful studio production exec and indie producer well before meeting Craven. She came up in the eighties with the late Roger Corman and was something of an auteur whisperer during her tenure at Disney, working with Wes Anderson, Spike Lee, Jonathan Demme, and M. Night Shyamalan on their films with the studio.

"I was juggling seven, eight projects at a time, which is what we all did," she says. "I was known as a director's executive. I could calm things and make them feel supported."

Craven and Labunka were set up by a mutual friend in

2003, the only blind date she's ever been on—and a black cat literally crossed her path on the drive there. She wasn't expecting the handsome, funny, and intensely focused Craven, and she immediately knew she was in the best kind of trouble. Despite their contrasting personalities—a vibrant, extroverted daughter of Ukrainian refugees and an introverted WASP born in late 1930s Cleveland—they were a "perfectly imperfect" match and got married over Thanksgiving weekend the following year.

They'd been together for the better part of a decade by the time he asked her to work with him on *My Soul to Take*.

"He had already started making the moves to separate himself from a lot of the people he worked with. It was just time to move on," Labunka says. She avoided getting dragged into the fray, but she was aware she'd become gossip fodder and that some people blamed her for Craven not just continuing on with the producing team from the first three *Scream*s. "I certainly have been told that I was the reason, I'm the fuckin' Yoko Ono. It was so ridiculous. It was like, 'Are you kidding me?'"

It's not like she leapt at the opportunity either.

"He actually came to me and said, 'Would you do this with me? I trust you implicitly,'" she recalls. "There was a series of very, very long and deep conversations. I had seen too many relationships destroyed; I had seen too many people losing sight of what the job was. So, we talked about it for a very long time and we both made a pact that the marriage came first. That was the most important thing."

The first movie they worked on together wasn't a walk in the park, but they proved a good team on set. So, when *Scream 4* came along it was natural to continue.

"I actually ended up in this crazily wonderful position because I didn't need the job and I wasn't afraid of Bob on any level," Labunka says. "I was only there to support Wes, help make the picture as good as possible, and, frankly, manage Bob. That became a full-time job. He was a bully, but if you were in a position to push back like I was, he would crumple. He'd have more respect for you if you held on to your own ground."

For the returning crew, like director of photography Peter Deming, the studio's meddling and disorganization were frustrating.

"It definitely wasn't as fun," Deming says. "Coming back after that amount of time, there's more at stake. If you're going to unearth this movie there must be a reason besides making a quick buck. Wes was always the one to nitpick about the script and make it better and—I know it sounds weird, but make it make sense. He wasn't getting the support from the studio that he really wanted, and there were definitely some screaming matches going on. They were usually after hours, but I would get the CliffsNotes about it. If that goes on for too long it works its way into the psyche of everyone who is working on it. We were sort of like, 'Well, listen to the guy who got you here.'"

"There were some blips, you know, but it's not a brand that was ever treated carelessly. Wes loved making these movies because Wes loves working with people that he loves," says Julie Plec. "He really developed a bond with everybody who made the first movie. So, then we all went and made the second movie, and then they went and made the third movie and the fourth movie. It becomes almost, in its own way, like a long-running TV show."

In this particular episode of the stabby procedural mystery drama, Craven was tasked with reviving a franchise that had been dormant for a decade and integrating the next generation with the legacy characters.

"It was such a wonderful experience with these incredibly fresh, excited, and exciting young actors. They bonded in such an extraordinary way," Labunka says. "It was lovely. And I think Courteney and David and Neve were so happy to be reunited with Wes. No matter what went on in other aspects of their lives, when they all got together with him, there was magic in the air."

He made an immediate impression on the new cast members too.

"This man was responsible for giving me nightmares for the majority of my life and I assumed he would be intimidating, unapproachable, and dark. It was the extreme opposite," says Erik Knudsen, who plays Robbie. "He was kind, happy, and brought a stress-free attitude to set. I was lucky enough to get to work with him and learn that you don't have to be deranged and hard to work with to make horrifying masterpieces."

Hayden Panettiere had been acting since she was a child, but *Scream 4* was her first horror movie—and who better to learn from than Wes Craven.

"It was amazing how he taught me the timing of being in a scary film. He said that it might seem uncomfortably long," Panettiere recalls. "Like when Trevor calls and it's really Ghostface and I'm with Jill in her room and I'm walking to the closet, freaked out that he might be in there. It was all about how slow you can walk to build up to the ba-boom, open the door and he's not there. The relief—and then the 'Oh my God, he's next door and our friend is being murdered and we have to watch.' It was all about the timing that I had to get used to."

———

WHEN RORY CULKIN WAS PREPARING FOR HIS ROLE AS CHARLIE, WHO turns out to be one of the killers, he wanted to differentiate his character from the Ghostfaces who'd come before him.

"Ghostface is truly scary because he plays with his food. He wants to scare you, almost like it feels better if you're crying when he kills you. Whereas with Jason and Michael Myers, I don't know if they give a shit about your fear level," Culkin says. "Ghostface seemed to kind of get off on fear. Ghostface just is fucking with you, and he can't wait for you to realize the call is coming from inside the house. Yeah, I think the playing-with-his-food part is the really unsettling thing. It's less about the knife plunging into you and more about the fucking with you mentally that freaks me out.

He continues, "I was thinking maybe Charlie is more desperate and frantic and unsure about what he has been doing. I would like to bring a sense of guilt and remorse to him. Maybe he didn't want to be doing this. Maybe he had a hard time sleeping after he would commit these murders because those screams keep ringing in his ears when he puts his head down at night."

The moment in *Scream* when Stu realizes, "My mom and dad are going to be so mad at me," was an inspiration. As funny as that line was, Matthew Lillard really grounded the moment and reminded the audience that these are high schoolers. They're still kids.

"I was trying to inject some reality into it," Culkin says. "Charlie is just a teenager in love, and maybe he's not the brightest guy and he is just listening to this Jill girl. Charlie's commitment to killing these people was a love letter to her. He's a cat that brings the mouse to the doorstep thinking, 'This is what you wanted.' I like the idea of him struggling with himself."

He sat down with Craven before filming the reveal. "I was like, 'Why am I doing this? Why am I killing people?' And he was like, 'Hmm, that's good. That's good.' Almost acting like he was talking to Charlie, he was like, 'If you're struggling with the guilt of all this, think of yourself as a soldier. When a soldier puts on his uniform he might have to kill people, but he's not a killer because he's wearing his uniform. When you have that mask on, you're not killing people. You're in uniform.'"

That struck a chord with Culkin. "I left his trailer, and I was like fuckin' ready. In my mind I was like, 'Maybe that's something Jill said to him, "Put on your uniform, Charlie. Look at me, you're not a killer. You're doing your job."'"

Charlie does look like he feels conflicted while he's stabbing Kirby, right after she thinks she saved his life by outsmarting Ghostface with horror sequel trivia. That wasn't just a product of his character development. In real life, Culkin and Panettiere were childhood friends.

"We grew up having sleepovers," Panettiere says. "He would sleep in my brother's room. It was across the hall from me, and my brother had two beds. We've been like family for years and years."

"I've known Hayden since we were little kids and I remember always having a crush on her when we were little,"

Culkin says. He tapped into that with his performance. "Because maybe if Kirby didn't reject Charlie, he wouldn't have gone to Jill. 'You were my first love, Kirby, but you didn't notice and now I have to kill you. That sucks. This all sucks, but it's too late. I'm in too deep.'"

Culkin pushed himself not just mentally, but also physically, to make Charlie seem disturbed and tormented.

"I was kind of torturing myself a little bit, thinking that's what you need to do to get a good performance," Culkin recalls. "I have since grown away from that, but I was kind of starving myself and listening to fucked-up music. In my trailer, when they would call me to set or give me a five-minute warning, I would start slapping myself. I wanted to feel something weird. I remember just wanting to feel like beaten, a little bit."

To keep that momentum going, he'd sneak out of sight between takes and slap himself again.

"I kind of talk it down now like it's silly, but maybe there is something to that. You have this weird, primal feeling when you get hit. That was probably the peak of my self-torture for a performance. Now I think I can get to that place without beating myself physically," Culkin says. "And I remember never wanting to stand still. They're setting up for the next shot, you're gonna have thirty minutes, just keep pacing. If crew or anyone is a little unsettled, good."

Culkin even worked to keep that vibe steady while socializing with the cast and crew. Neve Campbell had rented a place on a lake and invited everyone over one weekend. When people talk about their memories making *Scream 4* it often comes up as a communal experience cooking and eating together in a beautiful locale—but Culkin lived it a little differently. He kept his distance and used it as another opportunity to develop his character.

"I remember kinda disappearing into the woods by myself and using it as an opportunity to stalk them, look at them through the woods," he says. "They couldn't see me because I was far enough away and I put myself in the shoes of the killer, which is creepy to say."

For the folks who weren't trying to get in the mindset of a serial killer it was an opportunity to bond—as was his pal Panettiere's twenty-first birthday.

"I was with Wladimir [Klitschko] at this time, and he was in training camp," Panettiere recalls. "So, he enlisted one of my friends, Jeff Beacher, and David Arquette to set up this massive party. They went all out. They rented an entire building and invited the whole college town. Then they took me out at the end, and they had set up fireworks. They set them off and it spelled 'Happy Birthday, Hayden.'"

"I think we threw the biggest party Ann Arbor has ever seen," Arquette remembers. "It was bananas."

"It was like being in horror movie college," says Knudsen. "The new cast all stayed in the same Holiday Inn together. We went from room to room to hang out. Nico Tortorella reading our fortunes with tarot cards in his room. Or listening to music and playing guitar in Hayden's room. I have countless great memories from working on that movie. Learning how to drive a stick shift, passing a kidney stone, and getting stabbed by Ghostface. It was a project I will never forget."

In the prank-friendly culture Craven created, there was no shortage of memorable on-set experiences too. Dane Farwell, a stunt performer who plays Ghostface, remembers prop master J. P. Jones donning the costume and scaring one of the actors, which happened to just about everyone.

"One time on *4*, he literally chased an actress through a room or two of the house, and everybody was just cracked up laughing. I had no idea it was even happening, and I look up and I see Ghostface chasing the girl and she's screaming out loud. It was hilarious," Farwell says. "Toward the very end of the movie, I think it was the last day, they did it to me. Somebody is on the front porch of the house and they're knocking on the door. Right in the middle of the scene, I opened up the door, expecting the actor to be on the other side, and it was J. P. He had the knife raised and was screaming at me. I didn't move an inch, but I have to admit that it raised the hair on the back of my neck. They were actually filming it, too."

For Roger L. Jackson, the voice of Ghostface, one of his core memories happened while he was sequestered away from the rest of the cast during filming of the additional footage that lengthened the chase scene in the opening sequence. "My wife came with me for the retakes," he remembers. "I'm up in a bedroom off to the side where Ghostface chases [Jenny Randall] up the stairs, and my wife is with me. She's knitting and reading and eating potato chips while I'm threatening to kill somebody."

———

TO THE ENVY OF MANY *SCREAM* ALUMS WHOSE CHARACTERS ARE TOO dead for them to return to the franchise, Hayden Panettiere's contract specified that her character *couldn't* die. So they consulted with doctors about how to make her

Ghostface attack seem fatal in the moment but also believably survivable.

"I remember having conversations with a family friend that works in the ER. I knew he would know where you can be stabbed and be okay," says Carly Feingold. "And when someone went out and checked on her, she was still breathing and moving, because you also wanted to still think it might be a Billy-Stu thing where they're faking her death and she's gonna come back and she is the killer. We wanted to keep that belief alive too until the absolute end."

They also left Jill Roberts's fate a bit up in the air. Williamson's initial plan was for Jill to survive so her wish of becoming a celebrity victim could become her torment in the future, but the additional hospital scene closed that door. Unless it didn't.

"If you watch it very, very, very closely her eye does twitch at the end," says Feingold. "She looks dead, but there is a little twitch, and that was on purpose so it can be ambiguous if they needed her to survive for the next one."

There's one person who unquestionably did not survive the Woodsboro massacre of 2011—Jill's neighbor Olivia, who was played by Marielle Jaffe. In one of the most brutal and bloody deaths of the franchise, Sidney finds Olivia's body amid an explosion of unmitigated gore.

Want to know what the best part is? That's not CGI blood Jackson Pollocked all over Olivia's bedroom—nor is it a set. They did that to a real house in Ann Arbor, Michigan. (I can't think of anything more Midwestern than being like, "Sure! Splatter that room someone in our family actually sleeps in with as much fake blood as you want! I'm sure it won't be too hard for you to paint over, or give said family member lucid nightmares for the foreseeable future.")

University of Michigan lecturer Mark Kligerman, who both visited the *Scream 4* set and hosted Craven in his film class during the shoot, says the magic of practical effects like the ones used in this franchise is underappreciated now that so many things are done digitally in post-production.

"Especially with graphic violence, digital effects tend to totally whitewash and banish the rawness of analog effects," Kligerman says, explaining that over the years the way audiences engage with on-screen violence has changed because of CGI. He says it doesn't have the same kind of psychological or visceral impact when it's computer-generated. "There's something really insincere and dishonest about creating splatter effects with zeros and ones. At its very core, it's also a disavowal of the implications of that violence."

This scene was another classic Craven "more blood" moment, and the room even looked jarring in real life. "I remember it was really, really bloody," Feingold says. "It felt gorier, like going into *Saw* territory rather than being in *Scream* world. It was going to be a lot to reset so you had to get it right. We had a couple cameras on to do the main shot. Once the blood was everywhere, you couldn't go back. That was in a real house, so it wasn't like it was a set that you could just change over really quickly."

There's an Easter egg at the beginning of that bloody scene that has a pretty sweet backstory. Right before Kirby gets her Ghostface call, she and Jill are relaxing and watching *Shaun of the Dead*. That brief clip was a continuation of a long-running gag among horror filmmakers, according to the film's director, Edgar Wright, and as a big fan of Craven and *Scream* it was something he was honored to be part of.

"While the intertextuality of *New Nightmare* and *Scream* was a surprise to some, there was a winking side to Craven's movies that goes all the way back to 1977's *The Hills Have Eyes*. That film began a series of funny self-references between horror film directors that became a game of one-upmanship," Wright explains. "In the first *Hills Have Eyes*, there was a ripped poster for *Jaws* on the wall of a ravaged trailer, as if Craven was saying, 'That's not scary, *this* is scary.' Then, in response, Sam Raimi featured a ripped *Hills Have Eyes* poster in the cabin in *The Evil Dead*. Craven's reply to this was to have his characters watching *The Evil Dead* on television in *A Nightmare on Elm Street*. Finally, Raimi responded once again by putting the iconic razor glove of Freddy Krueger in the basement of the cabin in *Evil Dead 2: Dead by Dawn*."

Wright was thrilled when Craven reached out about including a *Shaun of the Dead* clip in *Scream 4*. "We did ask to see the pages in question just to make sure we weren't being made fun of. When I saw we weren't, I was more than flattered to be mentioned," he says. "I can't tell you how jazzed I was when I saw our film being watched in *Scream 4*—with Ghostface actually saying the title aloud. My face lit up with glee when I saw the finished scene in the Cinerama Dome on opening night."

WHEN IT COMES TO EXPLAINING WHY EXACTLY GHOSTFACE IS SUCH AN effective villain, *Scream 6* editor Jay Prychidny points to one of Kristen Bell's lines in the *Scream 4* opening: "I like the *Stab* movies. They're scarier. It's not aliens or zombies or little Asian ghost girls. There's something real about a guy with a knife who just snaps. It could really happen."

"And it's not just a human snapping, it's someone close to you," Prychidny says. "How much do you really know your own friends? It destabilizes your relationships with all people because if one person in your life can fool you that way, who can you really trust? Can you trust anyone? That's what happened to Sidney, that's what happens to Sam. They have trust issues—and with good reason—because they have been through this kind of trauma. I think that's really relatable, maybe not in a murder way, but that sense of betrayal and people having hidden colors. That's something that people experience in their lives."

Scream 4 isn't perfect, he says, but it kept him guessing more than any of the other sequels.

"You can really see a lot of the behind-the-scenes drama going on there because it's not a perfectly constructed movie by any stretch. You can see the seams of it a little bit, the squabbling over the content of the film," Prychidny says. "But, other than the first one, *4* is the best killer reveal for me. Jill's plan, her motivation, it makes sense all the way through, and her acting is unbelievable. As a filmmaker, you're thinking about how to vary up the formula and give the audiences new surprises, and I think that is so clever, to not end in the house with the killer reveal. At the time, you thought it was perhaps going to be the last *Scream* or that they would be moving on with new characters. So, I believed that Sidney was down and out. I believed that Emma had won. It was just such a shocker that the movie kept going, in a great way."

Tyler Gillett, half of directing duo Radio Silence who helmed *Scream 5* and *6*, says the social commentary was on point too. "Scream movies always managed to be weirdly ahead of their time, either perfect in the moment or they're prophetic," he says. "We talk so much about how *4* was almost a sci-fi movie when it first came out—but we're living in the aftermath, like the wasteland of what *4* was essentially talking about."

Roger L. Jackson says it reminds him of an Oscar Wilde quote: "Man is least himself when he talks in his own person. Give him a mask, and he will tell you the truth."

Jackson says, "One of the reasons I liked number *4* in particular was the whole idea of social media as the mask that people hide behind to do awful things."

The idea that teens would livestream their day-to-day life online, and do literally anything to become famous, is no longer fictional in a world where a billion people are on Tik-Tok, YouTube outperforms Netflix in viewership, and more than half of Gen Z aspire to be professional influencers.

"It was a pretty cool plot," Cathy Konrad says. "The idea of legacy kids related to the cast, with everybody having secrets and lies tucked inside what was iconic about those characters that people loved, was a great story. I thought it was very smart."

Patrick Lussier, who edited the first three films and wasn't involved in *Scream 4*, has one big issue with the movie: "My biggest challenge with the reveal in the fourth movie is that both killers are too short. One of them has to stand on the shoulders of the other one, and I don't believe either of them did those killings at all."

They tried to make all of the teens appear roughly the same height, but alas.

"We had to have lots of apple boxes around because Hayden and Emma were shorter," Carly Feingold remembers. "You want them all to appear the same height so anyone could be the killer, anyone could be in the Ghostface costume. That was a little difficult because they were significantly smaller. Nico was pretty tall. So, I remember following them around with the apple boxes to stand on."

The stature issues bugged Lussier enough that a decade later, when Radio Silence reached out while prepping the reboot, he brought it up. "Early on with Matt and Tyler, I remember having a long Zoom chat with them and talking about Wes, and talking specifically about that issue of the fourth movie. How its failure is in its casting of those two as the killers. Not that the actors aren't great, it's that neither of them have the height or the stature to believe that they did it. All the other movies, before or after, when you get the reveal of the killer you believe it. The *Scream 4* reveal creates, in my mind, an immediate disconnect. It's like, 'Nope, this was fun but I'm out.' It's really easy to lose the audience at that moment. You have to earn the reveal in so many ways." (In case you were wondering, *Scream 5* killer Mikey Madison is an entire inch taller than Emma Roberts.)

Lussier also says *Scream 4* was hurt by another franchise—and the call was coming from inside the Dimension house.

"When we made those first three movies back-to-back, we were ahead of everybody. We were setting that bar, whereas I think the fourth one suffered from being outside for too long. It also suffered from the *Scary Movie*s existing. The first *Scary Movie* especially hurt the fourth film. It made it a joke."

The *Scary Movie* franchise—which Dimension produced, capitalizing on the fact that they owned the name from Williamson's original screenplay title—spanned five films from 2000 to 2013 and brought in more than $450 million at the box office. "We were able to use that title because it sounds like a silly, goofy, and, in some cases, stupid spoof," Richard Potter says. "It specifically parodied *Scream* because we owned *Scream* and we were like, 'We'll do it before someone else does.'"

The parody didn't sit well with the *Scream* creatives, who had to undo a decade of damage.

"I remember Wes being really annoyed by *Scary Movie* and feeling that he should have gotten directing credit on it because they just stole so many sequences wholesale," Lussier says. "The opening of *Scream 4* is a gimmick, it's the one kill after another after another. It is so self-aware and it's both good and bad because it is falling completely in the steps of *Scary Movie*, which is a big weight to shuck. That mask has now been turned into something that's been used for laughs. That movie made a fuckload of money, but you had to buy back the jeopardy."

He continues, "With *Scream 5* and *Scream 6*, there was

enough distance and time that *Scary Movie* is largely forgotten. They weren't shackled to any of that. Also, none of the people who made it had anything to do with *Scary Movie*, which was not the case with *Scream 4*. All those studio people had something to do with *Scary Movie*. I think for the makers of *Scream 4*, *Scary Movie* was in its own way both a betrayal and a stick that you were beaten with because it was so successful."

———

REGARDLESS OF WHERE YOU RANK IT IN THE FRANCHISE, *SCREAM 4* HOLDS one distinction that no other film has: It was the last movie Wes Craven made before he died.

No one knew that at the time, of course, which makes the memories even more meaningful in hindsight.

Hayden Panettiere says Craven's "check your ego at the door" mentality created an atmosphere unlike any other.

"He had this very calm face and he made you feel like he was excited for you to be there," she says. "He was never frantic or like, 'Come on, guys, we've gotta get the shot.' It was always like, 'We'll get this, we're gonna get this.' That scene where I had to rattle off basically every horror movie that Kirby knew, he came down after the first take and he was like, 'Whoa, that was impressive. I didn't know how we were gonna have to do that, but you got them all.' Him being complimentary and proud, it was blissful. The anxiety of getting it right went away immediately." Craven also infused the film with his trademark humor, which brightened the experience on set.

"He got such a kick out of all his actors and he was great

with adding ad-lib lines spontaneously," Marley Shelton says. "In the moment where I'm wearing the protective vest when I get shot and I say, 'Wear the vest, save your chest,' Wes came up with that off the cuff. He really was a good leader. There was such tremendous love and respect for him."

"I've worked on a lot of movies, and I've been on a lot of sets. This one had this lightness and levity and fun," Iya Labunka says. "It was really extraordinary. I'm really, really grateful to him for insisting that I work on that film."

"I don't know if any of us thought it was the last one," assistant director Nick Mastandrea says. "We certainly thought it was the last *Scream*. We were all friends beyond the moviemaking. We'd have dinner together, hang out, watch games together. He started spending a lot more time on Martha's Vineyard, so we didn't see him as much, but I don't think anybody thought that was going to be his last movie."

"That was the furthest thing from anyone's mind when we were making it," Deming says. "I'm glad I was there. All that came out of left field for me. I had no idea that he was even sick. So, when I heard about it, I was truly shocked. I obviously wish we had gone on to make more films."

That's a sentiment shared by many close to Craven.

"I feel like he wasn't done. He had other stories he wanted to tell and visions he wanted to share. His time was cut short, for sure," Feingold says. "It was a great experience, but I don't think he thought it was his last, you know. I remember when they called the last shot. We all gathered together and popped champagne and celebrated, not knowing it was going to be his last film."

"The last time I saw him, we were doing retakes on number *4* in winter in Michigan, so there was snow everywhere. We were snowed in, practically," Jackson says. "My work was wrapped and we were coming back to the hotel at like two, three in the morning. As we were driving up, I look out the window and there's Wes out in the snow with his camera, taking pictures of the snowbirds at night because he loved birds. He'd been working the whole night just like all the rest of us, but he took the time to go out and follow something that he loved."

CHAPTER FOURTEEN

WES

It's stunning, at first, the way people talk about Wes Craven. No one expects an icon to be a regular guy—especially in Hollywood—and a deeply thoughtful, kind one at that. He didn't yell, he genuinely cared about input from cast and crew, and he was remarkably funny. After dozens of people express the same feelings, lighting up and often tearing up while talking about him, it becomes quite apparent that he was much more than a genius filmmaker.

"Everybody was always surprised when they'd meet him because they think he's going to be this crazy, outrageous, flamboyant horror maven, but he was just this self-possessed humanities-professor type," Julie Plec says.

"Wes had so much to share. He clearly was able to really tap into all the things he loved. He loved music and nature," David Arquette says. "I remember him watching these Korean action movies and old anime at video village. He was like, 'Sometimes it will give me an idea for an incredible shot.' That just blew my mind."

"Wes was special. You really felt you were talking to a family member. He really brought you in," Kevin Williamson says. "It's extremely unusual to have that sort of relationship from the get-go and to have that trust and to have his ear. I just loved the man. He is such a part of my beginnings of my career that I can't think of him without getting emotional. He was so influential to me. He taught me camera, he taught me angles, he taught me staging, he taught me framing. I was absorbing as much as I could. He was my hero."

"He was not your typical Hollywood director and certainly not someone you would think was out there terrifying the world," says Skeet Ulrich. "There are several of his movies that just continue to enrapture audiences. I think he just had something figured out psychologically that has transcended decades."

Craven's calm presence stands in stark contrast to his dark filmography, which stems from a traumatic childhood. His father died not long after leaving his family, and his suddenly single mother immersed herself deeply into the fundamentalist Baptist Church. That was one of a handful of truly formative events in his life.

W. Earl Brown remembers Craven telling him that he was the weird kid at school who handed out religious pamphlets and wasn't allowed to watch TV, and *A Nightmare on Elm Street*'s Freddy Krueger was named after a bully who used to beat him up. "Wes was dealing with his own nightmares that went back to his entire life," Brown says.

Craven went to Wheaton College, a self-described "explicitly Christian" school in the Chicago suburbs, thinking that he'd become a Baptist minister. Those plans changed after he penned an essay in the school paper, of which he was the editor, that questioned church doctrine using ideas from Voltaire's *Candide*.

"They had chapel every week and the dean of the school, from the pulpit, denounced Wesley Earl Craven as a heretic and he canceled publication of the school review because of what Wes had written," Brown says.

Craven was convinced he was damned, and someone at the college referred him to a therapist. When he got there, he found that the waiting room was filled with Wheaton students who had, presumably, been made to feel the same way. Brown recalls Craven telling him that the therapist explained he needed to learn to discern between good people who believed what Wheaton was teaching and evil ones.

That's when he started stepping away from religion. He wanted to believe, but he just couldn't reconcile what he'd been taught with reality.

"Wes was a person who had incredible curiosity and was very open to the world, but he also wanted to do the right thing," says Iya Labunka, who was married to Craven for more than a decade, until his death. "He was a deeply, deeply spiritual man and very much in touch with that aspect of human existence. He studied philosophy, he studied psychology, he really examined the unconscious."

Craven's own mind was stretched to an unimaginable place when he was nineteen. He woke up one morning to an unexpected and unexplained paralysis moving up his body.

"He got up from bed, fell down, and started losing feeling gradually from his toes up. They thought he was going to die because it was going to suffocate him," Labunka says. "It was this creep over twenty-four hours of literally a horror coming up his body and it stopped at his underarms. He spent a year paralyzed. It rewired his physicality and his psychology and the way his brain worked and the way he looked at the world."

"Wes brought up to me multiple times how much his mind changed in that time," says his longtime assistant Carly Feingold. "He went to a dark, dark place and he was able to crawl out and use it years later."

"Wes was able to just completely laser in on what was important in any given moment and distill it to its essence, and I do not know whether that was an ability he had before the paralysis, but I do know that the paralysis helped him develop that," Labunka says. "What's important, what do you pay attention to, what matters? Because he came so close to death, he truly saw each day from that moment as a gift. He lived his life with the knowledge that every day since then was to be appreciated and used in a way that was productive. That could be joy, that could be happiness, that could be taking care of yourself, that could be concentrating on things that matter to you."

That's also how he met his first wife, Bonnie Broecker. She was a candy striper at the hospital. Not only is she the mother of his two children, Jonathan and Jessica, but she's also the sister of Wallace Broecker, a prominent scientist who helped Craven get into an ultracompetitive graduate program at Johns Hopkins University, where he earned a master's degree in philosophy and writing.

By this point, Craven had seen and fallen in love with movies—his first was *To Kill a Mockingbird*, and then he saw the 1966 thriller *Blow-Up* at least half a dozen times—and bought a thirty-five-millimeter camera. He was teaching English at Clarkson College (now Clarkson University) in upstate New York and some students asked him to advise their film club. It didn't sit well with his dean, who gave him an ultimatum: Get your PhD and publish scholarly works, as professors do, or go make movies.

———

IN PURSUIT OF HIS FILM CAREER, CRAVEN MOVED TO NEW YORK CITY, where he drove cabs and briefly made pornography under the pseudonym Abe Snake.

"Look, it was the '70s in New York," Labunka says. "It was a way in for a completely neophyte person. Storytelling is storytelling."

The people he met during that time changed the course of his career: Harry Chapin (yes, the folk singer) and an aspiring filmmaker named Sean Cunningham. Through them, Craven got a job as a messenger for a production company and learned film editing. It wasn't long before Cunningham came to him with a proposition to make a low-budget movie.

"He fell into horror," Feingold says. "Sean Cunningham was like, 'We have some money to make a movie. You grew up fundamentalist Baptist, pull all the skeletons out of your closet and let's go.' That's how he wrote *Last House on the Left*. He just went there."

The movie, which Craven has said was a reflection on

the violence of the Vietnam War and how Hollywood movies tend to gloss over the horrors on screen, was unlike anything anyone had ever seen. It was a brutal, graphic story about parents who take revenge on the psychotic killers who kidnapped, raped, tortured, and murdered their teenage daughter and her friend.

"It is so hard for me to put together this kind, intelligent, sweet-natured, loving person that I knew with *Last House on the Left*," Brown says. "That movie is so fucking brutal and ugly, and it just intrigues me that a person like Wes even had those thoughts."

Craven and Cunningham tried making a handful of other stories outside of the horror genre, but no one was interested. Eventually, he caved and made *The Hills Have Eyes*.

It was a hit and he was branded a horror director.

"He was a classic. He was a pioneer. But he didn't want to be only known as that one thing, as Wes Craven the horror guy," says producer Cathy Konrad. "He went on to do a few other things, but he was never really let out of his box from an audience's point of view. I think they really just wanted to keep him for their own over here."

"There were moments in his life where he had great success because [his work] was shocking and unusual and it put him on the map, and then he'd fall off a cliff. That happened with *Last House on the Left* and it happened with *The Hills Have Eyes*," Labunka says. "Then he couldn't get anybody to buy *A Nightmare on Elm Street*. I mean, he could not get arrested trying to sell *Nightmare*, which is one of the reasons that Bob Shaye got the kind of deal that he got. Nobody else was willing to look at it. He had great success, he had failure, and he just would not be vanquished by the defeats."

As is often the case, much of the cultural appreciation of Craven's career happened in retrospect. Now he's revered for those films, as well as *Swamp Thing, The Serpent and the Rainbow, The People Under the Stairs, Wes Craven's New Nightmare*, and, of course, *Scream*.

"He was able to build a career from two dollars, a reel of film, and some really fucked-up ideas," says Plec. "That is the true spirit of independent filmmaking. He was able to then take that for a span of thirty, forty years and have not just one but multiple massive successes, to have a name that everybody knows. We call it the *New York Times* crossword puzzle clue. When you've really made it is when you're in the crossword puzzle."

———

DESPITE THIS SUCCESS, CRAVEN CAUTIONED KEVIN WILLIAMSON AGAINST following in his footsteps. With a brilliant screenplay that was breathing life back into the slasher genre, it would have been easy for him to get caught in the trap too.

"Wes said, 'Don't stay in horror films. Do something else. You don't want to get typecast,'" Williamson remembers. "That's why I really wanted to do *Dawson's Creek*. Because it wasn't a horror film. He always felt that he had been typecast, that he had been stuck in this world he couldn't get out of. Being called the master of horror isn't always a good thing when you want to direct Meryl Streep, which he ultimately got to do in *Music of the Heart*. That was a big deal. That was really important to him."

Music of the Heart, Craven's 1999 film about an inner-city violin teacher that landed Meryl Streep an Oscar nomination, was a creative trade-off for the first two *Scream* films.

"That was a labor of love for him, which was great, to see him doing something nonhorror," says assistant director Nick Mastandrea. "That was pretty special."

"He was really excited to make a non–genre film," director of photography Peter Deming says. "He didn't change at all, but it was a different artistic process. I think it spoke to the range that I wish he had time to show, because he had a lot more stories to tell."

Madonna had been slated to play the lead but had to back out due to a scheduling conflict, so he shot for the moon and reached out to Meryl Streep.

"Wes wrote me a lovely letter," Streep says. "His letter explained that this was a passion project for him, that teachers were crucially important in opening up his own mind and creativity and he wanted to pay that back through Roberta's story. My hesitation initially had to do with the fact that there was no time to prepare. I did not know anything about the violin, and I would have six weeks to learn—to go from zero to playing the Bach double concerto on the stage of Carnegie Hall alongside Itzhak Perlman, Joshua Bell, Mark O'Connor, and Isaac Stern. His letter convinced me the project might collapse if someone wasn't insane enough to try, and I decided to try."

She spent every spare minute on set practicing because she was "so anxious to not screw it up for Wes," whom she describes as "a generous soul."

"Because of his almost courtly patience and kindness,

and the people he surrounded himself with, who demonstrated that same grace, I kept having to remind myself that he was responsible for the *Scream* franchise, he invented Freddy, was the horror king!" Streep says. "He was disarmingly low-key, witty, with a sly sense of humor. He was unfailingly respectful managing both the accomplished cast and all the completely fresh children. Most high-profile, big-ticket franchise-film directors I know would've run screaming away from this particular challenge—but he arrived daily with a smile that never left his face. He was doing something he wanted to do, he was happy doing it—or did a pretty great impression of someone who was. It wasn't just me; everyone loved working on his set."

"I don't know any other adult human who could do what she did," says script supervisor Sheila Waldron. "The first scene where she was playing and talking at the same time, which was understandably very difficult, there were a couple of times that she messed up. Wes just goes, 'Cut, cut, somebody call Madonna!' And Meryl goes, 'Go ahead! Call Madonna! See how it goes!' They were very funny together."

Craven was a consummate professional, but he loved to joke around too.

"Wes had a wicked sense of humor," remembers Courteney Cox. "So, besides being in awe of his talent, I loved his genuinely beautiful heart and his surprising silliness."

It often manifested as dad jokes and pranks on cast and crew—including an epic one on Peter Deming, who was the director of photography on *Music of the Heart*.

"Meryl's character was dating this guy named Dan. In front of Peter, Wes said, 'Harvey called about the Dan scene.'

Peter said, 'Dance scene? What dance scene?'" Marianne Maddalena recalls. Without missing a beat, "Wes goes, 'Yeah, Harvey wants a dance scene. Can you believe it?'"

Craven couldn't resist leaning into the mix-up and it became an elaborate prank.

"They got a choreographer and they had Meryl on board with the gag," Deming remembers. "This went on for weeks. We had wrapped for the day, and we have a rehearsal of the dance number in the bathroom set. So, I grumbled and went over there. Everyone was there and the choreographer was going through the dance."

"Meryl runs all through the apartment and ends up in the bathtub, behind the shower curtain, opens up the shower curtain, runs back through the brownstone, jumps over the sofa, and sits on the sofa," Maddalena says. "She knocked her leg on the marble coffee table, and she completely cut her leg open. She looked at Wes, she kept in character, and she goes, 'I told you this scene wasn't a good idea!'"

At the end of the day, Deming appreciates the effort, even if there was a little too much of it. "It's probably something they could've done in one day instead of several weeks," he says with a laugh.

Labunka says Wes never got tired of telling people that story, and as silly as it is, it shows how he tried to bring light and humor into his life.

"Wes battled with depression. He had faced death. He was very open about being suicidal at points in his life," she says. "He definitely had demons. There was a darkness to him, which he thought was inherent in the human condition, that he worked to understand. But he also made a conscious choice to at least start out happy, to start each day positively."

Beginning each day with a positive mindset is the kind of thing most people would make as a New Year's resolution and forget about well before Valentine's Day—but Craven wasn't most people. Labunka says he made it a priority and saw it as a way of dealing with the darkness in the world. Every day, for thirteen years, he made her laugh first thing in the morning.

"The day could go to hell after that," she says, "but he made the choice to start it out in a good place."

———

NOT EVERYONE USES THE WORDS "FATHER FIGURE" WHEN SPEAKING ABOUT Craven, but even the ones who don't are describing that sentiment. It's remarkable when you remember that he didn't have someone who modeled that behavior for him.

"The death of his father at five years old had a profound effect on him," Labunka says. "That will mark you hugely. That was something that stayed with him until the end of his life. Somebody asked him before he died what he wanted to be remembered for and he said being a good father—even though he seemed to, from some people's perspective, leave his family in pursuit of a career because he went out to California. It wasn't working in New York, and he also, frankly, wanted to give Bonnie room with her new husband, because she was creating a family that he thought would be nurturing to his own children. That was a lifelong wound for him. He thought he was doing the right thing for them.

"I think he worked at that for the rest of his life, both consciously and subconsciously. Being a director is such a maternal and paternal position. You're the person who everybody looks to for every answer. He managed to do it without being autocratic, which is freaking amazing. It speaks to who he was as a person.

"His guiding principle was to treat everyone with respect and to understand what they bring to the table but without ever ceding his position as the leader. He was an alpha male. He was a quiet alpha male, but you felt steel. He would not have survived in the business as long as he did without having steel in his backbone."

Neve Campbell says you want a director who sets a tone of professionalism on set but also does it with kindness and a sense of humor, and Craven did exactly that.

"We're not saving lives. We need to have fun doing these kinds of things and we have to have gratitude," she says. "He always seemed very grateful and also cared deeply about doing a good job. When the person at the top sets that tone it trickles down, and not every director is like that. He set an example of how to behave in this business in a way that is wonderful and admirable and professional, and we will remember forever."

He made it a priority to learn the name of everyone on set—with the help of his assistant and Polaroids—and kept a list of people's birthdays so he'd remember to reach out.

"He was the same no matter where you were on the scale of life," says Stuart Besser. "He didn't treat you different because you were an Oscar winner. He treated us all equally."

"He made some great movies that entertained a lot of people, but I think for me personally his legacy is the atmosphere he created, the camaraderie, the loyalty he had," says Mastandrea.

"I loved working with Wes," Scott Foley says. "He was quick to smile and easy to be around. We both did the *New York Times* crossword, and we'd often ask one another about our progress for the day. *Scream 3* was my first feature film and I consider myself fortunate to have done it with Wes."

As friendly as he was, Craven was an introvert and didn't care for small talk, so during downtime on set he'd be off bird-watching or sitting in his director's chair doing those crossword puzzles.

Deming recalls Mastandrea poking fun at the hobby and joking that the director would respond to "What did you think of that take?" with "I need a six-letter word for . . ." as if he wasn't paying attention. "We would tease him a little bit," Deming says, "but he was always prepared, always knew what he wanted, but was open to ideas to make the film better."

"There was no hugging and backslapping," says set designer Bruce Alan Miller, "but he was very appreciative of people who bring something to the table."

"The best moments with Wes were usually the quiet ones where the two of us sat at the editing console experimenting with different scenes, checking different performances, and tweaking the minutiae of each film's moments," editor Patrick Lussier says. "I learned so much from him during those times, asking about the decisions, the challenges, the why this versus that. We'd shoot the shit about news and politics and coffee and squids and old movies and why this story worked versus that and how insane the suits always were because they'd give the most ridiculous notes. Wes was very thoughtful about storytelling and always came at it from a simple yet primal place. He always tried to avoid overcomplicating an emotion or on-screen event that could have more impact in close-up."

"Not once but twice he changed horror completely," Craven's assistant Carly Feingold says. "We wanted more from him. It's just sad that he was taken way too soon. He lived quite a life, and many different lives within his life."

"I feel like I almost took him for granted and I didn't really realize how brilliant he was," says Maddalena, who worked with him for more than two decades. "There's not that many people like him."

"You would think his demeanor might be a little more intense or macabre, but he wasn't that," says Tina Anderson. "I learned so much about how to take care of the crew. You have to understand when you're pushing too hard or when someone needs a pick-me-up or simply a better piece of equipment to do their job."

"There was just something about Wes that made people want to do their best," says Waldron. "Some directors like to hear themselves spew about how brilliant they are, but Wes would go in with few notes and he just knew it when he saw it. He loved being there and it was infectious. We loved making the movie because he loved making the movie and he loved his crew. He loved actors, he loved the process, he loved the form. It all meant something to him. So, it was easy to work for him. He just loved making movies. It wasn't just something he did, it was something he *was*."

———

WHEN IT CAME TO WORKING WITH ACTORS, CRAVEN WAS IMPRESSIVE WITH-out being intimidating and helped them pull out what they needed for a performance without coming off as demanding or impatient.

"He had integrity and was a wise soul—generous and a lovely vibe with directing such scary movies," says Parker Posey. "Even his name sounded like a horror movie director, and then you meet this man who is unassuming and gentle. He made you feel comfortable and accepted."

"He is this titan in film, but he is just a nice man," says Rory Culkin. "There is no venom to him. There's no real edge to him. You could just tell he was a good guy by looking at him. He had kind eyes."

"He wasn't an effusive guy, but I immediately felt weirdly seen in some way," says Emily Mortimer. "Sometimes you get people who you can feel that they're terrified you're going to fuck it up and then you do. Whereas with Wes you felt that he believed in you and knew you could do a great job and that made you feel like, 'Oh, maybe I can.'"

"I can't even begin to explain how impactful working with Wes was," says Sarah Michelle Gellar. "So many of his notes I still think about and use to this day. He was so much more of a nuanced director than he ever got credit for. He noticed everything and paid such close attention. Everything you saw on screen was something Wes had already thought of in his mind. That's one of the secrets to why *Scream* was so good. Before, no one cared about performances in horror movies, but Wes did. The acting was equally as important to him as the jump scares were. I am a better actor for having worked with him."

"What comes out of that man's imagination, you could've knocked me over with a feather. It's wild. You never know what is going on in the complication that is somebody else's mind," says Henry Winkler. "His demeanor never changed. He knew what he wanted, which is the key to making great stuff. If you know what you want without ambivalence it will explode in front of you. It will be like fireworks. He wouldn't settle, and he was a gentleman and a gentle man."

"What you are informs what you do," says Roger L. Jackson. "He was able to do what he did because he was a good man. Anyone who has been through enough pain realizes how important it is to reach people, to make them feel better, to entertain them."

"He was such a gentle giant, just a laid-back guy," says Elise Neal. "Everything that he did in the horror space is so legendary but he himself was just a regular guy."

"Because he was so grounded you implicitly trusted him," says Matthew Lillard. "A lot of times directors' own egos are wrapped up in the creative process. I don't think he had that same sense of ego. It was like, best idea wins, best line wins, best take wins. I don't think he was worried about the result of any given choice on any given take, and I think that he cherished giving you little nuggets to build into your performance. He had a trust in me that allowed me to be the best version of me, and that doesn't happen very often."

There's one moment on set that Lillard goes back to during low points of his career. He was looking for the set phone to call his mom on her birthday, and walked past

Craven and Maddalena while they were talking about him. They were saying how they thought he'd win an Oscar someday, and Lillard asked Craven to tell that to his mom.

"I picked up the phone. I'm like, 'Mom, happy birthday. Hold on a sec, Wes Craven wants to say hi.' He's like, 'I just want to tell you your son is very talented. We were just sitting here saying that one day your son's gonna win an Academy Award,'" Lillard says.

"There have been times where I don't think I'm ever going to work again. That I'm garbage. The trajectory of the ebb and flow is really brutal to survive. You have to hold on to these little moments. That phone call with Wes Craven has gotten me through the times when I go, 'Oh, fuck. I suck.' That somebody that I revered and loved had that to say to me in passing is incredibly powerful for me. I think about it all the time."

___

"I WOULD ALWAYS ASK WES, 'HOW DOES IT FEEL TO BE THE MASTER OF horror?'" Williamson remembers. "And he would go, 'Ask John Carpenter.' That was his answer."

Carpenter, who considered Craven both a contemporary and a friend, is similarly humble about their impact on the culture.

"We were all just trying to make a movie. None of us were trying to change anything and to be iconic," Carpenter says, describing Craven as hardworking and a very nice man. "Like how people expect comedians to be funny all the time, they expect us to be horrifying all the time. 'Mwahahaha.' That kind of thing. We're just people trying to make a living directing movies. The nicest people I know were horror directors. They're the sweetest. The horror writers, too, amazingly nice. I think we work out all our demons and then we don't have to worry about it."

Eli Roth agrees: "You can't underestimate Wes Craven's impact on the genre, and I think it's because he was such a sensitive person. Wes was a really, really beautiful soul and a generous person and I miss him to pieces. Only someone with his level of sensitivity, a transcendental meditator who is a bird-watcher, could be that insightful about humanity and terror and fear and scares. He was the opposite of dark. He was this beam of light. We're lucky we still have his movies. I always say time is really the only critic that matters and it's nice that forty, fifty years later these films are still being enjoyed and horrifying audiences. All you can hope for when you make a film is that it lives on."

"Most directors would be lucky to have one talking-point watershed horror film. I would argue that Wes had three," says Edgar Wright. "For me, one of Craven's stand-out films is *The People Under the Stairs*, which blends an urban treasure-hunt storyline with a creepy Brothers Grimm atmosphere and an anticapitalist streak. This film, often overlooked, reflects Craven's political and social commentary. His ability to create nightmares that resonated with audiences and his willingness to push the boundaries of the genre have left an indelible mark on the world of cinema."

"These movies that he has made are timeless," says Hayden Panettiere. "Forever people will know his name and his legacy of creating these magical films, these terrifying films, and characters that hopefully only exist in your nightmares. He was simply a treasure. It's heartbreaking that he is not with us anymore, and I just felt life was very unfair when it took him. It made me question a lot of things, but I'm so grateful that I got to work with him."

"I tell people *Scream* is not going to be one of the greatest horror movies, it's going to be one of the greatest movies," says Jamie Kennedy. "Wes is known for horror, but *Music of the Heart* is an amazing movie. He directed Meryl Streep to one of her Oscar nods. That's just incredible. His imprint on pop culture is huge."

"Wes was a very cerebral director. I think that's what made his movies resonate. They were grounded in this intellectual style. He still gleefully enjoyed dumping buckets of blood on people, but there was a reason for it," says special effects makeup artist Greg Nicotero. "Between *Nightmare on Elm Street* and *Scream*? I don't even know how to really put it in words what he has left us."

———

WES CRAVEN DIED IN AUGUST 2015 AFTER A SEVEN-MONTH BATTLE WITH brain cancer.

It's been both a blink and a lifetime since then for his wife, Iya Labunka.

People who fall in love later in life often say they wish they'd met their person sooner—but she isn't one of them.

"We met at exactly the right time. We met at a point in both our lives where we could give each other the best that there is in terms of a loving, supportive, amazing relationship, perfect in its imperfection," Labunka says. "I think that eased the end of his life immeasurably, to be surrounded by love. He was able to get to a place where he could love unconditionally and know that he was loved unconditionally. I feel absolutely lucky and blessed to have shared even a small portion of my life with him.

"He was an extraordinary person who didn't think of himself that way. He knew he had achieved things that very few people achieve, and he was very respectful of his own place in the business. So, there was no humblebrag bullshit. Toward the end of his life, he was an elder statesman and he took that very, very seriously and was very grateful to his fans."

Labunka says there was an interesting paradox with Craven because, on one hand, he saw himself as an everyman and thought anyone had the potential to do what he did—but he also realized that he saw the world in a way most people didn't, which helped him tell stories in a way no one else could.

It's a bit surreal for her that he's remembered primarily as a horror director, and it would be for him too.

"He never, ever thought that he would get put into the box of being a horror director and it was something he struggled with for most of his career—because it wasn't until toward the end of his life that horror became viewed very differently," Labunka says. "He really thought that *Music of the Heart* was going to be *the* film that changed the trajectory. Harvey, in front of me, apologized to Wes about how they handled that movie and how they marketed it. He actually took responsibility for not taking care of that film the way that it should have been to both give the film a better, bigger audience and to give Wes a different kind of platform."

Craven also directed one of the vignettes in *Paris, je*

t'aime and his thriller *Red Eye*, which starred future mega-stars Rachel McAdams and Cillian Murphy, but they're often viewed as outliers in the career of a horror icon.

When it comes to describing exactly what his legacy is, though, even Labunka struggles to put it into words.

"He was a towering figure in cinema. I certainly hope he's known for bringing into the mainstream the fears that we all deal with on a daily basis as humans—because that's what was interesting to him: facing your fears through a medium that helps you do that.

"With *Nightmare*, connecting the subconscious mind and the other side of the world into this world is an incalculable legacy. Very few people have been able to do that. Great literature does it in some ways, but he brought it into popular culture in a way that had not been done as widely as he managed to do. *Nightmare on Elm Street* is one of the most recognizable titles, phrases, cultural touchstones the world over."

The human mind was a bottomless well of curiosity for Craven.

"He did everything and anything to examine the mind and consciousness. He read, he met, he experimented. LSD, lucid dreaming—all the stuff that people are doing now, he was doing with Timothy Leary," she says. "Tapping into the subconscious and how it controls or doesn't control our lived experience was a fascinating, never-ending source of discovery and exploration for him. That never stopped."

At the end of the day, it all comes back to fear and how Craven turned the terrors in his real life into stories that helped people deal with the horrors of their own.

"People really, really reacted to the way that he saw the world, and how he experienced the things that we're so afraid of, and how he helped people face their fears—in many ways, with laughter," Labunka says. "He was not acknowledged for it in almost his whole lifetime. Maybe toward the end things started changing, but he really was not acknowledged for the depth of experiencing a horror film as a way of externalizing internal horror. He really believed that it helped people to work it out rather than put it out into the world.

"Now there is so much work coming out about him, and he's being studied in a way that he never was, which I think he would be totally chuffed about.

"In terms of horror filmmaking, he was both a pioneer and a beacon," Labunka says. "I know he wished he had done more different kinds of films, but he loved what he did as well. He loved it.

"It was not a choice. He was completely driven to put out into the world the things that he was trying to work out in order to help other people work them out. It is a cathartic experience. It is a way of working out our fears. We have an existential need for that, and he felt he provided it. Until his dying day, that's what he was doing."

CHAPTER FIFTEEN

SURPRISING
BUT INEVITABLE

There's a phrase the creatives on the new *Scream* films use a lot: "surprising but inevitable." That's the sensation they're trying to create for audiences, that what happens on the screen isn't expected but feels like it was fated. It also might be the best way to describe the franchise coming back to life after being dormant for a decade—and why that happened.

Despite having his name on everything Dimension Films made, Harvey Weinstein had very little to do with the first four *Scream* movies—but he was collaterally instrumental in the franchise's revival. His downfall and the dawn of Me Too in 2017 led to the Weinstein Company declaring bankruptcy. Lantern Capital, which specializes in investing in distressed assets, came in as the stalking horse bidder and walked away with the company's assets—including *Scream*—for about $289 million.

Lantern Entertainment was formed and operated for less than a year before making a deal to hand the reins to someone with Hollywood experience: Gary Barber. The former MGM CEO brought in investors, rebranded to Spyglass Media Group in a nod to his first entertainment company, and hired execs to run it. Spyglass sold off most of its feature film library to Lionsgate in 2021—but Barber made it a point to keep *Scream*, knowing there was more life in the iconic franchise.

Producer William Sherak, whose late father, Tom Sherak, was close friends with Barber, jumped at the chance to bring *Scream* back to the screen. He and his partners at Project X, Paul Neinstein and James Vanderbilt, set up a meeting almost immediately.

"We went to have lunch with Gary when he had just gotten the library—they didn't even have offices yet," Sherak remembers. "At lunch we said, 'We want *Scream*!' It was that simple. We knew it was in the library. We knew that nobody had gotten to him yet to ask for it. Gary is one of those supersmart people and knew he had something special in that title. I think he also knew that we would be great partners and be mindful of the greater good of the franchise."

"For us, looking at it from the business side, it was never designed to just be one movie," says Neinstein. "It was designed to have something that we can keep going and going and going. We've been blessed to be involved with this franchise for the period of time that we're overseeing it. So, we're going to try and make sure that we're setting it up for success."

While trying to bring something back after a decade is

never easy, Sherak says the time lapse was actually beneficial because of how cultural appetites had changed. Horror became intensely macabre for a while, and in the years leading up to *Scream 5* humor was making a comeback.

"We saw the pendulum swing really far one way and then come back, and I like to think we were at the forefront of it with *Ready or Not*. Let's have fun again, not just torture people," Sherak says. "In those ten years the genre went full circle. I don't think *Scream 5* works midway through."

Neinstein agrees, adding, "Everything had gotten so gory. You look at a lot of the movies in between and there was no sense of relief at all during the process. I think *Ready or Not* is a great example, like *Scream*. There are intense moments of suspense and gory kills, but then you get a sense of relief all of a sudden. It's fun for a minute and it gives you breathing room and then it starts again."

So, it made sense that Vanderbilt wanted to bring in his longtime friend Guy Busick, who was one of the scribes behind *Ready or Not*, to cowrite the *Scream 5* script with him. They pitched their idea to Barber, who loved it, and they were off to the races—almost.

There was one person they didn't want to do this without: Kevin Williamson.

"We put all of our effort prior to developing the script into sitting down with Kevin and saying, 'We only want to do it if you are involved and you are our North Star,'" Sherak says. "It took him a minute to really believe us and know it's not a money grab. We genuinely love what he created."

Remember, Williamson gave up his rights to the franchise in order to walk away from his deal with Dimension. He had said goodbye to *Scream* and made peace with that.

Williamson met with Spyglass, but he wasn't entirely sure why. He was sharing some ideas but found out they already had Vanderbilt on board. He remembers thinking, "They don't need me. Why am I here? Is this just sort of a courtesy? You don't owe me anything. I'm good."

Vanderbilt called him and asked him to lunch. Williamson had met him years back and remembered him well. "He had written one of my favorite spec scripts of all time and I was a huge fan of his," Williamson says. "So, I went and had lunch with him. He started talking about *Scream* and he said, 'We just don't want to do it without you. We can't do it without you.'"

Williamson was hesitant, for a lot of reasons. He didn't know where he fit, or if they were just worried about the optics of not having him on board. He felt like he'd outgrown it, and he didn't know how to make a *Scream* without Wes Craven. So, he said no.

"He was very honest," says Vanderbilt. "He said the experience on *4* hadn't been great. He was sort of like, 'I would never stand in your way, but I don't know if I want to be involved.' We talked a lot and then he passed."

Eventually, like Craven had with the original *Scream*, Williamson changed his mind.

"A month went by, and I was talking to someone who said, 'Do you really want to go buy a ticket to the cineplex and sit in the seat and watch *Scream* as an audience member? It's your franchise. You birthed this with Wes.'"

That struck a chord, so he called Vanderbilt. "I said, 'I'm sorry. I know I've spun you in a circle, but can I please be a part of it? I'd like to be a part of it if you still want me,'" Williamson says.

"It took me a while to get round to that because, at first, I was like, 'How dare you make a *Scream* movie without me?' Then I became part of it and I fell in love with these guys. They were kind of infectious. They got me excited about *Scream* again and I thought, 'Oh, I can do this without Wes. I can be the connection to Wes for them.'"

———

ONCE THE WEIGHT OF WHAT THEY WERE ABOUT TO DO SET IN, BUSICK'S reaction was incredibly relatable—and he wasn't alone in feeling it. "I don't know if I can do this, but if anyone's gonna fuck it up, let it be someone who loves it as much as we do," he says. "It was a very weird tightrope act: Let's give it a path forward but let's not break it."

Vanderbilt likes to say that he and Busick share a *Scream* brain, but that minimizes their weird, remarkable mind meld to an astonishing degree. They started by watching the first four movies together, separately taking notes. They kept them secret until the end because they wanted to honestly reflect on what they'd like to see in the movie without influencing each other. And, well, holy shit.

"It was staggering how close those lists were," Busick recalls. "It's the next generation, it's the illegitimate daughter of Billy Loomis, it's Woodsboro. We both had that. We knew we wanted the big three, the legacy cast, to return."

"We also had an opening where the person lived," Vanderbilt adds. "We both came up with Dewey dying. As fans, we hated to do it, but as writers we were like, 'This is what the movie needs. Sorry, David.' We knew we wanted Sidney Prescott to come back. We knew the movie took place in Woodsboro, and we were like, 'There is no fucking way if I'm Sidney Prescott I will ever set foot in that town again.' It's the one thing that would bring her back. That's the fulcrum point that *5* really turns on."

MATT BETTINELLI—OLPIN AND TYLER GILLETT, THE DIRECTING DUO KNOWN as Radio Silence, might as well have been custom-made for *Scream 5*. They'd just directed *Ready or Not* and were already part of the Project X creative family—plus watching the original *Scream* was a formative moment for each of them, and fandom has been a key ingredient in the new installments.

"We always had them in mind," says Busick. "They were the only choice."

"We knew the tone you have to hit to make a *Scream* movie is such a small bullseye," says Sherak. "We went in going, 'We can't screw this up. So, every piece has to be built with a megafan.' They were megafans, and we like working with people we like."

The Project X guys set up a general meeting between Radio Silence and Gary Barber, which was out of the ordinary, but they didn't really think about it at the time.

"We knew Guy and Jamie were working on something together that they couldn't tell us about," Gillett says. "At some point in that meeting, Gary let slip that Jamie was writing *Scream* for them. At the time, we were just like, 'Holy shit, friends of ours are writing a *Scream* movie!' We got on the elevator, and we looked at each other and then we shook our heads. We were like, 'No, no, no, no. There's no way. That'd be too cool for them to ask us to be involved.'"

A few days later, they were invited to the Project X office to read the script.

"We took like three and a half hours to read it because we didn't want to miss anything," Bettinelli-Olpin says. "I remember Jamie kept popping his head in: 'How's it going in here?'"

"'Are you guys still reading? Do you guys know how to read?' I think Jamie said at one point by the two-hour-and-forty-five-minute mark," Gillett says, laughing. "The script is so good. As fans we were so excited."

They'd been attached to *Cocaine Bear*, which was written by Samara Weaving's husband, Jimmy Warden. She sent them the script during the press tour for *Ready or Not* and they loved it. When the opportunity to direct *Scream* came along, though, they couldn't pass it up.

"It sucked but we loved, loved, loved the *Scream 5* script and were such *Scream* fans. It felt like this is truly a once-in-a-lifetime opportunity," Bettinelli-Olpin says. "And then of course we were super nervy about it because we were like, 'What if we fuck this up? We're fucking up something that we love and that would hurt.'"

SCREAM 5 COULDN'T JUST BE A GOOD MOVIE. IT ALSO HAD TO BE A bridge between the past and the present, to have enough nostalgia to hook longtime fans but enough freshness to bring in a new generation. No pressure there.

Blumhouse exec Ryan Turek, the longtime *Scream* fan with a Ghostface tattoo, says he was apprehensive when he heard the franchise was being revived because he didn't love *Scream 4*.

"I was super excited that Radio Silence was directing because the spirit of filmmaking in *Ready or Not* was a great audition for *Scream 5*. It was perfect," says Turek. "But the question always is, What's it gonna say? What is *Scream* gonna say?"

So, when he got his hands on a draft of the script before it started shooting, he couldn't help but dive in.

"I was hesitant to do that because I didn't want to have it spoiled but I really wanted to see where it was gonna go," Turek says. "And I was *so* happy. I was like, 'Okay, they found a voice, they found a theme, they found a message, the killers are great.'"

For the existing fans, there were enough nods to the past to remind them of where the franchise had come from—they worked in little touches like Dewey having Tatum's ashes, and the Meeks-Martins having a fireplace shrine to Randy—but for the most part the nostalgia was built into the villains' story. By making the killers frustrated fans of the *Stab* franchise, who were essentially setting out to re-create the original movie within the movie, they could lean into references without it feeling forced or alienating people who were new to *Scream*.

"It's not even really low-key, the genius of what Guy and Jamie did on *5*," Gillett says. "They fully made the plotting

of the original matter in a way that was completely necessary in terms of the motive and the characters."

They took a big risk in writing a story that featured
Sidney Prescott, Gale Weathers, and Dewey Riley without
knowing if Neve Campbell, Courteney Cox, and David Arquette would be willing to come back to the franchise after
a decade had passed, and without Wes Craven.

"It was 'If you build it, they will come,' you know?" says
Busick. "We didn't know if we could get any of the legacy
cast back. You write your story and you hope for the best.
We said that we had built it so we could remove those characters if need be—but we would have been screwed, to be
honest. Especially Dewey. He was such an integral part of
it. It was a Hail Mary. So, we just tried to give the actors
something different to play than they had in the first four
movies."

Williamson was especially concerned about where Sidney would be at this point in her life.

"I want to make sure that whatever she's doing in life,
she's thriving," Williamson says. "When I sat down with Jamie and Guy, I was like, 'Can she just please be happy? Can
we just see that she is not a victim and she's not just traumatized and that she has found the light?' In the fourth,
she had written a book and she was a successful advocate
for survivors. I wanted to make sure we continued that.
That's when we decided to make her married, they have
children, and so forth."

Neve Campbell was hesitant to make another *Scream*
movie without Craven.

"That was a hard decision to make," she says. "Obviously, we were all really sad to lose Wes. He meant so much

to us, he meant so much to these films, and he knew how to make these movies. These were his and Kevin's. So, the idea of doing it again without him felt both sad and scary."

Radio Silence was able to ease some of that apprehension by reaching out to her and explaining why they were passionate about taking on the project.

"They told me they had become directors because of the *Scream* movies and because of Wes Craven, and they really were going to honor him and honor his films. That meant a great deal," Campbell says. "I decided if it was going to be in any hands, theirs were the right hands."

The directors also had to convince Skeet Ulrich to return as Billy Loomis, who appears in the form of his daughter's hallucinations. Ulrich was, understandably, worried that he'd look like an idiot trying to play an eighteen-year-old again. Their story, and appreciation for Craven's work, resonated with him, too.

"I got an email from Matt and Tyler, and it was beautifully written," Ulrich says. "It talked about their love of horror, their love of Wes, their love of the franchise. I decided it was worth trying. And I'm glad I did. I thought it was a very brilliant way to bring Billy back."

One of the deeper cuts in reference to the earlier films was bringing back Martha Meeks, sister of dearly departed Randy and mother of two new characters.

"This is maybe gonna sound macabre and I don't mean it to, but really, genuinely, I have very low expectations when it comes to this industry. I have high expectations for myself, but low expectations in terms of people's memories," Heather Matarazzo says. "I never in my wildest dreams thought that I'd be asked back. Who the fuck's gonna remember Martha? Boy, how wrong I was."

━━━━━

WITH THE LEGACY ACTORS SIGNED ON, CASTING DIRECTOR RICH DELIA knew he had a lot to live up to when filling the new roles in *Scream 5*. Not only was the original cast incredible, but the fan base is so passionate—and it seemed like everyone in Hollywood wanted a part.

"I can't think of another franchise, or film, that I've worked on that has had that volume of incoming interest from all angles," Delia says. "We have had existing characters, whether they're dead or alive, their agents call and say, 'Just so you know, they would love to come back.'"

Throughout the process, none of the actors saw the real script or had any idea whether they'd be playing the killer. "It was a little bit of detective work, which was really fun," Delia says. "You wanted actors who could play a scene in a way that you thought they could be Ghostface or that you thought they could be a victim."

They built an ensemble, starting with Sam and Tara Carpenter. "We did a chemistry read with Melissa Barrera and Jenna Ortega and they immediately had a vibe between them," Delia says. "'We're sisters at odds and yet we really care about each other.'"

"You were just like, 'Oh my God, this is remarkable,'" Sherak remembers. "You just knew it—on a Zoom. Forget being in person. You saw it on a Zoom."

Then there were the twin bridges to Randy, his niece and nephew, Mindy and Chad Meeks-Martin.

Jasmin Savoy Brown had never seen *Scream* when she booked the role of Mindy, and she wasn't entirely sure it was different than *Scary Movie*.

"I'm not super drawn to horror," Brown says. "I love a thriller. I love the chase. I love everything about horror films except the blood and the stabbing and the gore, which is pretty ironic considering the career I have had."

She did watch it before they started filming and the significance of the job quickly sunk in: "I was like, 'Ohhh, this is a really big deal.'"

Mason Gooding was at the total opposite end of the spectrum. He had seen *Scream* for the first time at fourteen as part of a deal with his parents to prove he was mature enough to handle an M-rated video game called *Dead Space*. It made such an impact that he wrote a paper in college about why *Scream* was ripe for a revival, which he mentioned during a meeting with Radio Silence and Project X.

"More so than any other franchise, I feel like it has a level of timelessness given the satirical content of the IP," he says, explaining part of his thesis. They asked to read it and must have been impressed. "You could argue it was the deciding factor in my casting because I never actually auditioned for Chad."

After a costume fitting in Wilmington, Sherak asked Gooding to check out the latest draft of the script so they could talk about it. "I got to the end, and there's the little Chad thumbs-up," Gooding remembers. "I called him. I was like, 'I could've sworn Chad was dead!' And he was like, 'We'll see you on the next one. Just make sure this one turns out as good as we hope it will and we'll have you back for a sixth,' which is hilariously bold considering we hadn't even begun production on the fifth."

Scream 5 broke with franchise history in one major way. While the all-white cast of the original *Scream* was initially a send-up of horror film characters in the '90s, times have changed. This film's cast is more diverse than those of its predecessors and better reflects the world we live in.

"It's really cool that in the new movies our Core Four are Black and Latino characters," says journalist and horror expert Richard Newby. "The films are not inherently about race, which I think is a really important thing. In the post–*Get Out* world, everybody is looking to recapture that success in some ways. A lot of times the idea is that in order to have minorities in horror movies, the film needs to be specifically about race. With *Scream*, it's still a slasher movie, but we have these characters that look like the audience that continues to support these movies."

Brown's character Mindy is also the franchise's first queer character, which meant a lot to Williamson. (He had nothing to do with Robbie's throwaway "You can't. There's rules. I'm gay!" plea to Ghostface as he's being stabbed in *Scream 4*. So, I think it's fair to say that doesn't count.)

"Of this new iteration, Mindy is probably my favorite character simply by the fact that she is a representation of who I am as a gay writer," Williamson says. "I want her to stay a part of the franchise. I'm a huge fan of Jasmin."

The feeling is mutual, and the significance isn't lost on her.

"It's a huge honor to me and I take such pride in it, and I really want to protect the character and protect the legacy,"

Brown says. "Seeing ourselves reflected on screen always means a lot to anyone, but specifically to people who haven't seen it very much. That's people of color, queer people, and especially that combination. Then, you take it a step further, and it's a queer, Black horror nerd. People have expressed to me how much this character means to them, and that means so much to me."

Another heir to *Scream* characters past is Stu Macher's nephew Vince, played by Kyle Gallner. He met with Radio Silence in a Zoom meeting that was set up by his agents, and was thrilled because *Scream* was a stepping stone into his love for horror. When it came time to audition, he was getting ready to move and sleeping on a blow-up mattress in an empty house.

"I actually read for Richie," Gallner says. "I was obviously bummed I didn't get the role, but then I got a message from my team saying Radio Silence would like to still have me in the movie. They offered me the role of Vince. If you can't be Ghostface, the next best thing is getting killed by Ghostface, and I consider it an honor to have been cut down by such an iconic character."

Gallner knew Vince's fate from the start, though the scene changed from the initial script he read. "In the beginning it was a little more involved, with Vince driving away and then stopping on the side of the road and getting attacked," he says. "There was a bit more of a fight and a struggle. I think, in the end, the simplicity of Vince's death is kind of great. That knife goes into his neck so fast and he's just left standing there looking dumbfounded."

When it came to casting the killers, poster children for toxic fandom Richie and Amber, they had to figure out whether the actors could be convincing in those roles without giving anything about the story away.

"I think Amber was probably the most challenging to cast because she goes full psychopath," Delia says. "You need to see it. In my experience, actors will rarely go further on set than they go in the auditions. We really fought for Mikey Madison to get that role. We gave her a Billy Loomis scene to read in her audition for fun and she just went with it, without us telling her that she was the killer. She trusted us enough to go to those places."

———

JACK QUAID SUSPECTED HIS CHARACTER, RICHIE KIRSCH, MIGHT BE THE killer when he was asked to submit a self-tape doing Timothy Olyphant's monologue from *Scream 2*. Given his previous filmography, he rightly suspected they were testing him to see if he could pull it off. "Before that, I'm Hughie on *The Boys*," says Quaid. "I'm very much a scaredy-cat character, cowering in the corner."

It turns out Vanderbilt is friends with *The Boys* showrunner Eric Kripke and was able to get some intel on the sly.

"I called Eric and I was like, 'We want to cast Jack in the movie, I think.' He's like, 'Oh, he's the best. He's wonderful.' And I was like, 'Um, what's his range like? Let's say he had to play *not* funny and charming Jack Quaid?' And he's like, 'I got it. You're gonna be fine.'"

Not only did Quaid have the acting skill to bring the character to life, but he was also an epic overachiever when it came to prepping for the role.

"Amber and Richie met in the *Stab* subreddit. I wanted

to make sure I knew what being a toxic fan on Reddit was like, so I made an account called Stabhead with the bleeding *Scream* Ghostface mask as my profile picture. I still technically have it," Quaid says. "It was just character research. What is Reddit like? What is a person who spends most of their time on here like? I also waded into the deepest, darkest waters of YouTube. There's some people that are truly in their bones angry—name a franchise, they're angry at it—and I really wanted to delve deep into those things."

Quaid didn't just immerse himself in Reddit and YouTube. He rewatched all the previous *Scream* films, listened for every movie they referenced, and tried to watch all of those. *Halloween*, *Psycho*, *A Nightmare on Elm Street*, *Friday the 13th*, you name it, he probably watched it—along with *The Strangers* at the suggestion of Radio Silence.

And, as if that wasn't enough, he also created a playlist that is absolutely unhinged in the best way. It's something he often does for characters he plays, but Richie's playlist is one of his favorites and he still listens to it.

The cover image is, naturally, Woody from *Toy Story*, which Quaid imagines was Richie's favorite movie as a kid. He reads off some of the tracks: "Red Right Hand" by Nick Cave and the Bad Seeds, obviously; "Serious Things Are Stupid" by Cayetana; "Everybody Wants You" by Red Hearse; "Beautiful Stranger" by Madonna; "Season of the Witch" by Donovan; a cover of "Bang Bang (My Baby Shot Me Down)" by the Monophonics; and a few songs from the *Scream* soundtrack. "There's a shit-ton of songs in here," Quaid says. "'Tiny Dancer' by Elton John. I don't know why."

His secret to cracking Richie was making sure he actually

does genuinely care for Sam. He's with Amber too, of course, and Quaid thinks he gets a little too much pleasure from having two girlfriends because he has abandonment issues and fucked-up ideas about romance. "None of this is necessarily apparent on screen but it really helped me in the moment," he says. "With this playlist I wanted to make sure there was a hint of that. Besides 'Monster Mash' it's a very good playlist."

———

WHEN IT CAME TO THE MUSIC FOR THE FILM, THE PROJECT X TEAM turned to composer Brian Tyler, whom they'd known for years. He was part of "the graduating class of *Darkness Falls*"—the 2003 tooth fairy tale that was the first feature James Vanderbilt cowrote and William Sherak produced—but his work with Sherak dates back even further to an indie called *Four Dogs Playing Poker* released around the turn of the millennium. He had done *Ready or Not* with Sherak, Busick, and Radio Silence, and happened to be a fan of the *Scream* franchise.

Tyler considered *Scream* to be a musical Möbius strip. "You're going forward and going backwards into a world that exists at the same time," he explains. He needed to create a sound that fit in the existing universe while both updating it and making sure it still felt familiar—and navigate the psychology of musical red herrings.

"We are pattern-seeking mammals and problem solvers. We get dopamine hits when we solve something, and it's exaggerated by the amount of surprise that it would have elicited," Tyler explains.

There's a balance between using suspenseful music to build tension and playing something calming as a misdirect. Trying to subvert expectations and trick the audience every time becomes an impossible exercise in mindfuckery.

"I actually have to randomize it sometimes," Tyler says. "When I jump into a scene and there's a suspense thing and something may happen or it may not, I am not going to do it by reading the script or having seen the scene before. I will decide ahead of time, or I will just roll the dice, and there is a ratio I have built in. So, basically, it makes it impossible for someone to guess what I'm thinking."

Meanwhile, set designer Chad Keith was tasked with creating the physical mood of the film and re-creating Woodsboro—including a scale replica of Stu Macher's house on a soundstage in Wilmington, North Carolina. He was able to connect with Bruce Alan Miller, his predecessor on the earlier films, who helped him with minute details and exact measurements.

"I would be like, 'All right, how thick are the rails going up the steps?'" Keith recalls. "I didn't want a bunch of *Scream* fans on my ass for doing something wrong—because they are picky, picky fans."

So, they focused on intricate details like hand-painting the tiles in the kitchen to exactly match the original, re-creating the stained glass window above the front door, and making sure the room where Mindy relives her uncle Randy's encounter with Ghostface while watching a movie was identical.

Because the Machers' house had been the site of grisly murders, they had some leeway.

"The last time we had seen the house, it was a blood-bath," Keith says. "So, we finally settled on the idea that the colors could change and the carpets could change a little bit. We weren't going to be tied down to assuming that all the blood disappeared and the house still looks great."

It's an ironic twist of fate when you think about the fact that Wilmington was scouted for the original *Scream* but didn't work because they couldn't find the right houses, only for them to re-create Stu's house there decades later.

"It was pretty cool to be around when Kevin came to see it, and when Courteney and Neve and everybody saw the house for the first time," Keith says. "They were all freaking out about how close it was. I knew I had done my job well when the actors felt like they were in the original house."

"I cried when I first walked on that set," Campbell says. "They had put up the sign 'For Wes' and it was moving and touching and so surreal. They did an immaculate job of matching the original."

CHAPTER SIXTEEN

5CREAM

When it came to making the new *Scream*, there were unintentional and uncanny parallels to the experience of working on the original. No one could predict how audiences would react to the film, the cast and crew stayed in the same hotel and spent all their downtime together, and they legitimately worried about being shut down. On *Scream*, the positives stemmed from the environment Wes Craven created on set, and the negatives were caused by mercurial studio execs. On the requel, a global pandemic was raging and they were sequestered in a Wilmington, North Carolina, Homewood Suites. The circumstances were very different; still, the bonds the *Scream 5* team forged are a lot like the ones made in wine country, where castmates and crew became family while living in a DoubleTree and hanging out in a barn.

Jack Quaid affectionally calls the movie *5cream*, pronounced "five-cream." It was a joke on set, and they even had T-shirts made with Ghostface holding milk cartons.

"This is such a cliché, and you hear everybody say this all the time, but it was like summer camp," Quaid says. "I will cherish those relationships for the rest of my life. That cast was so incredibly cool."

Director Tyler Gillett agrees.

"Honestly, it seems shitty to say, but the way COVID shaped that experience was really fucked up and scary but also really beautiful and singular," says Gillett. "Like, 'We're in it together. We don't know what the fuck this is gonna be, or if it's gonna get shut down.'"

"Unlike most movies where people go, 'Oh, it's war and we're in the trenches,' this was literally life and death," says director Matt Bettinelli-Olpin. "Everybody involved got really close and became a very tight-knit family in a way that I don't think would've ever happened without the pandemic."

The movie was filmed in the fall of 2020 before a COVID-19 vaccine was available. They were masking, social distancing, and dealing with pandemic protocol enforcers who didn't understand the practical realities of filmmaking.

"We didn't have the budget of these giant movies from other studios where you could literally take out an entire city block and quarantine everybody in place," says producer Paul Neinstein. "Nobody could come, and nobody could leave."

Neve Campbell says filming during the pandemic was challenging for her because she likes to be able to watch the monitors and get a sense of the tone and what the DP is doing with the shots. "I like to see how things are coming across. I like to be listening to the director and the team at video village and I wasn't allowed to sit in video village. I had to sit in a room by myself with the door closed, which was depressing," she says. "I love that part of making a film, the group effort and the creative conversation that happens. None of us were really allowed to have that. So that was disappointing. I still enjoyed working with the actors and I enjoyed working with Matt and Tyler. I think we all felt the same. During COVID some of the magic was missing, not from the film itself but from the experience."

When they weren't filming, they did whatever they could to bring some of that magic back—like taking over the hotel conference rooms and dubbing it Camp Sherak.

"I put in a pool table, a Ping-Pong table, a dartboard, an Xbox, a PlayStation, and two commercial-size refrigerators filled with White Claw," producer William Sherak remembers. "I flew in bagels and lox every Sunday from a different bagel place around the country."

They'd go to the beach or go on hikes, and David Arquette taught painting seminars.

"David is a certified Bob Ross painting instructor," says Quaid. "He led us all through a class where we made happy little trees and a lake. I think I still have my painting. For a movie about murder, it was such a wholesome experience around it."

Jasmin Savoy Brown says living in their *Scream* bubble was the time of her life.

"Every single person is so successful and brilliant and talented in their own right and it hasn't gone to anyone's head," Brown says. "That's pretty rare in this industry. We love each other dearly and had so much fun."

It was almost *too* fun.

"We were like, 'The movie is probably going to suck,' because that's often the stereotype in the industry: If it's fun and easy to make, it'll flop. And if it's absolutely the worst thing ever, then it'll be a huge success," Brown says. "There really were a couple days where we were like, 'Shit, this movie is gonna be bad,' because we had so much fun."

FOR LONGTIME FANS OF THE FRANCHISE, WORKING ON A *SCREAM* MOVIE with people who'd been there from the start was surreal.

"All of a sudden Kevin Williamson, Neve Campbell, and Courteney Cox were all there, just talking. It was like an out-of-body experience to watch that," Bettinelli-Olpin says. "Courteney took a selfie with us, and Kevin took a picture of Courteney taking the picture. I remember being like, 'What is life right now?'"

That sense of wonder and gratitude remained throughout the shoot.

"Matt and Tyler were great. They were like kids in a candy store. They were so excited to be a part of it," Campbell says. "The first scene that I did with them they forgot to say 'cut' because they had a moment of feeling like they were watching a *Scream* movie and they forgot they were directing it. It was adorable."

For Skeet Ulrich, reconnecting with his character was easier than expected, but nothing else about the project felt quite as familiar.

"It was weird in a lot of ways," Ulrich says. "They saved it for the last thing they shot. Most of the cast was wrapping up, but they were all new. Neve was not there. Davey wasn't there. So, it felt foreign. It felt like a different job completely."

Craven's presence was also missed. "It was sad in some ways, and yet in other ways I felt like it was such a tribute to him," Ulrich says. "It was very bittersweet."

This time around, he didn't re-create Billy's bedroom in the hotel—but he did leave something special behind. "At the end of filming, the art department gave me this mock-up poster they had made. I didn't have any way to travel with it without ruining it," Ulrich recalls. "So, I wrote on it, 'Whoever finds this, I stayed in this hotel while I shot *Scream 5*, I hope your life is going well,' et cetera, and I put it behind the dresser that the TV sat on."

As far as he knows, no one has found it yet, but he hopes someone will.

THERE'S ONE LEGACY CHARACTER *SCREAM* JUST WOULDN'T BE THE SAME without: Ghostface.

The killer beneath the mask is someone different each time, yet when they're in the deathly garb it's like they become a separate, demonic entity—one with a mean streak and a haunting voice.

"I've never seen a full script," says Roger L. Jackson, the actor who voices Ghostface. "I never see anything but my own scenes. So, I don't know who the killer is."

That means there's never any temptation to add layers that might differentiate one Ghostface from another, which allows him to be both no one and everyone at once.

"I like to remember the line Goethe said, 'I firmly believe

that with the slightest shift in my character there is no crime I could not commit,'" Jackson says. "There are inner motivations that drive each of these characters to want to kill people. When you put on the mask, you are hidden. The demon can come out."

"Someone coined the term 'domestic horror.' We don't control, nor do we have the full context of, the people around us," Mason Gooding says. "Because of that fear of the unknown, the things we can't control, sometimes the scariest things in our vicinity are the people we see every day."

Unlike other slasher villains—Jason Voorhees, Michael Myers, Freddy Krueger—there's no supernatural lore to make the killer seem unrealistic or out of place in our world.

"With Ghostface it's always really grounded," Gillett says. "It's a real person under the robe, and that's always going to be more terrifying to us than a character that has some magical capability that ultimately breaks from reality."

While I was talking to Radio Silence about why Ghostface is such an effective character, the conversation took a weird left turn.

MATT: Ghostface is also very sexy. I think we all know that.

TYLER: Ghostface makes people horny. We have learned that.

ASHLEY: Wait, what?

MATT: Oh yeah, it can't be underestimated.

TYLER: It cannot.

ASHLEY: Is there dirty fan fiction out there that I'm unaware of?

MATT: Ohhh, go down that rabbit hole at your own peril.

TYLER: I also think that's part of what the slasher language is though, right? When we fell in love with these movies, we were all pubescent teens learning about our bodies and relationships, and there is a soapiness to all of the *Scream* movies. They are intrinsically sexy. But, yes, Ghostface makes people horny. If there is any quote that ends up in the book, let it be that.

ASHLEY: Oh my God, I was not prepared.

TYLER: Nor were we.

MATT: Yeah, and nor were we.

THE SUBVERSIVE AND SCARY OPENING SEQUENCE IN *SCREAM* THAT WAS conjured by Kevin Williamson and brought to life by Wes Craven is iconic and impossible to top.

So it was a bit insane, and more than a bit ballsy, to bring the franchise back after a decade-long absence with a new take on the teen who's home alone when the phone rings. When the *Scream 5* team got to work on their version, their focus for that opening sequence and the movie as a whole was honoring the original while bringing the story into the modern world.

This time it's Tara Carpenter who's home alone. She's

texting her friend Amber, trying to lure her over with the promise of an unlocked liquor cabinet, when someone calls the landline.

A stranger, pretending to be an acquaintance of her mother's, starts a chat about scary movies.

"What's your favorite scary movie?" the voice asks.

"*The Babadook*. It's an amazing meditation on motherhood and grief," Tara answers, before talking about how she prefers "elevated horror" and isn't into the *Stab* films.

The man on the phone reminds her about the plot of the opening scene, which she realizes she's currently living when he asks, "Would you like to play a game, Tara?"

"It was a major callback to Drew Barrymore's scene in the original," Ortega says. "It was my first go at a slasher like that, and I understand how respected the franchise is, so I felt pressure to do it right. Fortunately, being stabbed several times, I think the displayed emotion has the freedom to be subjective."

Unlike Casey Becker, Tara has a healthy dose of skepticism from the start and, despite the bone-chilling circumstances, keeps her wits about her. And, unlike the targeted characters in the opening sequence of every other *Scream* movie, she survives.

"The opening was pretty wild on *Scream 5* because it was the first three days of shooting, and it was Roger L. Jackson calling in on the phone," Gillett says. "So, the opening of our experience with making these movies was the opening of *Scream 5*. It was every bit as scary and fun and nerveracking as we expected it to be."

The success of the opening is in no small part due to Ortega's acting chops.

"It was our first time working with Jenna," Bettinelli-Olpin says. "That was one of those experiences, which we've been lucky enough to have a few times now, where you watch someone and within five minutes turn to each other and go, 'Holy shit. We got so lucky. She's incredible. Our jobs just got a lot easier.'"

And that job was making a *Scream* movie—which hadn't fully hit them until then.

"It felt like we had arrived in our careers, in a weird way," Gillett says. "As fans of the movies, to be there shooting a *Scream* opening was surreal."

———

WHEN KEVIN WILLIAMSON AGREED TO JOIN THE TEAM ON *SCREAM 5*, HIS only request was that the film be dedicated to Wes Craven.

Everyone was thrilled to oblige, and they went well above and beyond just dedicating the movie to him. They named a character after him—who, of course, is murdered in a tense and heartbreaking scene—and the big killer reveal happens at a wake being held in his honor, which includes a "To Wes" toast that a number of alumni from the franchise recorded audio for.

Because they admired Craven and his work so deeply, Radio Silence tried as hard as they could to get inside his head. They watched the director's commentaries of the previous movies on repeat and read every interview with him they could find.

They weren't alone. All the creative forces behind *Scream 5* either loved or idolized Craven and wanted to do right by him.

"That speaks volumes and is more important than anything else. That actually makes me feel really, really wonderful," says Iya Labunka. "I think Wes's spirit hovers over."

The back-to-back deaths of Sheriff Judy Hicks and her son, Wes, who was played by Dylan Minnette, really tuned in to the suspense and emotional pull that marked Craven's films.

"It was so brutal," Marley Shelton says. "It's this beautiful bright blue sky, middle of the day, *of course* Ghostface isn't going to kill you right now—and then boom. All bets are off in the *Scream* universe."

Fictional Wes was killed just moments later, but they built in what felt like eons' worth of false alarms before he ultimately met his demise.

"The scariest thing for me in a movie is the anticipation of something that you think might happen," says *Scream 5* cinematographer Brett Jutkiewicz.

That sounds an awful lot like the nothing is scarier than a dolly into a closed door wisdom Craven had shared with his crew, which may be why the emotion and pacing of that scene felt a little familiar.

"What I think is such a testament to the screenwriting and the direction and the camerawork in the original *Scream* is that it is so tense and so scary without being super dark," Jutkiewicz says. "That was something that inspired us for *Scream 5*, just thinking about ways we could use the camerawork to build tension."

And also like Craven, Radio Silence set a positive tone and encouraged the cast and crew to share their feedback.

There's one moment that stands out for Jasmin Savoy Brown. It happened while they were filming Wes's memorial party at Amber's house. In the movie, Mindy is sitting on the couch with her girlfriend and they kiss—but that wasn't scripted.

"Originally, Mindy just said, 'I'm gonna make out with Frances' and then then it cut, and we never actually saw them kiss," Brown says. "I said, 'It's really important that we see it, even if it's a quick moment. It doesn't have to be anything more than a kiss, but I think that representation is huge.'"

The directors immediately agreed, and she says that interaction is just one of many where she felt like she was heard and her opinion mattered.

"That speaks to their character. That speaks to their egoless-ness and their brilliance," Brown says. "I think that's part of why the movie was so successful, the fact that they were open to everyone's notes. They hired us all for a reason, they were interested in all of our takes, and the movie is better for it."

───────

ANOTHER HALLMARK OF *SCREAM 5* IS THAT IT INCLUDES ONE OF THE most emotional and controversial moments in the franchise: Dewey's death. Even if you agree that it was necessary to the story, it's heartbreaking.

It was especially brutal for David Arquette.

"I'm reading through this script and I was like, 'Oh wow, Dewey's got a great role in this one.' I kept going and I was like, 'Ohhh, that's why.' I had to sit down," Arquette remembers. "It never occurs to me to say, 'No, I'm not doing it. I'm not gonna let Dewey die.' That's not my place, really."

He did have other notes. His biggest concern was that there was too much emphasis on Dewey being a drunk, which Arquette says just didn't feel right for the character. So, they dialed it back and showed his struggles with more subtlety.

"David, rightfully so, was like, 'I'm happy to play that texture, but I want to make sure that, even though Dewey is on hard times, he still has that sparkle.' He's that character that still feels like he's gonna survive everything. His resilience is still the thing that makes him *him*," Gillett says. "I think that he was really right to want to preserve that."

Heather Matarazzo had a similar reaction to the scene where her character reunites with Dewey.

"In the original script Martha is like, 'Dewey, hiiii, you look like shit.' It didn't feel right to me for her to say it because it felt mean," Matarazzo recalls. She didn't want to overstep, so she was relieved when Radio Silence asked her to do another take with a variation on it. "I just looked at David and I was like, 'Dewey, you look . . . ,' and I didn't say the rest of the line. That felt right, and they loved it.

"Radio Silence was really open to trying different things," she says. "I felt at home in the house of Wes, this church that Wes had created. They were very similar priests."

True to his character, Dewey dies trying to protect the people he loves.

After he, Sam, Tara, and Richie escape a close call with Ghostface, he goes back to put an end to it. In a cruel twist, the person he loves most seals his fate. A call from Gale distracts him for a split second and that's all the killer needs.

"I remember that day," Quaid says. "The doors of the elevator close and so Melissa and I are off camera. We just looked at each other. That destroyed me."

The emotions surrounding Dewey's death weighed on Arquette during the shoot, and it seems like they still do.

"The whole time I was reluctantly kind of upset about it," Arquette says. "Plus, you have to go on and keep a secret for a long time, lie to people about it, put the smile on your face, which is hard to do. It was hard. I thought about Wes a lot on that movie, just in general, and the time we had spent together."

Ultimately, he understands the impact of that moment.

"There is an element that I liked," he says. "It's why I wanted Dewey to be injured after *Scream 1*, because you never see the characters in the next one have any sign of the pain they'd gone through. I just wanted to make it real. It grounds it."

It was the first death of a major character since *Scream 2*, when Randy Meeks was brutally murdered by Mrs. Loomis. It was shocking, and it was sad. You felt like you were losing a friend, and you worried for the safety of the other characters you cared about.

Dewey's death created a real-life meta moment for Jamie Kennedy while he was watching *Scream 5* at a movie theater in Thousand Oaks. "I didn't know the impact my death had on the audience until I saw David get killed," Kennedy says. "It really made me sad. It really hit me, and I was like, 'This is not just a movie.' It made me realize how much of an effect it has on people, so I try to honor it as much as I can."

THE REVEALS IN *SCREAM* ARE AS IMPORTANT AS THE OPENINGS, IF NOT more so. After all the bloodshed, and all the guessing, the audience finally gets to understand why this is happening. It needs to feel earned but not obvious. In other words: surprising but inevitable.

"I have a theory that Ghostface can't die when they have their mask on," says Mason Gooding. "The idea that you have to identify Ghostface, you have to put a name and a face to the murderer, to be able to defeat them is terrifying narratively because it requires your characters to investigate internally what they could have done that would compel someone to murder."

In this particular case, Sam Carpenter is paying for the sins of her parents (and whoever gave Ghostface a flamethrower in *Stab 8*). It's totally unreasonable to assume her boyfriend would know or care about any of that—but when Richie stabs Sam and says, "I know, it's a bummer it's me," it still feels like a gut punch you should have seen coming.

Since nearly all of his castmates didn't know who the killers were, Quaid had to be sly in the story *and* on set.

"My North Star was Allison Williams in *Get Out*, because you didn't suspect her and then you thought, 'Well, how could it have been anything else,'" Quaid says. "I had a plan with Matt and Tyler to essentially give three takes for every moment. One where I'm playing it like I'm just Richie, a very innocent character; one almost over-the-top in terms of how secretly evil he is; and then a third one that's kind of a blend in the middle. Movies are really found in the editing room.

So, if they want a shot of me looking a little dastardly, or one where I look really innocent, they have those options."

Quaid also built in some subtle physical clues, like every time Richie kisses Sam he's holding her face. "Richie is in love with Sam. Yeah, he has been playing her this whole time but he's starstruck by this person because she is the daughter of Billy Loomis. He grabs her head in a very 'you're my property' kind of way," he explains. "We planned this: When she slits my throat at the very end, she is grabbing my head in the same way. I love that little reverse."

Like the opening sequence, the kitchen face-off was a tribute to the original film.

"At that moment, the masks are off literally and figuratively," Jutkiewicz says. "So, it just felt right that it's a bright kitchen space and we're getting to see the intensity of the performances."

"Shooting the whole kitchen scene, we're literally fans making a movie about fans re-creating a movie that we're also kind of re-creating," Bettinelli-Olpin says. "It was meta upon meta. We're in there with Neve telling us about when they shot the original and what we could do to improve. I remember Neve telling us that the big reveal was way too much."

"I hesitated to say that, but I did," Campbell says with a laugh. "The monologue was way too long. I remember standing there during the scene and going, 'This can get cut. We're losing the audience. We're losing *me* right now.'"

"She was a hundred percent right," Bettinelli-Olpin says. "We ended up cutting it in half."

What remains is a tight, bloody exposition on toxic fandom and obsession.

"Richie is a character who has always wanted to be Ghostface and have this killer monologue. So, he's leaning in hard," Quaid says. "He can be a little campy with it. A lot of that came from Matt Lillard and how much he embraced the absurd. I love that he is clearly a psycho the entire movie, but you don't realize that he's *the* psycho 'til the end, and he's just so funny. I tried to bring as much humor as I could during that monologue. It's gotta be menacing, but it's gotta also be kind of funny."

In true *Scream* fashion, it ends with the heroes winning and the killers getting their due. Quaid, for one, really enjoyed watching his on-screen girlfriend get her revenge.

"Richie gets stabbed twenty-seven times, or something insane," Quaid says. "She is not stabbing me, obviously, it's a sponge. I'm tucked away on the staircase just watching her do it. I remember being like, 'Holy shit.' It was just like one after the other and they kept most of them."

It was a cathartic moment for Sam, and for the audience too.

"I love when Melissa Barrera goes nuts with the knife. I could watch her stabbing some dude because he deserved it all day," says Blumhouse film exec Ryan Turek. "She commits to that role really well. It also just dives into her psyche, like there is something itching to get out and the only time she lets it out is when she's taking some dude down."

———

SCREAM 5 BROUGHT IN $30 MILLION AT THE BOX OFFICE OPENING weekend, which certainly wasn't bad for one of the first movies back in theaters after the COVID-19 shutdown. It wasn't quite what the studio had been expecting, but they got unlucky with weather as a snowstorm hit the northeast U.S. and Canada. Normally, the Canadian box office would account for up to about 12 percent of theatrical revenue, but nearly every theater in the country was closed. Still, the overall success of the film reassured them that reviving the franchise was the right call.

It's hard to fully quantify what fans thought, since online reviews are a small sample size and easily manipulated. But, for what it's worth, *Scream 5* has a B+ CinemaScore, which comes from in-person polls taken as people leave the theater opening weekend.

"It's one of the first movies that welcomed people back to the theaters in a big way," says horror screenwriter Michael Kennedy. "Post-pandemic, people were really wanting something comforting, and weirdly, *Scream* is that."

"Audiences that grew up watching these films get to come back and see the familiar faces they know and love, but a whole new generation of people get to jump in as well and fall in love with a new batch of characters," Kyle Gallner says. "It truly is a testament to the staying power of Ghostface, the *Scream* movies, and horror in general."

"I'm a little jealous, to be candid," Matthew Lillard says, describing it as like watching your ex move on with someone else. "Every Christmas you get their Christmas card, they're a happy family going forward. I'm the old family, that's the new family. You're happy for them, but you're still jealous."

As for the movie itself, Lillard is a fan.

"The movie is like a love letter to Wes Craven," he says. "In a way, it's sort of given more weight to the first movie.

There is an elevation of those characters that we see at conventions and a whole new generation of kids finding it that are really excited to meet us. It was super lovely the way they gave homage to Wes and celebrated him, and celebrated what the movie was back then."

Not everyone loved it, and some people were pretty hateful about it, as has unfortunately become all too common in the internet age.

"We've gone from fans being people who just love and adore a certain series to people who are wannabe film execs and directors. They think that they can do it better than people who have actually been hired to do these jobs," says critic and horror fan Richard Newby. "Richie and Amber's whole mentality is very much that. They're wannabe studio execs."

For the most part, Radio Silence isn't bothered by people who don't like *Scream 5*, but they were surprised by how some fans expressed that.

"I think we underestimated the intensity of the fan base," Bettinelli-Olpin says. "There is definitely a very small subset that is vitriolic, and that was a little shocking to us. But at the end of the day, ninety-nine percent of it is awesome and supportive and lovely.

"We made a movie. We like it, and if you like it, great. If you don't, totally cool. It's the personal attacks that feel a little uneven."

Scream films comment on not only horror movies but also the zeitgeist. The fact that "fans" lashed out over a movie that criticizes toxic fandom proves that its meta-take on that moment in culture was spot-on.

"Under all of this is the idea that 'I want something that

feels exactly like what I loved in the previous thing. I want it to be safe,'" Gillett says. "What has always been interesting about *Scream* is that it fucks with your expectations. It challenges the notion of what you think the movie is going to be at every turn. For a *Scream* movie to be a successful *Scream* movie, it has to be that before it's anything else. It has to be subversive and weird and challenging. So, this idea that it's gotta be this thing that you expect it to be is such a strange fallacy."

Bettinelli-Olpin notes, as did several others, that except for the original—and, to some degree, the second movie—audiences didn't necessarily love each of the *Scream* films right away. They all gained popularity through rose-colored hindsight.

"I saw all four of them in the theater and loved every one of them but I remember the general reaction among audiences and critics was diminishing returns, especially to *3* and *4*," Bettinelli-Olpin says. "It was really interesting when *5* came out and suddenly it was like, 'There were four perfect movies. How dare you screw them up with your inferior movie?'"

They love that the entire franchise has grown in popularity over the years—and they'd rather make a movie that people don't necessarily like now but watch and talk about in a decade than make one that's instantly popular and just as quickly forgotten.

Ultimately, they were only truly concerned about an audience of one. As long as Williamson was happy and felt like they'd made a bona fide *Scream* movie, they were happy. They sent him a preview link on a Friday, but he couldn't watch it right away.

"I didn't realize this, but they were all sitting around going, 'He didn't call, he must hate it,'" Williamson remembers.

The next morning, he made popcorn and watched it with his fiancé, Victor, who was impartial because he grew up in Colombia and had missed the *Scream* mania while it was happening. He didn't have any attachment to it and hadn't seen any of the other sequels. He loved it, which was a relief, because Williamson did too. At first, he wasn't sure if it was because it was good or because he was just so happy to see the characters on screen again. With Victor's enthusiasm, he knew it was both.

"I remember watching the movie with a smile on my face," Williamson says. "I loved when Dewey died. I thought it was emotional, I thought they did a beautiful job with that. I teared up at the end because I was so happy there was another *Scream* and it was that good. I was so happy to call them to tell them. I was like, 'I don't know if you care what I think, but man, you've got a good movie.'"

Williamson loved it. And, in his own words, "It was only surpassed by *6*."

GHOSTFACE TAKES MANHATTAN

Before *Scream 5* even hit theaters, Spyglass knew it wanted another installment, and like the first sequel, *Scream 6* was fast-tracked to ensure it was released before the franchise lost its momentum.

"We were unbelievably proud of what we did. Then, like all creative people, you immediately go to self-deprecation and question every choice you've ever made in your life," says producer William Sherak. "Was it a fluke? How do we not screw this up? You have a little bit of success, they let you do it again, now you *really* can't screw it up."

Creatively, they treat each film as if it's their only shot at telling a *Scream* story—but, on the business side, there was never a question that they were building this thing for the long haul.

Since Sherak works on both sides of the filmmaking

equation, he says he bifurcates his thinking based on whom he's meeting with and why.

"There is the franchise management side of it and then there is each individual movie. You have to look at them separately at certain points and together at other points depending on who is in the room," Sherak explains. "When we started, when Gary gave us the ability to be part of this, it was always the goal to have fun making as many as we can. Inside the development meetings, when you dig down one layer deeper, you have to make every movie as if it's the last one you're going to get to make. You want to leave it all on the table. If you're worried about making six more, are you using all the best ideas for that one or are you holding things back? That's how you end up in trouble."

Of all the places they could have taken *Scream 6*, literally and figuratively, they went somewhere probably no one else would have: New York City.

Like *Scream 2*, the story follows the young characters—the Carpenter and Meeks-Martin siblings—to college. Instead of a typical college campus, they brought the story to a city of eight million people.

"I never would've taken it to New York City," says Kevin Williamson. "Did you see *Jason Takes Manhattan*? It was awful."

If they're using Williamson's opinion as their barometer of success, which many of them are, changing his mind about that is a massive win. *Scream 6* became his second-favorite film in the franchise so far—behind only the original.

"What a game changer it was," says Williamson. "They proved me wrong."

To writers James Vanderbilt and Guy Busick, *Scream 5* was playing the hits and *6* was the "punk rock B-side." They'd paid homage to what came before, successfully reset the universe, and were ready to take some big swings.

By setting the story in New York, they had the opportunity—and the obligation—to upend long-standing genre tropes about when and where characters are safe when a killer is on the loose. Thankfully, it's something this particular franchise is well-suited for. That you could be surrounded by people yet still vulnerable is a chilling idea that hadn't been explored in a *Scream* film since Maureen Evans's murder in a crowded theater playing *Stab* in the *Scream 2* opening.

"In these movies, you're trained that you don't want to get caught alone with the killer because you're in danger if you're alone. If you can get to shelter or other people, you are safe," says Vanderbilt. "This is the absolute opposite of that. You can run to where you think safety is—travel in public, you'll be safe if you're on a subway train with a hundred people—but, actually, no. It's the worst place for you to be in this situation."

Like the first time around, Vanderbilt and Busick were shockingly in sync.

"This is a very uncanny and weird thing," Busick starts off. "When Jamie and I had our first story meeting over Zoom, because we were still smack in the pandemic, we had our notepads and were like, 'Okay, blue-sky, what do we want to see in the next *Scream* movie? What would make us happiest as fans and what feels the most fun and risky and cool?'"

Busick went first. "I was like, 'I'm just gonna pitch you

this. You might hate it. We have a traditional Ghostface kill, a phone call, lure somebody from a crowded place, which we didn't expect, into a private place, kill. Then the killer takes off the mask at minute six and we follow the killer. Hopefully you're going, "Wait, what the fuck is this movie?" Maybe you're thinking we're gonna be from Ghostface's point of view the whole movie,'" Busick says.

Which, by the way, is exactly the reaction you'd have— unless, of course, you read the *Variety* review that spoiled it two days before the movie hit theaters. I saw *Scream 6* at the premiere and was floored by the opening, and I'm still pissed on behalf of anyone who read that first and was robbed of the surprise. Okay, rant over; back to Busick.

"I didn't pitch out the whole thing, but I pitched out a few signposts," Busick says. "Jamie gets this look on this face and I'm like, 'Oh God, he hates it.' Then he holds up his notepad and it says, 'Traditional kill, Ghostface takes off mask, we follow Ghostface.' And I'm like, 'Bingo! We're right back there again.'"

They start with what they call their "vomit draft," a version of the script that just gets everything down on paper so they can start picking it apart and fine-tuning the story. Busick says that process for *5* was "*fast* fast," somewhere between two and four weeks, and *6* was more like four or five weeks. Vanderbilt says *6* felt faster to him, but that could be because the pressure was on.

"It was like, 'Oh, they're looking at dates to release it. You should figure out what the movie is. You should figure out what happens because in March of next year it will be happening on three thousand screens,' which I actually think was helpful," Vanderbilt says. "It was really like, 'first thought, best thought.' If a screenplay is in development for ten years, everything has been second-guessed so much that sometimes it just gets watered down and the edges get shaved off more and more."

———

RADIO SILENCE RETURNED TO DIRECT, WHICH MAY SEEM LIKE A NATURAL move—especially in hindsight—but pretty much no one thought the directing duo coming back for another *Scream* was a smart thing for them to do.

"To lay the foundation, *6* is a movie that basically every single person we know or talked to was like, 'Don't do it. There's no reason to do it. You guys did *5*, it worked, move on,'" says Matt Bettinelli-Olpin. "But we had so much fun and we loved it and we wanted to do it again—and I think we were secretly hoping we could do a trilogy. As a film-maker, to be able to do a trilogy of something is the dream."

"Making your three movies, all of our favorite directors have done that," Tyler Gillett says. "There was something really tantalizing about an opportunity to achieve that with the people you love."

So, they ignored everyone and did it for themselves.

"We made sure that *5* was a love letter to Wes, to Kevin, to the original four movies, that it really felt like it lived in that world," Bettinelli-Olpin says. "With *Scream 6*, we all told ourselves, 'This one is for us. Let's make our version of *Scream* where it's really as much our voice as we can possibly make it.'"

There are some rules to making a *Scream* film, though.

"It's understanding tone and it's understanding that

you're making a movie in a franchise you didn't create," says Sherak. "You have to be okay with that. You don't get to go completely off the rails. That doesn't mean you can't do cool stuff. Matt and Tyler did it better than anybody. They made it their own without question, but they were *Scream* movies."

"They're honoring what came before them, but they are also presenting it in a very fresh fashion," says Kevin Williamson. "They have turned it into an artistic endeavor."

This time around, Radio Silence had two catchphrases: "Risk it all" and "Go down choosing."

"*Scream 6* was a leap of faith. 'Together we can do this,'" Bettinelli-Olpin says. "Just speaking for the two of us, we have this weird thing that I don't think we know consciously, or didn't know consciously. Looking back at the choices we've made, we've been told that's a bad idea every time on some level. Because there is always a risk. We already feel like we won the lottery because we're making movies for a career."

"It's all a victory lap at this point," says Gillett.

Still, working on this particular movie wasn't exactly a smooth drive, even with a team and cast that they love.

"When we were making *Scream 6*—I cannot stress this enough—all the way up until the first day of shooting, nobody had a clue what the fuck the movie was," Bettinelli-Olpin says. "Nobody had a clue how it was gonna work, nobody knew anything. A week before we were shooting, it was still like, 'Maybe Neve's gonna be in the movie.'"

Because they didn't know whether Sidney Prescott would be part of the story, they had to do double the planning.

"We were prepping two versions of it for weeks and weeks," Gillett says. "It was insane."

———

LEADING UP TO THE SHOOT, AND TO SOME EXTENT STILL TO THIS DAY, *Scream 6* was haunted by press coverage and fan complaints about Neve Campbell's absence from the film. To boil the situation down to its core: Spyglass had a budget in mind and Campbell felt her contribution to the franchise, and her character's significance, deserved more than the studio was willing to pay.

"I knew I wouldn't be able to walk on set feeling disrespected. I knew I wouldn't be able to walk on set feeling that I hadn't respected myself. And I knew I wouldn't be able to walk on set if I wasn't being paid what I deserve after decades of doing these films," Campbell says. "I love these movies and the idea of them carrying on without me made me sad, but it wasn't worth feeling disrespected. So, I didn't watch the movie, and I didn't pay any attention to how it was doing. I love all those actors. I have no ill will towards anybody who made the movie. I'm happy for anyone who gets to be a part of these films. But, for me, it wasn't the right decision to go and be in the film. And now, in the end, it's come back around and I'm very grateful."

"The situation with Neve, I mean, good for her is my feeling," says Iya Labunka, who remained close with Campbell even after Wes Craven's death. "Pay her what she's worth. What the fuck? She is so integral. Honestly, Wes would never have let this happen."

"Neve is supersmart. She has her head on her shoulders.

I think they should have offered her more," says William-son. "It was uncomfortable because they would say, 'Well, we offered her this,' and I'm like, 'And she said no. When you double that, you might have a conversation. You need to understand her point of view.'"

But, despite how much everyone involved respects Williamson's opinion, he really didn't have any control over the situation. "I'm not the man in charge and I'm not the man with the checkbook and I'm not the man who owns the rights," he says. "I'm the plus-one now to this new *Scream* franchise."

"Sidney Prescott is an amazing character and Neve is an amazing person who has crushed that role for a very long time," says William Sherak. "It wasn't the right thing for a host of reasons, and the storyline that we chose to tell works beautifully—and there is a version of that movie that would also work beautifully with Sidney. Let's be very clear: There is no version of a *Scream* movie that can't work perfectly with Sidney Prescott. You play out the cards you can play. We can only control what we can control."

On screen, they explained it in a straightforward, logical way. Busick and Vanderbilt didn't overwrite it and it worked.

After getting punched in the face by Tara, Gale tries to convince the sisters she's on their side. As they're walking away, she tells them she's talked to Sidney to get them to stop.

Gale explains, "She sends her love, but she's taking Mark and the kids someplace safe. She deserves to have her happy ending."

The typical movie plot thing would be for her to show

up. In the real world, if you're Sidney Prescott, at this point—unless Ghostface comes to you—the only reasonable choice is to stay away.

Horror screenwriter Michael Kennedy says people who criticized the scene are missing the point. "[Sidney is like,] 'I've done this once. I can't keep abandoning my family and risking my life when I have children and a husband,'" Kennedy says. "I love that Sam and Tara got that too. I think a lesser writer would have made them mad at her, or tried to create conflict with that, and they were just like, 'No, we get it.' I love that. It's such a really smart moment. I remember reading a review for *Scream 6* and the reviewer criticized that moment because it seemed too flippant and an afterthought. It's actually deep when you stop and think about it for ten seconds."

Patrick Lussier, who edited the first four *Scream* films, says the deal impasse was a godsend for the story.

"The luckiest thing to happen to them on *6* was to not have the baggage of Sidney Prescott," Lussier says. "Sidney is the biggest challenge because not only is she such a driving force in the first three movies but her story is so oppressive and unhappy. There is a moroseness and a melancholia and a seriousness to that character. Being able to shed that allows you to be light on your feet and charge ahead."

———

RICHIE KIRSCH'S FAMILY WAS CENTRAL TO THE STORY, AND IT'S FITTING that the second film in the new wave would nod to the theme of parental revenge in *Scream 2*. Richie's father, brother, and sister blamed Sam Carpenter for his death and they conspired to avenge him in the most brutal way they could imagine: infiltrating her life, tormenting her and her loved ones, and, ultimately, killing them all.

To really pull it off they needed the right actor to play Richie's dad, Detective Wayne Bailey. It had to be someone disarming and trustworthy who would shock the audience when he flipped the psycho switch during the reveal. Enter Dermot Mulroney.

"For that character, we wanted someone who America likes," says *Scream 6* casting director Rich Delia. "He is familiar enough that they're like, 'Oh, I love him,' but then they kind of forget about him. They have a positive association with him, so they're not thinking of him as the killer, but he's not so outwardly famous that he's pulling you out of the movie at the same time."

Mulroney got a call about the role out of the blue. He knew he was a killer, but he didn't know which character he was playing or anything about the story. The veteran actor hadn't done a major franchise film, so that alone was a draw.

"That's how it came to me: 'You are a Ghostface killer. Now, here's this script in three parts.' They sent it to me about thirty pages at a time," Mulroney says. "I was as perplexed as anybody. I was trying to figure out who Ghostface was, even though I knew it was me."

Mulroney is proud, in a morose way, of how much work his character did to set up his family's killing spree. Getting his kids into the same college and making sure they were living with members of the Core Four is no small feat. Then there's the theater rental with all the memorabilia, taking out the two other wannabe Ghostfaces, and faking his daughter's death. Mulroney describes it as a "diabolically precise and meticulous scheme."

"Once you have three killers it gets harder to justify that you're going to find three people who have the same willingness to cross a line and kill for the same reasons," Busick says. "Even with a family, you're kind of like, 'Really, the whole family are all psychos?' But when you see Dermot and his wonderful third-act monologue, you're like, 'Oh, I can buy that. Look at this guy. He raised psychos. That's just what he did.'"

Liana Liberato, who plays the Carpenters' roommate and secret Kirsch sister Quinn, had no idea what she was auditioning for. She sent in a self-tape right before leaving for a friend's wedding in Italy.

"I didn't realize that I had gotten a callback until I was on the second leg of my trip," Liberato says. "They were like, 'Hey, so, you're gonna be reading with Matt and Tyler and Chad for *Scream 6*.' And I was like, 'When did I audition for *Scream 6*? I would've definitely remembered that.'"

They gave her Amber's killer-reveal monologue from *5*, and she says the jet lag probably helped her act the part. "I love playing a crazy person," she says. "It just feels so therapeutic to me."

Little did she know, she'd get quite the catharsis from playing Quinn. She found out she got the job about a week later but only had the first two acts of the screenplay—and, at first, was a little disappointed with her part. Like the audience, she thought Quinn dies when Ghostface attacks everyone in the girls' apartment.

"I remember reading it on the plane and I was like, 'Oh

man, I'm dead, I'm really dead. That sucks,'" Liberato says. "When you're in a *Scream* movie you want to be the final girl, you want to be Ghostface, or you want to have a really epic death. I was like, 'Dang, I don't really get any of that.' I was kind of bummed."

That all turned around at her wardrobe fitting. She'd tried everything on and was about to leave when they told her the directors were on Zoom because they needed to see her in something else.

"Then they brought out the Ghostface outfit," Liberato says. "I can't imagine my face. I could not compute what was happening. They were like, 'Surprise! You're Ghost-face!' And I was like, 'Wait, what? I'm dead.' They're like, 'You're not dead!' Then I got to try on the outfit, which was insane. I left that fitting sobbing because I was so excited."

Her on-screen brother, Jack Champion, had a similar experience. He'd had a few meetings with Project X and Radio Silence and was worried he'd been a bit too much of a fanboy.

That may have worked in his favor.

"Jack Champion is so delightful," says Delia. "He brought this happy-go-lucky, 'I'm excited to be here' energy that was almost off-putting. Should we suspect you because you're so normal and nice?"

It's the perfect vibe for Ethan "I had Econ" Landry, which as far as Champion knew was the extent of the role.

"They only let us read the first three-quarters of the script and I was sus, obviously," Champion says. "There's no way I'm gonna be the killer—it's too good to be true—so, he probably dies. Before they let me read the third act, I had a wardrobe moment where Matt and Tyler come in with their phones and I'm like, 'What's happening right now?' Someone brought in the Ghostface costume and they're like, 'You're gonna be Ghostface, Jack!' I was just like, 'Shut up. You're lying to me. This is a game.'

"I was just completely flabbergasted. It was a shock. It's like, 'Oh my gosh, I'm going to be Ghostface, this iconic character. Me? Jack from Virginia? I have to live up to this legacy.'"

Devyn Nekoda, who plays Mindy's girlfriend Anika, didn't have any idea what untitled project she was going out for either. It was a short audition, which she recorded with her boyfriend over FaceTime.

"Then I get the callback and my manager goes, 'Hey, Devyn, by the way, you auditioned for *Scream*. Just thought you should know,'" Nekoda says. "I was not a huge fan of horror films. I'm a total scaredy-cat. So, I went to my mom and I'm like, '*Scream*, that's the guy with the mask, right? That's Ghostface?'"

The audition came at a low point, when she was thinking about giving up on acting after not getting any work in over a year. She remembers doing one of Jack Quaid's monologues from *Scream 5*. "I kind of went a little crazy. I feel like I blacked out for a minute doing that."

She flew to New York for the premiere of her latest film, *Sneakerella*, and tried to put it out of her mind.

"As I'm in the airport going home, I get the call. My manager is like, 'Do you have a minute?' I'm like, 'No, not really. I'm going through security.' She's like, 'Okay, just really, really, really quickly. Don't hang up yet. You booked *Scream*.' I put my phone in the bin and I'm bawling my eyes out. I will never forget that moment, it was so surreal.

"I was told that she was the cool one, the life of the party, and that she was in a relationship with Mindy, which I was really excited about because I knew that was the first time that the *Scream* franchise had had an LGBTQ relationship, so that made me extremely excited."

They also had an opportunity to bring back a fan favorite: Kirby Reed, played by Hayden Panettiere. They'd talked about it on the previous film, but they couldn't come up with a scenario that didn't feel forced.

"Then in *6*, when we came up with the FBI angle, it was like, 'She's gonna be a great red herring in the third act.' That made sense, so we pulled the trigger," Busick says. "There have been other characters [where] we've been like, 'How do we work in so-and-so? There's no way to do it that would make sense, so we gotta put that one back in the toy chest and sadly walk away.'"

———

JACK QUAID KNEW MORE ABOUT THE STORY THAN ANY OF THE ACTORS in the film because Radio Silence had called to ask for a favor. "Before they even started shooting it, I knew that the killers were going to be Richie's family. I was weirdly touched by it. Richie kind of lives on. It meant a lot to me, even though he was a psychopathic toxic fan killer," Quaid says. "They called me because they wanted to ask if I had any home movies that could be Richie's fan films that were going to be projected onto this screen."

Luckily, Quaid spent his teenage years making movies with his friends.

"We called it Epic Fest, and it was a Facebook group. Every summer, me and three other friends would do these little videos. They were essentially sketches, fake movie trailers and other kinds of things. For a week we would post a video every day and our whole high school would vote on which team submitted the best collection of videos.

"There was one where I'm sixteen, maybe younger, talking to camera, and I'm doing this dumb voice. I don't know how to be funny at all yet and I'm like, 'Hey, guys, I really wanted to record a Christmas episode.' I hadn't seen it cut into the movie until I went to the premiere in New York. My hair is insane and it's so long and I'm like teenager skinny. If you had told me back then that this video would later be used as a serial killer's video diary I would have lost my mind."

He met his on-screen family at a party before the premiere, which he also got a kick out of.

"They're all fuckin' psychos," Quaid says—about the characters, not the actors. "I love it. Jack, Liana, and Dermot, they're all really cool and I love that we're a part of a serial killer family. It delights me to no end."

It also delighted Busick and Vanderbilt to toy with the audience a bit.

"In the grand tradition of *Scream* movies trying to tell you who the killer is, we were like, 'You're gonna see Jack Quaid's face twenty times before we get to the reveal,'" Vanderbilt says. "Fun fact: Guy and I, in our two *Scream* movies to date, have never had a killer actually disguise their phone number. Literally like . . . it's Amber! It's Amber's phone! And then it's Richie's phone! I take a weird pride in that. The killer is calling you with their phone. Hiding in plain sight is always fun."

The Kirsch family also gave them the opportunity to

take Ghostface in a more primal direction; the killers were related but their motives were diametrically opposed.

"It was about movies for Richie, but for the family it was just about revenge," Vanderbilt says. "We loved the idea that if *Scream 5* is all about the *Stab* movies, *Scream 6* literally starts with the killer going, 'Who gives a fuck about movies?' That was really important for us too."

"'We're going after Sam for killing Richie, our son and brother, but we will kill anyone who gets in our way,'" Busick says. "This is our Terminator Ghostface. A Ghostface who doesn't fall down easily and who doesn't stop. You're not safe if you make it to the place where you're supposed to be safe. He is still going to come after you."

CHAPTER EIGHTEEN

A SECRET
ACTION MOVIE

While *Scream 5* was set almost entirely in houses and the hospital, the sixth installment has New York City as its playground. They drew inspiration from the city itself, turning typically mundane places into sites of unexpected attacks—with the help of cinematographer Brett Jutkiewicz, who grew up on Long Island.

"Knowing New York the way that I do, it felt like a lot of opportunity for Ghostface to be lurking around any dark corner," says Jutkiewicz. "He could be in any crowd of people."

"In a big city, you can be surrounded by people and something bad could happen and you could not get any help, which is terrifying to me personally. That kind of isolation in a busy area," says *Scream 6* editor Jay Prychidny.

One of the notes Kevin Williamson had about *Scream 5* was that there wasn't much running. They clearly took that to heart on *6*. "It was one chase scene after another. It was so wonderful," Williamson says. "I thought the set pieces in *Scream 6* were awesome and I loved it."

Those sequences—especially the bodega, ladder, subway, and theater—give the film a level of excitement and character that had been missing from the franchise for a while. When it came to finding the right person to pull it all together, producers called a Montreal local whose résumé included multiple *X-Men* films and the Project X comedy *Murder Mystery*.

But that production designer, Michèle Laliberté, almost didn't take the job. She stopped reading ten pages into the script because "all this alleyway slashing" was too much, and she turned it down. Producer William Sherak convinced her to watch the earlier movies so she'd fully appreciate all the Easter eggs in the film and to talk with Radio Silence, who won her over.

"What they wanted to do with the finale, the homage to the franchise and this vision they had of trying to make it really fun for the fans, they were just genuine in their approach to the project," Laliberté says. "And the relationship they had together, you wanted to be a part of it."

They had big ambitions for the film. As Prychidny remembers it, "They wanted this to be go-for-broke, almost like a secret action movie, with these set pieces that build on each other and escalate in this crazy way."

You can really feel that in the scene where Sam and Tara Carpenter run into the nearby bodega for help after being attacked on the street. Usually, a move like this would at least temporarily neutralize the threat—in real life or a slasher flick—but Terminator Ghostface follows them in, kills anyone who gets in the way, and swipes the shop own-er's shotgun.

In the script, the scene at Abe Snake's bodega—a nod to Wes Craven's porn pseudonym—was originally longer and included a car chase.

"Ghostface comes in, chaos ensues, they run out with Ghostface, they get in a cab, Ghostface chases them, the cab flips. It was a whole thing," Matt Bettinelli-Olpin re-members.

"Then we get up there and our wonderful line producer, Ron Lynch, was like, 'That's not happening. There is no way that works in this schedule.' Our instinct was we'll cut the cab stuff but make a real meal out of what happens in the bodega."

These small convenience stores are part of daily life in New York City. Probably not the first place you'd go in a cri-sis, but they're familiar.

"We wanted it to feel like they were being hunted," says Jutkiewicz. "That was really the first time we see Ghostface in this film be so brutal and so vicious. That was something we talked about from the beginning. This is our introduc-tion, in a way, to this new Ghostface."

The sisters crawl through broken glass in the bloody mess of a store before misdirecting the killer with a tossed beer can, tipping over shelves, and making a break for it. It reminded me of the scene in *Jurassic Park* where the two kids are crawling around a stainless-steel labyrinth of a kitchen trying to evade a pair of velociraptors—and it turns out that was one of the sources of inspiration.

"We definitely referenced that when we were thinking about that sequence and creating these different beats," says

Jutkiewicz. "I'll sketch out where the camera will be and what the path of the actors might be, while still being open to ideas from actors on the day. In that sequence, the beat where Sam throws the empty beer can to distract Ghostface was based on an idea that Melissa had when we were shooting it. She felt like there needed to be a little bit of a misdirect. Matt and Tyler, who are super collaborative, took that and designed this whole other beat, which I think is a crucial part to the story there. That misdirect gives them enough physical space away from him to start moving around."

Mason Gooding remembers the day well, but for a very different reason.

"I'll never forget, Tyler took a look at the shotgun and he was like, 'Can we plug the chamber?' I know it was decommissioned, as was protocol, but he was like, 'I don't want it to even look to us like something could come out of this end of the gun,'" Gooding says. "In addition to telling a story, in addition to directing, they care about safety, and they care about doing things cautiously and considerately. I just don't know if all people are willing to do that."

THE LADDER SEQUENCE—WHICH STARTS WITH A CHEESY BUT HEART-warming moment where Chad dubs their group the "Core Four" over dinner and ends with poor Anika being thrown face-first into a dumpster while trying to crawl to safety with her friends—was also reworked a bit during production.

Traversing a ladder from the Carpenters' window to Danny's apartment in the building next door several stories up seemed like it might be too complicated to shoot, so Busick and Vanderbilt wrote a new version that involved a drainpipe. Ultimately, everyone realized their initial idea with the ladder would actually be easier and they returned to it—but they did make some changes to the set design to add another layer to the scene.

"Inside the apartment when Ghostface busts in and breaks up the dinner party, there was less tension before you get to the ladder beat and we decided it would be cool if there was a Jack and Jill bathroom," says Gillett. "They get the one door blocked and then they realize *oh shit*, the banging has stopped, and there is another entrance into the room."

It also gave them the chance to show poor Paul 2.0 dead in the tub. Laliberté says figuring out the right amount of blood to splatter all over the white bathroom was a uniquely memorable moment of the shoot.

"I had on my iPad the bathroom with photoshopped versions of, okay, there's a little bit of blood. There's a bit more blood. There's more and more blood. There's all-over-the-place blood. This is you wouldn't believe how much blood there would be, and this is fully red," she remembers. "We were on the sidewalk, and it was a sunny afternoon, and we were just looking at them on my iPad choosing the amount of blood we would put on the walls. For a girl that wasn't a horror fan, that was something to remember."

Fan-turned-Ghostface Jack Champion is especially proud of that scene—even though you don't realize he's in it. "I have to flex this," Champion says. "The scene where Danny is screaming from the window and then Ghostface looks up and kinda tilts his head. That was all me. Being in the costume for a whole chunk of a scene was so special to me."

Meanwhile, his on-screen sister, Quinn, was playing dead—and her fake death gave Liana Liberato cover when it came to keeping that secret from family and friends too.

"I was completely bloody, fully acting dead, and they had a lot of pictures of me in that situation," Liberato says. "My friends would be like, 'I'm sure you're Ghostface, blah, blah, blah.' I am a terrible liar, but I had proof to show them. I was like, 'This is literally a scene that I filmed with me dead on the floor.' I'm like, 'Look, I'm stabbed. So sad!'"

Nekoda also has some pretty epic photos from filming that sequence, during which she's stabbed and falls to her death.

"I was there when they did the ladder fall," Busick says. "The first time I met Devyn was with the prosthetic after her mangled face has hit the ground. She was like, 'Hi! I'm Devyn!' I'm like, 'Hi, I did this to you. I'm so sorry.'"

"Yeah, that was pretty funny," Nekoda says. "I'm like, 'Hi, I don't normally look like this.' That was one of my first days on set and I feel like I met a lot of people that day."

The prosthetics took about two and a half hours, as she remembers it, but the shot on the ground only took about twenty minutes.

"I had someone walking around with me. I had to hold their hand because I could only see out of my one eye. They covered my ear and they poked my earrings through that fake ear, which I thought was really funny," Nekoda says. "I remember Matt and Tyler being like, 'Is there anything that you can do, like a funky way to lie on the ground?' I grew up dancing my whole life, so I'm pretty flexible. I grabbed my foot and I put it up to my head and they're like, 'Yup, that'll work!'"

Stunt performers crossed a ladder between the actual buildings, which were also re-created on a stage so the actors could film their shots closer to the ground.

"We took casts of the brick. So, it was exactly the same as what we had on the location," Laliberté says. They weren't sure they could pull it off, but they gave it a shot and it worked. I'm really happy they took the chances and pushed it, because it was a fun sequence."

If there's a quibble with the scene, it's Quinn's death, which Vanderbilt says is a nod to Agatha Christie's iconic novel *And Then There Were None.* No one explains whose body they substituted and how they got it into the building. If she'd been stabbed while out on a walk and thrown into the East River, no such problem. But, alas, there's no place for the logic police in the *Scream* universe. If you think about all the times the person should have heard Ghostface talking in the other room while on the phone with them, it ruins the fun.

Mulroney has some ideas about how Detective Bailey and Quinn pulled it off, though.

"When I was a kid, I was obsessed with Harry Houdini and he used to use squash balls under his armpit and then press really hard and it cuts off the blood flow to your wrists. So, I think that's what Quinn was doing upstairs. The coroner I probably paid off, so they'd take the body away and switch it out with another dead body."

Mulroney also put some thought into how Detective Bailey made himself cry on cue so he could seem appropriately devastated that his daughter had just been murdered by Ghostface.

"It's not in the script or anything, but I figure he put a

little Tiger Balm on the cuff of his coat. When he rubs his eye—which, if you check in the movie, it's in there—if you have the sports cream on your cuff, you'll cry. A lot of actors use that. So, there I'm using a B-actor trick in an A-plus movie."

ONE OF THE MOST TENSE AND MEMORABLE SCENES IN THE MOVIE HAP-pens on the subway. The Core Four and crew decide public transportation is the safest way to get to the theater so they can trap Ghostface, but Mindy and Ethan get separated from the group. They're surrounded by people decked out for Halloween—including Ghostface, which for some reason is still a costume people can just buy in a universe where serial killers wear it on murder sprees. The lights flicker on and off as a shadowy ghastly figure inches nearer to Mindy before very publicly stabbing her while muffling her screams.

"That domesticated horror, the fear of the known, that your neighbor could be a serial killer, New York is the highest degree of that," says Mason Gooding. "You interact with so many people on the day-to-day and have no idea what type of person they are, but you are locked into a subway system with them for forty-five minutes to get to class. It allowed Matt and Tyler to do something that I feel they do so effortlessly as visionaries, allowing characters to be affected by their surroundings in such a natural and visceral way."

It got a little *too* real for some of the audience.

"People told us after *6* that they weren't going back on the subway ever in New York," says producer Paul Nein-stein.

That's a testament to the job they did building a replica of a subway car. Because they shot the movie in Canada, they didn't have access to the actual New York City transit system and they couldn't rent a car and transport it because the available ones were in bad condition and the stage wasn't strong enough to support the weight.

So, the art department built one, along with the Ninety-Sixth Street subway stop, which took about eight weeks. They really needed two cars, but that wasn't in the budget, so they got creative.

"We made it look like it was two subway cars by putting a mirror in the set," Laliberté says. "It was really efficient and surprising to the guys when we did that. It was kind of magical. It ended up being a really expensive sequence, but the train car came out beautiful."

"That turned out to be one of my favorite sequences in the whole film," Jutkiewicz says. "Being from New York and knowing what it's like to ride on a subway and how creepy that can be sometimes, I thought it was such a great environment for Ghostface to be in. Creating that tension and that dynamism through the lighting was both a challenge and such a fun opportunity for me, and I'm really happy with how that sequence came out."

Scream 6 costume designer Avery Plewes describes the subway scene as the love of her life. "I was like a dog with a bone with that sequence," she says. "I love Halloween. To me costume-wise and suspense-wise it's the climax of the movie—and we love an Easter egg. 'Are you really a horror fan?' is kind of the vibe."

There are iconic characters like Freddy Krueger, Jason Voorhees, Michael Myers, and Pinhead, along with some noncreepy costumes, and you don't see it but there was a bedazzled Ghostface mask that was made by producer William Sherak's then twelve-year-old daughter.

"There are some really iconic New York characters on there. There's throwbacks and callbacks to Wes Craven's legacy and then there's also just movies that we were all fans of," Plewes says. "Grace from *Ready or Not*, which I designed, is also on the subway. I don't know if any other costume designer has done a costume version of a costume they've designed."

As much fun as it was, it's a terrifying scene—and Jasmin Savoy Brown's fear was real.

"When Ghostface covers my mouth, I really thought I was about to die. My brain and body couldn't understand that it wasn't real," she says. "There is some sort of magic in that mask, I swear. It is so scary in person."

MANY TENSE SCENES LATER, THE FILM'S CLIMAX PLAYS OUT IN AN ABANdoned movie theater, where the Kirsch family reveals themselves as the killers. They've built a shrine in memory of Richie that honors the ones who came before them, which gave the crew the chance to essentially create a museum of *Scream* history.

"There were so many callbacks to each of the previous films in the museum. I had to study each film. It's like I went to college for *Scream* in four months," Plewes says. "There's nothing in that museum scene that was from any of the original films."

It's easy to assume they just popped over to a storage

shed somewhere and grabbed what they needed, but that wasn't the case. It took painstaking levels of research, attention, and dedication; and it was an all-hands effort by the art, props, and wardrobe teams.

The theater itself isn't actually abandoned and dilapidated. So they created wallpaper to make it look like the paint was peeling, added spiderwebs, and just generally trashed the place to give it the creepy decrepit vibe.

"It was beautiful. All the lighting was really moody. It was all red, too," Laliberté says. "Through the whole movie we were sparing red, not using it at all in our sets, so that the blood spills were going to be super punchy. But at the end, they jump in a subway and take the red line and end up in this theater that's fully red and burgundy. For us, it was like the perfect color. It was the perfect location, really."

When it came to collecting Richie's memorabilia, they compiled a list of artifacts from the movies that would be fun to include—like the "Happy Birthday, Roman" banner and burned fax machine from *Scream 3*—and re-created everything.

The same went for the clothing they included. Jill's shirt from *Scream 4* is a children's Abercrombie that they found on Poshmark, while what they found to replicate Tatum's turtleneck from the original movie was the right texture but had to be dyed that distinctive neon yellow.

"There is a huge emotional attachment for people. My job is harboring the connection of emotional attachment and clothing. That was really important to me," Plewes says. "There were days where one of my assistant costume designers literally had a sheet over her head over her laptop, watching each movie still by still taking screenshots, because all of the work isn't online. That's the level of crazy I went to to get the details right."

Each of the nine Ghostface robes is a little different and some of the unique details proved problematic.

"Not a lot of people know this, but the original *Scream* robe, around the neck was a drawstring. In our script, Melissa originally took Billy Loomis's robe off on camera. And I was like, 'You can't do that. I'm sorry, guys. It's gonna look insane taking the *Scream 1* robe off over her head with the gloves that are attached. It's just not going to look good, and if you pretend the robe is not drawstring, we will all be ripped to shreds by the fan base.'"

With each of those robes came a hand-painted mask that was in a different state of degradation. Plewes struggled because the flaky, cracked appearance is not what would happen to one of the masks, even after twenty-five years. At worst, it would yellow a bit.

She paused her inherent need to be logical and realistic and focused on how they could create something that would "scare the shit out of people."

"I thought a lot about porcelain dolls. My grandmother gave me porcelain dolls growing up and I hated them. I thought they were horrifying," Plewes says. "Some dolls are the same silicone material of Ghostface. So, I started looking at super-old silicone doll faces and how the layer of plastic kind of separates from the face. We reverse engineered it from that. This one can have a crack here, this should have tarnish here. We added lowlights and highlights. The Billy mask is super sunken in, so it's really harrowing."

Fun World sent over dozens of masks for them to use.

They hand-painted at least ten of the ones that are worn in the film, and just a couple of the ones that were purely props. They were stored in unmarked shoeboxes so no one could stumble upon them on set, an added layer of security to ensure nothing got spoiled.

"Ghostface never gets dressed in their trailer," Plewes says. "We send the robe and the mask to set in an unmarked garment bag."

Plewes also snuck in some little hints: Quinn's necklace represents a family tree and Detective Bailey and Ethan each wear plaid at some point in the film, as have other killers over the years. And there were some sentimental nods too: Tara and Kirby both wear Wes Craven's birthstone, peridot, and Gale wears a signet ring with a "W" for both "Wes" and "Weathers."

IT'S IMPOSSIBLE TO KNOW WHAT *SCREAM 5* OR *6* WOULD HAVE LOOKED like with someone else at the helm, but it's a pretty safe bet that *6* wouldn't be a go-for-broke action flick. It's the kind of thing that requires everyone to be firing on all cylinders to pull off—and that success is in no small part due to the way Bettinelli-Olpin and Gillett run their shoots.

"They hit the jackpot getting Matt and Tyler to direct these movies," Liana Liberato says. "They are genuinely so caring and hold the other four films in such a high regard, and admire Wes's work so much, but then also they aren't afraid to take risks and reinvent things."

She continues, "You wouldn't think when you were on the film that you were a part of something so huge because everyone trusts each other. Matt or Tyler would come and sit down with me and be like, 'So what do you think about saying the line like this?' or 'How would you want to do it?' I was like, 'Wait, you care about what *I* would want to do?' I just didn't want to mess anything up, and they want you to do different things because they want to see different colors of characters and find that in the edit."

"I had never worked with two directors before. Hearing how they've been friends for so long, you really have to be two special people to want to continue to work with one another after twenty-plus years," says Devyn Nekoda. "I saw their connection. Their communication is unlike anything I have ever seen. And they really want the best for you."

Marley Shelton, who's one of the few cast members to have worked with both Craven and Radio Silence, says the experiences felt very similar.

"Matt and Tyler had such reverence for Wes and I think they really wanted to do right by him in terms of carrying on his legacy. They also created that same sort of family, fun, safe environment," she says. "They had this really fascinating shorthand of communication. They'd finish each other's sentences and you got used to them as kind of one entity. They were just this force of enthusiasm."

"On set everybody [feels] like their ideas are valued, which is all you really want from directors," says Brett Jutkiewicz. "They're so good at anticipating the feeling of a sequence in terms of the tension and the scares. They're so attuned to that, knowing what little pieces they might need to really round out a sequence, or to have the freedom in the edit to play with how much tension they may want."

CHAPTER NINETEEN

HAM SANDWICH

In order to really sell the fake-out in the *Scream 6* opening sequence and convince the audience they might be about to watch a first-person Ghostface story, they had to nail the casting.

Tony Revolori had the range and résumé, with everything from Wes Anderson movies to superhero tentpoles under his belt.

"Casting-wise, when that mask comes off, you have to believe that person would be in the whole movie," says producer William Sherak. "Tony is so perfect because you can't over-stunt-cast it where you go, 'Wait a second. Tom Cruise is in this movie?' You have to be careful. There is a very, very, very fine line where you go, 'Wait, this is a good Ghostface.' You know him, you know he could pull that off."

Revolori was hesitant because he doesn't really like scary movies—and he still hasn't seen a *Scream*.

"I am very scared. I am the perfect horror audience

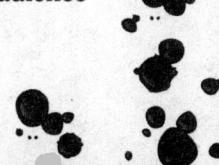

member, I jump, I scream, I cry, I get terrified for four hours afterward, and I can't sleep at night," he says.

Revolori probably would have said yes to the role without any intervention, but his friend Mason Gooding didn't leave him with much of a choice.

Gooding was on the phone with Sherak on the way to the gym, the same one where Revolori worked out, and the producer said they were really excited about a bait-and-switch character at the beginning of the film. When Revolori's name came into the conversation, Gooding couldn't hang up fast enough.

"I went up to Tony and I was like, 'Listen. I don't know if you know yet, but you're about to do *Scream 6*. Regardless of what financially or professionally needs to happen between now and then, I'm seeing you on set, whether you like it or not,'" Gooding says. "He was like, 'I heard. I was gonna talk to you about it, but you're so sweaty and you came in super aggravated.'"

"He's like, 'You're doing it! I'll see you in Montreal. Done,'" says Revolori. "The hesitation was only there for about thirty seconds before Mason pile-drived me into the film. So, I owe Mason my entire check—or ten percent."

Gooding personally would have gone with something more like "doggedly pursued," but regardless of how you describe his approach, it worked. "I knew that it was a mutual benefaction that I could involve someone I deeply care about and admire in the *Scream* franchise," Gooding says. "And I knew the movie would be better for it."

When it came to casting aspiring serial killer Jason's victim, *Ready or Not* final girl Samara Weaving was a no-brainer.

"Getting to pepper the film with actors I love that I don't think would normally do smaller roles like this, that's really fun. Because it was *Scream*, someone like Tony Revolori or Samara Weaving would come in and do kind of a cameo," says casting director Rich Delia. "There are actors who showed up to *Scream* who were like, 'I really want to do this movie. I just have to know, do I die?' And when you're like, 'Yeah, you die,' they're like, 'Yes!' People want a *Scream* death. So many people die in the movie that we were able to grant a lot of those wishes."

Revolori certainly won't forget filming his demise.

"The most memorable bit was the blood and just how sticky you are afterward," he recalls. "Like, 'Are you ready? We're going to pour a cup's worth of blood in your mouth and you'll scream and it'll all fall out.' Then afterward you're taking a shower to get it all off with shaving cream, but I had so much fun doing it."

He played around a lot during filming.

"There were lots of bits I threw out there that ended up on the cutting room floor, rightfully so because they were absurd and outrageous," says Revolori. In one take he kissed a photo of Richie Kirsch, who's played by his friend Jack Quaid. Another included a jab at superhero movies, which was funny because he played Flash Thompson in a trio of *Spider-Man* films.

"There was an MCU joke, similar to the first movie, with Jenna Ortega talking about high-class horror and *Babadook*, me talking about film students and being like, 'No one talks about these classic horror movies, everyone just watches dumb fuckin' Marvel movies.'"

When it comes to the dialogue that's actually in the

film, Revolori's Jason Carvey in a post-kill phone call has some of the darkest lines in the franchise. He's talking to his roommate, or so he thinks, and describes what it was like to don the Ghostface costume and kill their film professor: "It was even better than we could have imagined. And when the knife went in her, it's like she wasn't a human anymore. Just an animal. And every time when I went in, she was less . . . less human. . . . And then? She was . . . just meat."

It's deeply disturbing, even for a movie about serial killers.

"It's crazy—and this is gonna sound psychopathic, so I apologize to whoever is reading this, I promise you I'm not— those were the easiest lines," Revolori says. "It's easy to make them sound menacing and dangerous and you can feel the words coming out of you, at least being in the character. It was those moments that I'm like, 'Oh, this is where the audience will understand my pathos and why I do what I do.'"

"It's so bleak. The killer in the open, this incel kid on the phone talking about what it was like to drive a knife through Samara Weaving, I was like, 'Oh my God.' This is the darkest I've seen a *Scream* movie go, and I was appreciative of that," says Blumhouse exec and *Still Screaming* documentary writer-director Ryan Turek. "It was a step in the right direction. We're gonna go into new territory we've never seen before, beyond the New York City backdrop."

Revolori had a harder time filming the scene where he runs into Tara and crew on his way home, during which he and the audience know he's Ghostface but his on-screen classmates don't.

"That was the most difficult thing for me to shoot because I was trying to make it seem like Jenna and I have been friends for months going to college together, while at the same time being menacing and being creepy without tipping her off," Revolori says.

They tried takes where he was slightly more devious, and maybe Jenna was a little oblivious or naïve, but there's one note from the directors that sticks in his memory: "Be sexy. Be Ted Bundy."

We joke about the Ghostface fetish that Radio Silence had mentioned.

"My DMs are cursed now," Revolori laughs. "Horrible. Horrible. It's strange. I chuckled at it and I thought it was really funny—at first."

"Yeah, I can confirm," Quaid adds. It's something the friends now have in common. "Now that AI is a thing, I'm getting tagged in like Ghostface AI. You see Ghostface, he's not maskless, and he's doing every kind of sex act imaginable. There is so much horniness around Ghostface. I don't personally get it, but I understand it. Does that make sense? There is something about a serial killer. I mean, look at how many letters Ted Bundy got in prison. It's a very light version of that."

———

KEEPING THE MYSTERY ALIVE IN THESE META SLASHER WHODUNITS WITHout totally hiding the ball from the audience is always a tightrope walk—and this time they had to do it with three killers.

"You're dropping clues and it's like, 'Is this clue too obvious?'" says *Scream 6* editor Jay Prychidny. "Then it's this mind game, like, 'Well, maybe if we make it obvious, then it seems like that *won't* be the thing.'"

The actors, of course, are thinking about that too.

"If you say something really fast, people are gonna be like, 'Hey, wait a minute, that must have been important,'" says Dermot Mulroney. "The scene when I'm walking across a parking lot to get into my cop SUV, that's when I accuse Kirby. The camera is on the move, I'm on the fly, I'm opening the door and I'm snapping in, I'm talking on the phone. So, people got really suspicious about Kirby not because I said it but because I said it *fast*. They think we're trying to trick you by trying to fly it by you."

Quinn and Detective Bailey don't have any scenes together before the reveal, but she does have them with her secret brother, Ethan, and they were conscious of not giving away that their characters were leading double lives.

"The news reveals that someone has died, and I remember Melissa's character is like, 'We're leaving,'" Liana Liberato says. "I doubt this ended up in the final film because that would be too revealing, but Jack and I were able to share a look in that moment. Because we would, naturally. That's not a good thing for us. They need to stay in the city."

She didn't worry too much about people suspecting her, though, because she had cover built into the story.

"I got to hide behind a pretty classic trope—the hypersexual roommate—and I got to die early," Liberato says. "I was able to rely on what happens to my character and I knew people would just assume that I was going to be the promiscuous girl that dies."

Jack Champion dialed in to his natural positive energy and intentionally leaned into the vibe, like he was an actor trying too hard to play Jack Champion.

"If I'm just myself but I'm *trying* to be sweet or I'm *trying* to be nervous, then it adds a suspicious spice," he says. "I can be wholesome and sweet, or I can seem like I'm putting it on just a little bit. That's what I went for, being myself but almost like you can tell I was acting at certain times."

———

THE NEW WAVE *SCREAM* FILMS WOULD NEVER HAVE SUCCEEDED WITHOUT thoughtful character development and charismatic actors, and *6* picked up where *5* left off and built on those personalities and relationships.

"You get to know these kids. They're not cardboard cutouts," says Sherak. "The easiest note to give in the world is to take fifteen minutes out of the first forty minutes of the movie to get to the kills faster. Every studio will give that note. Every one of them. We didn't do that. In order to care if they die later, you have to like them. If you don't care about them, it's actually more fun for Ghostface to win."

Prychidny says Radio Silence was fiercely protective of those character-building moments.

"Those scenes were almost untouchable in a way," he says. "They were ready to go to bat if anyone came to say, 'Aren't these a little slow?' Luckily that never happened."

One of those was the dinner table sequence before Ghostface attacks in the Carpenters' apartment, the one where the Core Four get their name. Sam, Tara, Mindy, and

Chad are sitting around laughing, like normal friends who aren't being stalked by a masked psycho.

"A lot of that dialogue was meant to convey that we were a family and a unit," says Gooding. "Part of conveying that sentiment involves a level of messiness and incohesion in dialogue delivery that meant talking over each other or saying colloquialisms."

They improvised moments between the dialogue, and because they're close in real life, Jasmin Savoy Brown says filming the scene felt like hanging out with friends.

"We improv-ed so much. That didn't feel like acting at all," she says. "Sometimes when it was on Melissa or Jenna's coverage, I would say completely the wrong thing to get a reaction out of them. Jenna and I had this joke about pterodactyls flying outside. We would keep looking outside and being like, 'Oh my God! Did you hear that?! There's a pterodactyl outside!' We were just doing the stupidest shit, but it brought life to it. That's a testament to the guys. They let us do all of that and fuck around and waste time because they know that those little moments will make it more real."

Gooding says the most "off the rails" part was after they discover Sam has been secretly seeing their neighbor, Danny. They riffed on the kind of jokes sisters and friends would be making in that situation, and it got a little racier than pterodactyls.

"None of that made it into the movie," Gooding says, laughing. "Most of it was R, hard R, maybe NC-17, and so easily lent to what they did end up using, which were little laughs and smiles and glances at one another. That again is a testament to Matt and Tyler allowing us to find those moments and cutting around it to still get that sentiment across without having forty-five minutes of the most obscene shit you've ever heard."

Radio Silence definitely knew what they were doing, even if they didn't quite know what they were getting themselves into.

"I remember we were sitting at the monitors going, 'Well, this is gonna suck to edit,' because it's the most improv in either of our movies, but it's also the most authentic," Bettinelli-Olpin says. "It felt like they were really having that moment together. They got to cut loose and have fun and it wasn't about the dialogue as much as it was about the emotion and the relationships building in that moment and creating that tight unit."

"It felt like we had to treat it as natural and really live in how comforting it feels to sit at a table with your best friends," Tyler Gillett says. He adds with a laugh, "Just having a real fancy dinner, with place settings. Ya know, teens!"

Throughout the film, Prychidny made it a point to ground the story through love.

"I'm always on the lookout for love," he says. "It could be a murder, an action scene, the killer going off in demented ways, anything that shows the love between the characters. I'm always trying to carve that out wherever I can find that because that's part of what it's all about."

He jokes that the shared glances between the Carpenter sisters could have been a drinking game.

"We'd watch the film and we'd just yell out, 'Sister look!' because there are so many moments of just Sam and Tara looking at each other," Prychidny says. "It happens constantly and you can't get enough. So, it's like, 'Sister look! Sister look!'"

———

SCREAM 6 ALSO MARKED TWO MAJOR MILESTONES FOR LONGTIME CHARacters: Roger L. Jackson finally got a solo card in the credits for voicing Ghostface, and Gale Weathers got her first call from him.

Jackson didn't do all of the calls in *5* and *6* live, but he was on the line for that one.

"Roger never breaks character when he calls in live," Gillett says. "If you pick up the phone and say, 'Hey, Roger, we're gonna go ahead,' he just speaks to you as Ghostface and it is incredible. It's amazing how much of that character just exists inside Roger."

"I've never met him, but he is so funny and menacing," says Champion. "It wouldn't be Ghostface without him."

Gale and Ghostface face off in a condo that looks a bit like a Bond villain's lair—which, by the way, was someone's real home. The writers reworked the scene to make it fit the location and then Michèle Laliberté's team built padded columns and put down linoleum patches so the fake blood wouldn't ruin the floor. After a chase, Gale gets the best of Ghostface—but only momentarily.

"I really loved taking on Ghostface in *Scream 6*," says Courteney Cox. "One of my favorite lines was 'How's that for nostalgia, fucker?' I'm just thrilled she's survived this long."

Scream is sometimes criticized for keeping its main characters too safe, with the notable exceptions of Randy and Dewey.

Horror director Eli Roth says it's an easy trap to fall into with a franchise.

"The danger is you become too in love with the characters that you don't want to kill them," says Roth. "The later *Scream* films, the characters you love can get stabbed fifty times and somehow miraculously make it to the hospital. Billy and Stu stabbing each other once and playing it real, that's the difference between Wes Craven and everyone else. Wes will kill the character if it's important to the story whether he likes the character or not. That's the lesson I want to take on my sequels. I can't just keep people alive because I like them. If you're going to make it a real slasher film, you have to kill people."

Audiences didn't seem to have too much of an issue with Gale surviving the attack in *6*, since she was really only stabbed once and the paramedics were there right away.

But then there's Chad. Sweet, invincible Chad, who gets his first kiss with Tara and is immediately brutally skewered by two Ghostfaces—and still lives.

"When he comes out in that gurney in the end, in the test screening you could feel the divide in the audience," says Prychidny. "A very large portion of the audience cheered, but I was sitting next to a girl and she was like, 'This is fucking stupid!'"

"We got roasted for Chad," says Bettinelli-Olpin. "It's funny because we had the conversation where we were like, the problem is easily solved—*if* we agreed with there being a problem. We want the movie to be a thrill ride, and we want you to have a great time, and we want you to feel like that guy is fucking dead. Dead, dead, dead, dead."

Even Mason Gooding was surprised his character survived when he finally saw the scene during post-production.

"We were doing ADR and they were showing me the scene where Chad is getting filleted," Gooding remembers. "I was like, 'Is it believable that I walk away from this one in any capacity?' And they were like, 'Mason, I don't know how to tell you this. We had a cut before where it was at least twice as long.'"

"We actually stabbed him many, many more times," Gillett says. "We pared it way down in the cut."

Prychidny was torn. He didn't think it was super realistic for Chad to survive but didn't want to cut the scene short because of everything other than the stabbing.

"He has this great performance on his face in that scene," says Prychidny. "I feel like we could've lived in that emotion of Tara watching Chad getting stabbed longer—but, when they shot it, the Ghostfaces are just going nuts."

"There's a moment of tenderness that gets undercut in the most *Scream* way," says Gooding. "It's like, if you milk it, then you just think, 'Well, she was screaming over his body for a solid two minutes.'"

More emotion means more stabs, more blood loss, and a way less believable survival. They met in the middle so you could still feel the tragedy of the scene without totally leaving the plane of reality.

"We froze the Ghostfaces a little bit so they weren't stabbing him quite as much, but you could still hold on the emotion of it," says Prychidny. "We got maybe a little too obsessed. We'd be counting stabs. 'Okay, he's been stabbed fifteen, sixteen times, the audiences won't accept it—but thirteen times, that's okay.' We'd get in these debates about exactly how many stabs."

"One of our big jokes is that when you're shooting a

scene where somebody gets any kind of injury, everybody on set is a doctor and everybody has an ironclad opinion—not even an opinion, knows exactly where every vein is. Every single time. Everybody knows everything," Bettinelli-Olpin says. "These movies are a little heightened and they do live in this reality where people survive stabs. Obviously, Dewey broke that wide open in *Scream 2*, and there is a fun to that. The same way that Dewey felt like this invincible, lovable goofball, for us that's Chad. I think there's something really fun about having this character that you can't kill. That said, we joked that in *Scream 7* he would slip on a banana peel and it'd be goodbye Chad."

"The dude is just mincemeat by the time we're done with him," says Champion. "Then by the end of the movie he's still holding up the four. The Core Four, baby!"

It is a movie, after all.

"If we played either of the *Screams* that we did as real, they are way too mean and sad," says Bettinelli-Olpin.

"It's a balancing act. While Ghostface is a menacing, cruel character, the movies don't ever feel mean or cruel," Gillett says. "They always feel like they exist in a bit of a heightened reality. When it feels fun and when it feels cruel is a really thin line."

That's where the ham sandwich comes in.

Prychidny was the first person to mention the phrase, explaining that part of the charm of the franchise is the ability and willingness to suspend logic for the sake of entertainment, to some degree anyway. It came up while we were talking about Quinn's fake death.

"If you'd say something like, 'Where did he get the body?' Matt would be like, 'Oh, ham sandwich,'" Prychidny says.

"It's like the more you think about some of these things, the more they make zero sense."

Bettinelli-Olpin adds, "We always joked about 'ham sandwich,' but it was never an excuse to skirt logic."

It's a phrase they'd use when something worked in the moment and made sense for the story, but certain details might not be entirely plausible. It was a way to keep things light on set and not lose the forest for the trees.

They learned the term from Williamson, who first heard it years ago, but he's not sure where.

"It's like you're watching TV and you're totally satisfied and everything's great. The show ended, you get up to the kitchen, you make a ham sandwich, and you go, 'Wait a second, that didn't make sense,'" Williamson says with a laugh. "But we got you to the ham sandwich. You didn't think about it when you were watching the show. It's the idea that if we can just get the audience out of the theater before they figure out that it doesn't make sense, you're okay."

Ham sandwich is never plan A, though.

"The trick is to do really good storytelling and it's so tight there's not a ham sandwich. Even when they are eating the ham sandwich, they're like, 'Oh, that made sense,'" Williamson says. "I'm a logic-police person. I want everything to logically make sense."

———

TO SET THE KILLER REVEAL IN, ESSENTIALLY, A *SCREAM* TIME CAPSULE WAS surreal both on screen and during filming. It felt almost like the previous Ghostfaces and victims were in the room too.

"It was such a grand feeling because in past *Scream*

movies all the killer reveals were in a party setting or in a kitchen or in an enclosed area where it feels kinda intimate," Champion says. "Here, we were literally in a theater surrounded by all this *Scream* nostalgia."

He says Quinn and Ethan traded personalities as soon as the masks came off.

"She goes a little bit more serious and I'm a little bit more psychotic and goofy," he says. "In my brain, as soon as I took the mask off, *this* is Ethan Landry. I just felt natural, like I'm a killer and I'm here to kill you."

"I didn't want Quinn to be crazy," Liberato says. "As an actor, you try to justify your character's behavior as much as you possibly can, even if they're deranged killers. I was like, 'What is the most human approach to this? Well, her motive is derived from pure pain and sadness.'"

Meanwhile, their dad is heartbroken and out of his mind.

"That is such a plum cherry to get in a script and know that the assignment is clear," Dermot Mulroney says. "How the guy reveals his nefarious plot is in each of the movies, so it's really iconic. I definitely wanted those elements of the full lunatic breakdown that Lillard and Ulrich turned in in the first show."

"I love the reveal in *Scream 6*," says Patrick Lussier, editor of the first three films. "I love that the movie is so inside itself but at the same time not weighed down by the Hollywood-ness of it. I've directed Dermot as a killer before and loved it. He is the easiest guy on the planet to work with and an absolute joy."

Mulroney certainly gave them a lot to work with, some of which they didn't expect.

"Dermot really was no-holds-barred when it came to his performance. There was a huge variety for almost every line, different versions, different levels of insanity, different levels of emotion. He improv-ed throughout," says *Scream 6* editor Jay Prychidny. "That scene could very easily have gone completely off the rails. It was about trying to ground it. You try to find those moments where the audience can sympathize with the killers as much as possible, to make your villains as multilayered and textural as possible. One of the surprise emotional moments of the film is when Dermot reveals that he's the father of Richie Kirsch. The directors and myself, we'd have this emotional reaction to that scene of him saying that his son was killed, which I think wasn't planned or intended but came out in the editing."

Detective Bailey meets his end in spectacular fashion after Sam unleashes her pent-up rage while wearing her father's Ghostface garb—though Mulroney jokes that he could return with a high-tech eye patch—but it's nothing compared to what happens to Ethan. You'd almost feel bad for the kid had he not really, really deserved it.

"The part where he comes back at the end, I lobbied to take that out of the movie," says Prychidny. "I was severely outvoted. Maybe I was wrong, but at the time I felt strongly that it was just too much. And also, Jenna saying, 'Die a fucking virgin,' and ripping that knife out of his throat is one of the biggest cheers of the movie. It is so satisfying. I felt like to then reveal he didn't die kind of robs Jenna of that moment, but I was outvoted."

Champion was surprised by how resilient his character was when he read the script, but he's thrilled about how it ended.

"I don't know if there's another killer that has taken more damage and gotten up than Ethan. He got stabbed six times by Melissa and then he gets stabbed in the mouth by Jenna and then he gets a TV dropped on his head," Champion says. "Stu is my favorite killer. Matthew Lillard is such a master. To have the privilege to have the last scare of the movie and to die by Stu Macher's TV, I couldn't ask for a better death."

There's a lot of violence, but Radio Silence doesn't think the movie is any darker than its predecessors.

"We were really surprised by the reaction to *Scream 6* as being more brutal than the others," Bettinelli-Olpin says. "We tried to push the envelope a little bit, obviously, with the bodega and the shotgun, but all Ghostfaces are pretty extreme."

"It's easy to forget how brutal and fucked-up *Scream* is, all of them," Gillett says. "The original in particular. Going back and rewatching it, which we have done countless times over the course of making the last two movies, it's like the fun, the poppiness of those movies, the tone that you're left with, is very different than when you really get down to brass tacks and dissect what the movies are. They are incredibly brutal and very hardcore. We remind ourselves all the time we've gotta chase that Wes Craven dragon, and part of that means you have to be willing to go to an uncomfortable, dark place."

The film set a franchise record with a $44.5 million opening weekend and saw the third-highest global box office.

There's a measure of success that means far more to the people involved: how Kevin Williamson feels about *Scream*

6—and that's better than they could have ever hoped for. Not only is it his second-favorite in the franchise after the original, but back before he had any idea that he'd be directing the seventh film, he told me just how much the two new movies mean to him.

"Being a part of *Scream 5* and *6* has been a blessed experience," Williamson says. "I'm glad that it's living on because now I finally see a pathway that *Scream* can sit on the mantel next to *Halloween* and *Friday the 13th* as a franchise. With *1*, *2*, and *3* I never felt like it was a franchise. They made *4*, but *4* didn't do so well. Now, with *5* and *6*, and knowing that there's going to be a *7*, I truly feel like *Scream* is part of horror history."

CHAPTER TWENTY

THE *SCREAM 7* THAT WASN'T

When you look at the cadence of the *Scream* films, there are some eerie parallels between *1-2-3* and *5-6-7*.

The first of each triad exceeded expectations; the second was rushed to capitalize on the momentum and released the following year; and the third came more than two years later and was plagued with issues after the studio decided to forge ahead without some members of the team.

When it comes to *Scream 7*, there's a happy ending, but not without some heartbreak along the way—much like the films themselves.

Scream 6 set a franchise box office record with its opening weekend—but before it was even released, as soon as the studio had seen the finished product, it was eyeing a fall 2023 shoot for the next one. Then multiple once-in-a-lifetime events happened.

Guild negotiations are always a tense time in Hollywood, but I don't think anyone expected actors and writers to strike concurrently—something that hadn't happened since 1960. The industry was effectively shut down for half of 2023 as the guilds and studios battled over issues raised by the dominance of streaming and the emergence of generative artificial intelligence.

The WGA was on strike from May 2 to September 27, while SAG-AFTRA was from July 14 to November 9. James Vanderbilt and Guy Busick had cowritten a draft of *Scream 7* before their guild went on strike, which gave producers something to work with so planning could get underway.

"Making movies is one of those weird, crazy things where you don't get to live knowing what tomorrow looks like," says producer William Sherak. "It's just not the job. You put a plan together, you wait for the plan to get screwed up, and then you come up with a new plan. At any moment, something can derail a project. Had the strikes not happened, something else could've come out of left field."

And other somethings did.

The first major shakeup was with Radio Silence. Matt Bettinelli-Olpin and Tyler Gillett wanted to direct *Scream 7*—but as with Williamson wanting to write *Scream 3*, that wasn't enough. The studio had a schedule in mind and the directing duo were already in prep on *Abigail*, the vampire kidnapping heist movie that was cowritten by Busick and produced by Project X.

"We were like, 'We'll do it. We just can't do it in this window,'" Bettinelli-Olpin says. "And it was a friendly and polite, 'Okay. Moving on.' But it did sour us a bit, we're not gonna lie."

"It's not just a job for us," Gillett says. "It's never been just a job, particularly with *Scream* because we love the movies so much. We're such fans. So, to have it reduced to something that basic just was shitty."

"From the outside, there's this idea that movies in a franchise are made by machine," Bettinelli-Olpin adds. "That they are just destined to be what they eventually become, and that is just wholly untrue."

What they'd been through on *Scream 6*, after everyone they knew told them not to do it in the first place, was salt in the wound.

"Part of why the *Scream 7* situation stings so much is we put a lot on the line for *6*," Gillett says. "We went in like, 'All right, this is gonna be a labor of love because it's happening so fast and no one is really sure what it is.' The sand was shifting so fast day to day on it. There were times when we were like, 'What are we doing? This is crazy. There is nothing we can put a foothold in to actually get this thing through to production.'"

Gillett continues, "Having weathered that and coming out the other side of it with what *Scream 6* is, like Matt said, it's a lot of work. It's really handmade. We put it all on the fuckin' line to make that movie, and then to not have *7* work for scheduling reasons, it's just like, man, what a bummer."

"I remember those moments where we would be talking during pre-production on *Scream 6* where—full stop—everybody in our lives was telling us not to do it. Because what's the win? We already did a *Scream* movie, it worked, it was successful, take your W and move on," Bettinelli-Olpin says. "For us it was that we really do love everybody we were working with. Straight up, the only reason we were doing this is because we want to work with Mason and Jenna and Jasmin and Melissa, William, Paul, Jamie, Guy, the whole team, the family, Kevin Williamson. It meant a lot to us. We were like, 'We want to go do it with them and for them.' When it becomes really personal, and the only reason you're doing it is for love and for the personal reasons, to be told 'thanks but no thanks' sucks. All that to say, the movie we went and made instead of *Scream 7* was incredibly special to us." (Quick aside to note that the *Abigail* premiere was a full-on *Scream* reunion and absolute love fest, and it's clear that their feelings about their work family are 100 percent reciprocated.)

Radio Silence was replaced with *Freaky* and *Happy Death Day* director Christopher Landon, who'd been an intern at Woods Entertainment during the nascent stages of the original *Scream*.

"I was sitting in story meetings with Kevin Williamson when I was eighteen years old, so I have this very personal connection to the franchise," Landon says. "I was there while they made it. I was there for their first test screening, which was the first time I saw it. It was very rough, a classic first test screening, temp sound, temp music, temp color, et cetera, et cetera, but I remember how well it played and how into it the audience got. I was very excited and very inspired by that experience."

While Williamson would have loved to see Radio Silence finish out their trilogy, when he learned that wasn't going to happen, he advocated for Landon. When we talked about him back in the fall of 2023, Williamson thought Landon might be the future of the franchise.

"He knows how to do scares, he knows how to do comedy,

and there is always some emotional layer to what he does," Williamson says. "That's what I love about Chris's directing. Out of nowhere, he'll bring you that moment and your heart will melt and then he'll go right back into a big, bloody set piece. He finds his moments and that's what makes his stuff really, really sing. That's what I'm excited about with the next *Scream* because I've seen the script, those moments are in there, and I can't wait to see what he does to them."

Beyond the storytelling aspect, there was a personal reason he was happy about the choice too. "For me it's super special because *Scream* is written by a gay writer, and now the franchise has a gay director for the first time ever," Williamson says. "So, I can't think of anything more fitting. I do believe that *Scream*, in a lot of ways, has a gay sensibility."

Landon says it felt like a homecoming, especially since that internship at Woods Entertainment marked the first time he really believed he could be a filmmaker.

"I felt almost like I had a weird responsibility as a fan and as a gay filmmaker to say yes and go for it," Landon says. "I jumped back in time and was eighteen again, reading that script for the first time and just losing my mind. The beauty of it is when your older adult self gets to shake hands with the kid from a long time ago and say, 'Wow, this is pretty fucking cool.'"

It was a serendipitous moment, but it didn't last.

————

ALONG WITH RADIO SILENCE, *SCREAM 7* ALSO LOST HALF OF THE CORE Four: Jenna Ortega and Melissa Barrera.

While the actors were on strike, not only could they not do any work or negotiate deals for future roles, they also were barred from talking about pretty much any TV or film projects they'd ever made. So, when Ortega—who had become a megastar with multiple movies and a second season of her hit show *Wednesday* in the works—decided in the summer that she wasn't going to return for *Scream 7*, it managed to stay secret for several months.

Based on the way people were talking about the project in the early fall, I suspect they thought she'd change her mind and at least make a quick cameo in the form of a FaceTime call. In late November, right after the SAG-AFTRA strike ended, it became clear that wasn't going to happen.

News finally broke that Ortega wasn't returning a day after it was announced that Melissa Barrera had been fired from the franchise, which stoked speculation that Ortega's decision was made in reaction to her co-star's firing because the cast had grown so close while making the films.

While some media coverage implied Barrera was fired because of her pro-Palestine support in general, the statement released by Spyglass at the time pointed to language in social media posts she had shared about the war in Gaza that it felt crossed into antisemitic territory. Her deal wasn't yet in place for *Scream 7*, and the studio decided to part ways with her.

Barrera shared a statement in an Instagram story that didn't directly address her firing, but rather reinforced why she was speaking out and would continue to do so.

"First and foremost I condemn Anti-Semitism and Islamophobia. I condemn hate and prejudice of any kind against any group of people," she began before continuing on to explain that she feels a responsibility to use her platform to advocate for issues she cares about. "Every person on this earth—regardless of religion, race, ethnicity, gender, sexual orientation or socio-economic status—deserves equal human rights, dignity and, of course, freedom. I believe a group of people are NOT their leadership, and that no governing body should be above criticism. I pray day and night for no more deaths, for no more violence, and for peaceful co-existence."

The sense I've gotten from people in the franchise is that they wish the decision to fire her hadn't been made so quickly, that they think her heart was in the right place and feel sitting down and talking it out may have resolved the issue.

When I spoke with Jasmin Savoy Brown the next fall, I asked what the past year had been like.

"It's been really sad and stressful," says Brown. "Often actors are expected to know as much about politics as politicians. And, in today's day and age when everything is online, everyone thinks they're an expert in everything, which isn't the case. I also think there is a clear difference between talking politics and standing up for people who don't have a voice. It's not politics, it's human life."

The timing of Ortega's announcement set the internet's collective attention on the remaining members of the Core Four, which put Gooding and Brown in an impossible situation. No matter what they said, or didn't say, someone was going to be angry about it.

It was well over a year before their returns to the new version of *Scream 7* were announced, and still there were people angrily flocking to the comments, criticizing them for coming back, and openly hoping for the film to fail. There was also a lot of love, and the majority of fans expressed their excitement about Chad and Mindy returning, even if it's bittersweet.

"I can't imagine making this movie without Melissa and Jenna. It won't be the same. On the flip side, I do care about this character so much and I care so much about the people that care about her," says Brown. "I hope that someday—even if it's twenty years from now—the Core Four gets back together on screen."

———

AFTER THE CAST SHAKE-UP, 7 ALSO LOST DIRECTOR CHRISTOPHER LANDON. "I made my decision to walk away about a week after they fired her," Landon says. "There was no movie anymore. The whole script was about her. I didn't sign on to make 'a *Scream* movie.' I signed on to make *that* movie. When that movie no longer existed, I moved on."

There was an information lag between the time when all of this was happening and when it became public. When the news about Barrera's firing broke in late November 2023, a deluge of online anger was unleashed. Much of it was aimed at Landon, who people incorrectly assumed had been involved in the decision. Others speculated that the tumult would cause him to walk away, not realizing that he already had.

"I was still sorting through my feelings about everything that had happened. When it all went down, it was something I was trying to process in a private and balanced way," Landon says. "When you're a public-facing person, often people don't like that. People want an immediate reaction, and they want you to agree with them."

Landon was receiving death threats. They were credible and detailed, and he believed his family was in danger. Such threats are unfortunately not rare in Hollywood, and many people in the *Scream* franchise have lived through similar horrors. Through all of this, he still hadn't gone public with the news that he was no longer directing *Scream 7*, but eventually it became too much.

"I made the decision to announce that I had left after the threats got too intense. They were all screaming at someone who wasn't even on the movie anymore," Landon says. "There were a lot of people who thought I was some sort of villain. That really got in my head. It was painful, and it was painful to lose a dream job in such a sudden and bizarre way."

It was even more surreal because he'd had misgivings about taking on the project in the first place.

"It was a phone call that came out of the blue for me, and if I didn't have the personal connection that I do have to the franchise, I would have said no for sure," Landon had told me back when he was still on board to direct. "I love the franchise, but I didn't really feel like I necessarily needed to step into that kind of a pressurized situation. Especially because I think, critically and commercially, they just hit a home run. So, there is a very high level of execution that I have to pull off. That would have probably normally scared me away."

When we caught up almost a year after all this went down, I brought up how he'd been hesitant to take on *Scream 7* and how prescient that seemed in hindsight.

"Sometimes you have gut feelings about weird things," Landon says. "Strangely, in the background, I was developing this other movie that I ended up making. When the *Scream* thing imploded, I was ready to go make [*Drop*] and it felt like, 'This is the right thing.' The current movie is still a love letter to Wes. It's my homage to *Red Eye*."

The entire experience was filled with complex, sometimes contradictory emotions, but ultimately Landon is content with how it all panned out.

"There's no *Scream* movie for me to make anymore. It was a huge, valuable lesson to me too. Just because something seems so destined, written in the stars, doesn't make it so. Sometimes things happen that are so beyond your control, and you have to learn how to deal with it and move on. It took me a minute," Landon says. "It ended up being the best decision of my life."

———

THE YEAR ENDED WITH NO DIRECTOR, A SPLINTERED CAST, AND AN UNcertain future as producers went back to the drawing board and set out to reinvent the franchise for the second time in four years.

"I'm only one cog in the wheel. The only thing I knew going in, and still know, is that there is an appetite from Spyglass to make the next one—and a serious appetite," says Sherak. "Gary has been an unbelievable steward of allowing us to continue to deliver these movies for fans, and a partner in saying yes to the crazy ideas that we have. So, the one luxury I have is knowing we're going to make it."

Sherak wasn't deterred by the multiple unforeseen changes. He's been in the business long enough to know better than to stress over things he can't control.

"No movie gets made because it *should*. Movies get made because the planets align, somebody walked outside, spit three times, turned around, prayed to something, and the gods rained down light on them," Sherak says. "My desk is littered with scripts that were about to be made and weren't, or scripts that I never thought would get made that are on the fast track now for no reason other than circumstance. You can't will something into existence, unfortunately."

They decided to start from scratch instead of attempting to salvage bits and pieces of the first *Scream 7* story.

"What makes these movies good is character development, not plot. The plot is an engine, but caring about the people is what makes you love it," says Sherak. "When you start from a character perspective, a new character with a new way of thinking might not end up in that same plot because they wouldn't walk into that room that way, they wouldn't allow themselves to get chased that way, they wouldn't answer the phone that way. Trying to Frankenstein a screenplay from something previous, if characters aren't going to be in it, ends up creating a problem if you actually care about character development versus just what's a cool story to tell."

The good and bad news is that by the time they needed to get to work, James Vanderbilt was heading to Budapest to film his directorial debut, *Nuremberg*. So Guy Busick continued on solo.

"I've been involved in many projects where the powers that be just decided to go a different direction. Sometimes you're brought along for that new direction and sometimes you aren't," Busick says. "In this case, it was a bummer to lose the story that we wanted to tell and had planned to tell, but it did offer an opportunity to step back, rethink things, and build something that was really exciting to us. If we're looking for a silver lining, it's that."

Despite the initial rush from Spyglass that resulted in Radio Silence being left behind, after everything that had transpired during the course of 2023, the studio slowed things down.

It was the right call.

Without a story, you can't do anything. Or rather, you shouldn't. But too often the prospect of continued financial success outweighs artistic ambitions.

Or, as horror icon John Carpenter puts it: "It's all about money. Hollywood runs on money."

Scream is often compared to *Halloween*, a series with thirteen slashers spanning six decades, but Carpenter didn't set out to create a franchise.

"I never thought that *Halloween* had any more story to it," Carpenter says. "I sat down and wrote one sequel to *Halloween*, *Halloween II*. It was a horrible script. Horrible, horrible. I didn't do a good job, because I had no ideas. It was an assignment. If you don't love what you're doing and you don't have a great idea—you don't have a great story—you're fucked, so to speak. That's a Hollywood term: You're fucked."

Busick is very well aware and has no interest in writing a movie under those conditions, especially not a *Scream* film.

"There is no point in a cash grab or a rush job, because the fans will smell it. Nothing ends a franchise faster than if you feel like they are just treading out the tropes to make a buck," Busick says. "And I don't know how to write that. I care too much about what Kevin and Wes created to treat it like that. Whether it ends up being a good movie, there are a lot of factors. We put our heart and soul in there and if you don't like it, you don't like it, but at least we know we did our best."

Not long after we had this conversation, Busick pitched a new story centered on Sidney Prescott, something the franchise hadn't truly seen since *Scream 2*.

With Neve Campbell not yet convinced to return, it was one hell of a blue-sky idea.

CHAPTER TWENTY-ONE

A CRIME OF PASSION

Scream 7 was never truly in jeopardy. Kevin Williamson had created a brilliant concept that could be picked up and reset in any place and any time. The longtime fans who have become the creative forces care deeply about the legacy he and Craven had established and are fiercely protective of the franchise. The new creative team wouldn't make a half-assed *Scream* movie. Full stop. It might not be the story you personally were hoping to see, but they'd put everything they had into it and walk away with no regrets.

"Anyone can put on a Ghostface mask and start killing," Williamson says. "That's what's great about the franchise; it has that mystery element. You can always create a new whodunit."

Because the blood-soaked soap opera has a new villain each time, each with their own unique motive, they have creative freedom that some other franchises are lacking.

"We don't have the challenge of trying to explain how our bad guy is still killing people," says producer William Sherak. "Every movie it's a new Ghostface. The genius of what Kevin created is that it is a serial killer who buys a dime-store Halloween mask. It's not a werewolf, it's not the mummy. It is a friend of yours that has gone fucking crazy. What makes it fun, scary, and awesome is that anybody can put on the mask—and because anybody can put on the mask, you can tell any story."

"It really lets a writer tie Ghostface to the personality of the character and writing the story around that character," says *Scream 5* and *6* director of photography Brett Jutkie-wicz. "It's a different person in the mask every time who has a different story and a different complex set of emotions and reasons for doing what they're doing."

A few people described *Scream* to me as a State of the Union for horror and the cultural zeitgeist. It's first and foremost a slasher, but there's always some kind of social commentary built into the story. The faster the world changes, the easier it is to differentiate that aspect of the films.

"These movies are not timeless. They are moments in time," Sherak says. "You know exactly when each *Scream* movie was made. They are commenting on what is going on at that moment in fandom, in pop culture, in technology.

"What is different today than in the late '90s is that pop culture references change so much faster. That helps situations like this, because you can choose to comment on something completely different than what the previous one commented on and have a natural reason; it's a different group of people."

The original concept for *7* was a continuation of the

story in *5* and *6*, but the new one is going in a very different direction.

"This is going to be a standalone, but it'll probably feel more like the original *Scream*s than any of them, which is what I love about it," says Williamson.

Just like with *5* and *6*, Guy Busick shot for the moon: "Once again, we have one more *Scream* to make. What do we want to see?"

The answer was simple in theory and more complicated in practice: a true Sidney Prescott story.

———

KEVIN WILLIAMSON HAD ALWAYS WANTED NEVE CAMPBELL TO COME BACK to *Scream*. He understood why she passed on *6*, but he felt like there was so much more story left for Sidney. He deeply wanted her to feel connected to the new films and the creative team in the same way he had since he'd changed his mind about rejoining the franchise in the lead-up to *5*.

"I expressed that to Neve. I was like, 'I wish you could have the experience that I'm having with it,'" Williamson says. "I was very hesitant. I didn't want to jump in. I said, 'No, no, no'—until I said, 'Yes.' Once I said yes and I gave in to it, it's been a wonderful ride. I've met all these new people, and they've sort of become a new family for me."

Before Busick pitched his idea to Campbell, he ran it by Williamson via Zoom. It struck exactly the right chord with the franchise's creator, which made them confident to approach their star.

"We all sat around William Sherak's dining room table,

Neve, her manager, me, Guy, Jamie, and William," Williamson remembers. "They pitched it to her and it was even better than when he pitched it to me. She goes, 'Well, guys, I love this. I think this is amazing.' She had a couple questions. She wanted to discuss a few things. Creatively she is so smart. She knows exactly who Sidney Prescott is. She knew exactly who she wanted Sidney Prescott to be in this next version and it was very much in line with what Guy had pitched, and she even added to it. She was so in sync with it. She said, 'If we can work out the rest of it, I'm in.'"

"The rest of it" being an offer from Gary Barber at Spyglass that reflected her impact on the franchise.

"She was so lovely and so professional," Williamson says. "She handled herself so much better than I could have. It was really exciting for me to watch, quite frankly, and then Gary did the right thing. I didn't ask Neve the details. I just said, 'Are you happy?' She goes, 'I'm very happy, and what I am so very happy about is how he handled it.'"

Hollywood negotiations often start with a lowball offer, but Barber skipped ahead this time and they started in a place that allowed them to work out the details quickly.

"I had big conversations with the studio when they approached me about it. We had some apologies, and we had some honesty, and that was really great. So I feel good about coming back," Campbell says. "When they approached me, they said, 'We're going to come with a number that is starting in a much more appropriate place.' Then we negotiated and we got to where we needed to be, which is what should have happened on *6*, but it's okay. We live and learn."

Not only is she back as the lead, but she's also producing.

"Cooler heads prevailed and everyone was smart about what they were doing," Williamson says. "I was so thrilled to have it all fall into place."

———

THEY HAD A NEW STORY, THEY HAD THEIR STAR, BUT THEY STILL DIDN'T have a director.

Williamson had been disappointed when Christopher Landon walked away, even though he understood it, and he'd hoped maybe Radio Silence could be talked into coming back.

Around this same time, Williamson had sent Sherak a script for a project called *The Audition*, which he got back after Netflix sat on it for too long. Project X had just signed a new deal with Radio Silence and indie studio MRC that was geared at mid-budget, original horror films, and it seemed right up their alley.

"William Sherak called me up and goes, 'We love it,' and I go, 'I want to direct this. I think it would be great. I'm really passionate about it,'" Williamson says. "He goes, 'Let me get back to you,' and he just went kind of weird."

Williamson was baffled by why Sherak would suddenly go quiet about a script he seemed to love. He started to think maybe he didn't *really* like it.

What Williamson didn't realize was that he'd set off a lightbulb for Sherak: Their *Scream 7* director was right in front of them, and had been from the start.

"When I looked at the landscape of people you would go to, there was nobody else that checked every box," Sherak says. "It was [like,] 'Keep it simple, stupid.' We went, 'Oh my

God, this is an amazing idea.' Then it was just a function of would he want to. Would he actually say yes?"

About a week before they offered him the job, I asked Williamson if he'd ever direct a *Scream* movie. He said no, unequivocally, and he had good reasons.

"I meant it," Williamson says. "I didn't want to do it."

What changed?

"I got asked, I guess," he says. "I honestly didn't think it would ever happen. Then when Neve called with William and she officially asked me, I just got very emotional. I was like, 'Abso-fuckin-lutely I would. I would do it in a heartbeat. I want to do it right now.' I got very excited."

Campbell called him on February 22, 2024. He made a point of writing it down so he wouldn't forget it, not that either of them would.

"I got to ask him, and he just burst into tears," Campbell says. "And I started crying too because I was happy for him and happy that we're going to get to have this experience together. It was a very beautiful, very sweet moment and *of course* it should be Kevin. Absolutely he should direct one of these. He knows these characters and these films better than anyone."

"I cried. I mean, I got off the phone and just sobbed," Williamson says. "My fiancé thought I was nuts. He wasn't around during 1996. He doesn't know how difficult this road has been, the experience that I have had with this franchise. How hard it's been and how wonderful it's been. He hasn't seen any of that. So, when I finally just sort of unleashed, he was like, 'Wow.'"

All of the hesitation he'd felt melted away, even if some self-doubt crept in.

"I was like, 'You had me at hello. I'm not gonna say no to this.' I thought about it for all of two seconds," Williamson says. "As I got off the phone, I did have a moment where I thought of all the reasons not to do it and tried to look at all the cons. And it's like, 'Fuck it, there is no reason not to do it. Just stop thinking. Don't overthink this. Just say yes and do it and have the time of your life. What if I don't do a good job? It doesn't matter. Just do it. Just say yes.'"

There's no doubt in my mind he will do a good job, and I tell him as much.

"I will. Yes, I will," Williamson says. "I live in fear of failure, but you know what, failure is not an option with this one."

"I do believe it will be the best version the movie can be," Sherak says. "I genuinely believe that. I don't know a better love letter to the franchise and the fans. Whatever happens from this point forward, after 7, this one got made. Do I believe and hope that we will be successful and that we will make more? Without question. Regardless, for a moment in time, I get to have Kevin direct a *Scream* movie starring Neve. That's cool!"

With Campbell on board and Williamson at the helm, they turned their attention to Gale Weathers.

"We had a Zoom with Courteney," Williamson recalls. "We pitched the movie to her, and they said, 'Kevin is going to direct,' and Courteney's like, 'About fuckin' time.'"

They wanted to be very intentional about how they announced Campbell's return and Williamson directing, so they took some drastic steps to avoid leaks—like not bringing his agents into negotiations.

"Basically, Gary called my lawyer and we did it all within

two phone calls and texting and just made the deal. It was really important for Neve to announce it. So that's why we did it the way we did it."

Campbell, on March 12, shared the cover page of a script with her name watermarked on it. It was for *Untitled Scream 7*, written by Guy Busick and directed by Kevin Williamson.

"I'm so excited to announce this news!!! Sidney Prescott is coming back!!!!" she wrote in the caption. "I'm very happy and proud to say I've been asked, in the most respectful way, to bring Sidney back to the screen and I couldn't be more thrilled!!!"

She then went on to share Williamson's news too.

"I've dreamt for many years of how amazing it would be to make one of these movies with Kevin Williamson at the helm. And now it's happening," she wrote. "Kevin Williamson is going to direct *Scream 7*! This was his baby and it's his brilliant mind that dreamt up this world. Kevin is not just an inspiration as an artist but has been a dear friend for many years."

You could say it was surprising yet inevitable.

"Kevin Williamson is now making the movie I think he always should have made," Landon says. "It was a giant 'duh!' It all crystallized and made perfect sense."

And, even though it happened in a way Williamson didn't see coming, he got what he'd hoped for: The *Scream* franchise finally has a gay director at the helm.

"He always wanted a queer filmmaker to make one of these movies. No one understands it better than he does. It feels kismet," Landon says. "However messy it got, it got to the place it was supposed to get to. I will be there opening night. I'll be so excited to see what he does. I'll always be a fan."

It's impossible to ask Wes Craven what he thinks about Williamson following in his footsteps in this way, but people close to him are unanimous in thinking he'd be elated. And proud.

"This is a brilliant move and I think Wes would be thrilled," says Iya Labunka. "And Neve, I am so happy for her. I've been in touch with her and with Kevin and I just think it's the best thing that could've happened. I really, really do. I think it's wonderful."

I tell her that, based on everything I've heard up to this point, *Scream 7* has the potential to be the best film since the original.

"It could be. Obviously, that's the hope, and I think Kevin understands the weight of that," Labunka says. "He takes it really, really seriously. He understands it better than anybody, except maybe Wes, and he and Wes were such a great team. They just complemented each other so well, in so many different ways. It's brilliant and I'm just thrilled."

———

THERE WON'T EVER BE ANOTHER WES CRAVEN *SCREAM*, BUT WITH KEVIN Williamson directing, the seventh movie may feel like one.

"I hope what Kevin would do would be what Wes would do. I hope I'm in sync with that a little bit," Williamson says. "I learned so much from Wes."

Williamson loves *Scream 6*, but his movie won't be as

violent. It's something he and Campbell talked about outside Sherak's house right after Busick had pitched her the story. She wanted to have a candid, private conversation and hear Williamson's thoughts.

"I go, 'I really like the pitch and here is why,' and I walked her through it," he says. "He gave Sidney a real conflict, he gave her a real life, he gave her a real family, he gave her real obstacles, and then someone gets killed. He really set her up very well and this is why I like this story."

Campbell agreed, before sharing one big concern. When Sam turns the knife on Richie and goes berserk in *Scream 5*, it stopped feeling like *Scream* to her. She told Williamson that she started to feel disconnected because she was still living in another *Scream*, namely Craven's.

"Neve wants to go back to the first one and find the suspense and really concentrate on scary and not bloody," Williamson says. "She was smart. She goes, 'This is the time to do it because we're moving away from New York. We're going back to Sidney's life. This is the time to reset a little bit.' And I'm like, 'Yup, let's do it.'"

Campbell wants to dial things back a bit and focus on the storytelling and character building.

"This is a whodunit," she says, "but not *just* a whodunit. It's who are we following? Who are we caring about? I want the audience to feel engaged with the characters enough that they care what happens to them."

"I want to make it emotional," Williamson continues. "The most important thing in a horror film is your emotional connection to the movie, because you can't scare someone if you can't make them care."

It's the moment after the scare that matters; Williamson learned that from Craven.

"What's the moment where the audience is catching their breath?" Williamson says, explaining the thought process. "How do we want them to be relieved and how long do we want them to be relieved? How long do we want them to breathe? Do we want to double-scare them? Do we want to pull the rug out from under them? How are they going to feel?"

It's not all about putting yourself in the mind of the audience, of course, but the characters' minds too.

"What's your character thinking? Really concentrate on what your character's reaction is in the moment after the scare because that is going to propel you into the next moment," Williamson says. "Wes was always thinking moment to moment, which related to me because I came from theater. I studied acting, of all things, when I was in college because I got a scholarship. I studied the Meisner technique and Meisner was very moment to moment. Live in the moment, live in the now, right here, right now, that's all we have. When I write, I try to go from moment to moment to moment. That's how I create a beginning, middle, and end of each scene. What does a character want? What are they going to do to get it and how do you resolve that scene and how does it push you forward?"

To push the *Scream* story forward, he's going to have to stay in the moment as a director too.

"At the end of the day, you can't pretend there's going to be another movie," Williamson says. "This could be the only one. So, everything has to be in this film. If it works, then there'll be another one, but we can't just think we're going to get another film. I mean, I'm sure the studio can, but I can't. This will probably be the only one I'll do, so I've got to do everything I want to do."

On the most basic level, he's already doing what he wants to do: telling Sidney Prescott's story. Instead of centering on things happening in her orbit, the focus is her life.

"That's the story I care about," Williamson says. "That's the *Scream* I've been wanting to see.

"I am really excited that we're going to be able to touch on some themes and ideas and go back to some origins of *Scream*. It'll be a little nostalgic but we're also going to have a lot of fun. I think it moves the franchise forward. I think it does cap off *Scream 5* and *6* thematically, but it does it with Sidney. And Gale, of course, and a few other surprises."

I'm making a point not to get too spoiler-y here, but I brought up that Craven didn't kill his heroes and told Williamson that I don't feel like he would either.

"I have made it very clear, I think publicly too, that Sidney has been through so much torment, and she has been through so much trauma, that to give her anything less than a happy ending is mean," Williamson says. "It's just sacrilegious."

Before Williamson had decided to direct *Scream 7*, I had asked him what the key is to ensuring these movies stay good. What advice does he have for anyone who makes one?

"Everyone who has succeeded with *Scream* either loves horror movies or loves *Scream* or loved Wes," Williamson says. "Whoever does *Scream*, it has to be a crime of passion.

You have to be passionate about the franchise. They just need to love it, and be talented, and I think they'll be okay."

Williamson wasn't talking about himself, but when it comes to finding someone talented who loves horror and *Scream* and Wes, there's no one closer to the mark.

FULL CIRCLE

No matter where *Scream* goes from here, Kevin Williamson's creative return as a director is the best thing that could have possibly happened to the franchise in this moment.

"*Scream* gave me my career; it gave me my life," says Williamson. "I'm so grateful for it. I'm so blessed because of *Scream*. I'm so proud to be a part of it to this day. It truly has been a gift. It has made me very, very happy."

The arc of the franchise so far feels a lot like those of the movies themselves. The story has an unexpectedly strong opening and it ends on a relatively high note, despite the unexpected physical, emotional, and psychological challenges along the way.

"They are all sort of secretly feel-good films," says *Scream 5* and *6* writer James Vanderbilt. "At the end of it, you come out the tunnel on the other side and there is some sunshine there. These characters you cared about,

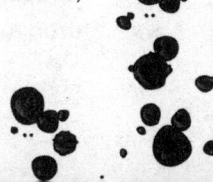

some of them made it, some don't, but the people you love are probably going to be okay and there is something really wonderful about that."

Mason Gooding says he's thrilled to see Campbell back on her own terms and working in tandem with Williamson "to create a labor of love that I'm hoping puts fandom and appreciation first in a way that makes *7* a very loving horror film, one that—for Neve, for Kevin, for the people that enjoy this franchise—feels like a homecoming."

With its return to Sidney Prescott's story, *Scream 7* will feel like coming home for longtime fans of the franchise. After watching her grow up, and survive trauma after trauma, we're stepping into her life as an adult and meeting her family for the first time. Until now, we've known next to nothing about it.

There were references to a man named Mark in *5* and *6*, which led fans to think she had settled down with Detective Mark Kincaid, who was played by Patrick Dempsey in *Scream 3*. Dempsey entertained questions from press about *Scream 7*, which fueled the speculation, but he didn't actually return.

Would it have made sense for Sidney to marry a police officer who'd already lived through a Ghostface encounter? Sure. Could his absence from *Screams 4–6*, and any actual confirmation of that relationship in the scripts, be ham-sandwiched away? Sure. Was it necessary for this Mark to be *that* Mark? Absolutely not. (Around the time Sidney Prescott was born, give or take five years, there were about 165,000 Marks born in the U.S.)

Neve Campbell isn't plussed. I didn't catch the name-drop in *Scream 5* the first time around, and neither did she.

"Honestly," she tells me, "I thought it was just a random name."

Mark Evans, a.k.a. Mr. Sidney Prescott, is played by Joel McHale, who's best known for his role in *Community* and is expected to bring some much-needed moments of levity to the life of his perpetually haunted partner.

Casting a movie like *Scream 7* during a time when the franchise is under an especially honed microscope presents a unique set of challenges. So the filmmakers again turned to casting director Rich Delia, who's more than a little familiar with working "under a cloak of secrecy."

"People are trying to figure out every little thing," Delia says. "You want to honor the fans, and you want to keep things secret, so that they can go into the theater and experience it the way that they should."

He'd never reveal all his tricks, but they use code names and disclose as little information as possible to actors who are auditioning. It's a creative trust fall on both sides.

"You're looking for actors that have depth and have layers," Delia explains. "Actors need to be chameleons in a sense. Whether you're playing Mother Teresa or Hitler, the same actor could play both of those characters. They're just leaning into different aspects of the human condition. Finding actors who have a wonderful range and can lean into different facets of a personality without judging [the character] is really important."

As with the previous two installments, Delia was tasked with casting the offspring of legacy characters. With Sam Carpenter and the Meeks-Martin twins, you only knew one of their parents so there was quite a bit of latitude with casting the roles.

Sidney's daughter was a different story. The teen needed to be believably descendant from both Campbell and McHale, but it's not all about looks.

"Sometimes people look a lot like their parents and sometimes they don't," Delia says. "You really just want to make sure that they feel like they're a unit, that they have chemistry like they have known these people their whole lives and have been raised by them. It's more of a tone and energy."

As a producer on the film, Campbell had a voice in casting. When she saw Isabel May's screen test, she knew right away that they'd found her on-screen daughter.

"She's really open and has very natural instincts, and she's bright and talented," Campbell says. "She certainly has what we need for this character."

Along with Campbell, Courteney Cox is back as Gale Weathers, and Mason Gooding and Jasmin Savoy Brown are back as Chad and Mindy. Early casting announcements for new characters included Anna Camp, Mckenna Grace, Celeste O'Connor, Asa Germann, Sam Rechner, Ethan Embry, and Mark Consuelos. (Another Mark!) Some other familiar faces, including Matthew Lillard, David Arquette, and Scott Foley, will also return.

"Whatever project you're working on, it's a delicate balancing act and you try to find ways with the casting to elevate aspects of the script and maybe subvert audiences' expectations," Delia says. "Part of the challenge, and also the fun of it, is really utilizing the casting to help sell certain aspects of the story—or hide certain aspects of the story."

For an ensemble like this one, they'll see anywhere from

one to five hundred actors for each role. The inbound interest, both career- and curiosity-driven, remains intense.

"You get asked about everyone in *Scream*," Delia says. "People ask you, 'Is this person coming back? Is this person still around? Are you casting this person?' I don't think there has been a character in the *Scream* universe that I haven't been asked about. People love the movies so much that these characters become real people to them. They are invested in them. It is a privilege to be able to work on something that people care so much about."

WHEN IT COMES TO BELOVED CHARACTERS, THERE'S NO ONE WHO SPARKS as much spirited debate as Stu Macher. Is he really dead? It's a topic that comes up often, and even people in the franchise are divided on the answer.

He's Schrödinger's serial killer—and everyone is a hundred percent certain they're right.

"I don't think he dies under the TV," Matthew Lillard told me in the fall of 2023. "I think, if anything, he would have died from the bleeding out—but, for the record, he's still alive and he's very much available."

Williamson ran into Lillard around that time, not long after the movie adaptation of *Five Nights at Freddy's* made a huge splash on streaming and at the box office. He remembers the actor teasing that the *FNAF* filmmakers didn't kill him and he finally gets to be in a sequel.

As much as everyone adores Lillard, and Stu, in that conversation Williamson was pretty definitive.

"I was like, 'You're so dead. You're dead, dead, dead,'"

Williamson says. "And he was like, 'Awww, man. Maybe I have a twin brother.' He is so funny. He's like, 'But Skeet dies, and *he* gets to be in them.'" That was before this iteration of *Scream 7* existed, of course. Fast-forward a bit and Lillard was understandably floored when Williamson called out of the blue one afternoon.

"I'll never forget where I was when Kevin called me," Lillard says. "I was walking in the park on the phone with one of my companies, and Kevin Williamson is calling me. I was like, 'What is that?' So, I jumped off the call and answered the phone. We started small talk that we had recently seen each other at a party, and he's like, 'I wanted to say this at the party, but I couldn't. Do you want to come do *Scream 7*?' I was like, 'What?!' I sort of freaked out. It was a little like chasing that girl through high school and then all of a sudden she's like, 'Do you want to go to the prom with me?'"

He's thrilled to be back, but when reality set in, so did the pressure.

"The idea of Stu coming back is so synonymous with the movies. That question is always being asked—and now you're doing something about it," Lillard says. "Being back and walking on set, and realizing the weight you have in the franchise based on your legacy, is humbling and exciting and lovely. There's a weight to it that was not unbearable, but nerve-racking. There'll be a lot of fans waiting to see exactly how this shakes out."

Former Dimension exec Richard Potter points out that if Stu were alive, he'd always be a suspect.

"If Stu is alive—even if he is in a psych ward, even if he is in a coma and he is strapped to a bed—every time someone dies by someone in a Ghostface mask, the first thing that every investigator has to do is find out if Stu is still locked up. You can't do that off camera. You'd need to have a scene in every movie where they go to check to see where Stu is."

Meanwhile, David Arquette is on Team Stu Is Alive.

"You can suspend the disbelief. It's worth it for his connection to the fans," Arquette says.

That applies to his character too, of course. He adds with a laugh, "As long as I'm still alive, Dewey can still be alive."

Dewey's on-screen sister isn't opposed to a return either.

Rose McGowan says over the years fans who clocked that Tatum had two beds in her room have suggested she could have had a dark-haired twin sister waiting to avenge her death.

"She could have been the family secret. She could have been institutionalized. She would be a great killer," says McGowan. "I'm not that interested in acting anymore at all. That's not what my focus is, but for Tatum, I think that would actually be an amazing reprise. And I love Kevin Williamson. I've always deeply respected him."

Another fan favorite is rumored to have survived thanks to a decaying theater marquee that was promoting a Jennifer Jolie retrospective in *Scream 6*—and Parker Posey is totally on board.

"I've been asked about this before and I'll say it again: I never wanted to die—and the double-sided mirror is a great focal point for JJ to return into another realm of the *Scream* franchise," Posey says. "I'm not sure how Hollywood works, but I keep putting it out there, and *Scream* keeps following me."

Radio Silence didn't intend to make a statement about Jolie's corporeal status by doing that. They just loved the character and thought it would be a fun nod to Posey's performance. Matt Bettinelli-Olpin says they'll "defer to her" as to whether the *Stab 3* star survived.

The fact that so many stars would want to come back—not just those already mentioned but also Dermot Mulroney, Tony Revolori, and Elise Neal, among others, I'm sure—speaks to how unique working on *Scream* is. It's like the polar opposite of trauma bonding; everyone is having the time of their lives, and that shows on screen.

"At the end of the day, it's just about the people," Jack Champion says. "It doesn't matter how meta you get, how many horror references. If you have a cast that seem like they are genuine friends and you care about them as characters when they're in danger, I think the job is done."

"Casting is really important," Arquette agrees. "To find these groups of people that really connect with each other, that have these senses of humor, and they can think on their toes. That the cast really likes each other is important. That adds to the realism of it."

———

NEVE CAMPBELL AND I TALKED ON ZOOM THE DAY BEFORE SHE STARTED filming *Scream 7*. She'd flown into Atlanta just ahead of a snowstorm (the Southern U.S. kind, not the Canadian kind) and had spent the weekend working with her script and settling in for the winter shoot.

"I'm excited to put on Sidney's boots tomorrow," Campbell says. "I had dinner with a group of wonderful, enthusiastic young actors last night, who are so excited to be a part of this film, and that feels great. I love doing what I do. I love being an actor. I love being creative. I love storytelling."

Her producer boots were already well-worn by this point, of course.

"I've done a lot of work with Kevin on the script since we got to Atlanta, and in December as well," she says. "To have a voice in what direction we wanted this film to go is wonderful."

Working with Williamson as a director has felt like an organic evolution of their relationship.

"I just love that man. He and I are dear friends. He's an absolute sweetheart, and humble, and incredibly smart," she says. "Kevin has a great sense of humor, and he cares deeply about his work. What I'm excited about on this film is that he carries that same kind of energy that Wes had. He cares a lot about people having a good experience and making sure that everyone's doing their jobs, but also that everyone's being conscientious of one another."

When I visited the set a few weeks into filming, that was immediately clear.

It's still work obviously, but there was a steady stream of humor even in the middle of the night, and I found the dynamic between Williamson, DP Ramsey Nickell, and first assistant director Rudy Persico (a *Vampire Diaries* alum) to be almost as fun to watch as the shoot itself. And every single crew and cast member I talked to couldn't have been nicer. I imagine it's a lot like what a Wes Craven set felt like.

"The beauty of what Wes was able to build with the *Scream* franchise was that he built a community and a family," says Julie Plec. "To be able to bring that family back around to its origins with Kevin—and Neve and Courteney returning, and all the additional announced surprise cameos—really does bring it full circle to where it started in a narrative way, and in an emotional way, and in a nostalgic way."

The story they're telling is not going to be spoiled here, but there are some things that are obvious enough for Campbell to share.

"It would be nice for audiences to get a sense of where Sidney is at this point in her life," Campbell says, being playfully vague. "So we're going for that."

She pauses and smiles. "Amongst other things."

It's no secret that Sidney has a daughter, which creates a difficult full-circle moment for a woman whose own mother was brutally murdered when she was a teen. It's another layer to reveal in a character that has already proved to be surprisingly relatable over the years.

"Think about how challenging it would be to make the choice to even have a child if you were Sidney Prescott. Then, if you did have children, the stress and fear that you would live under about your history coming back to you," Campbell says. "I don't want to give it away, but how she chooses to parent is a big choice and perhaps different than how others might."

Each time Campbell reconnects with Sidney, regardless of how many years have passed off screen, she imagines how her emotional scars would be impacting her day-to-day life. That's how she keeps Sidney grounded in reality.

"Her challenge is to live in joy and live in peace despite her PTSD and despite the fact that she's always going to be looking over her shoulder. She's always going to be aware of everybody in the room. That will be her journey forever because that's not something she's capable of letting go of, and wouldn't, because she's a survivor," Campbell says. "Finding the few people in her life who she can trust and keep close, and finding the things that bring her joy, that's probably been her journey between any of these films. Having to rebuild her life each time and choosing not to give up despite all she's been through."

———

WHETHER THE FRANCHISE ENDS WITH *SCREAM 7, SCREAM 17,* OR *Scream 75*, as long as it continues to play by its own rules, lightning will continue to strike.

Some of the *Scream* rules are obvious: You need Ghostface, but Ghostface can't win. You need a creative opening sequence and an equally clever reveal. It's a slasher, so people have to die. It needs to be funny enough to defuse some of the tension, but not to the point of lowering the stakes. There needs to be a reason why this particular movie is happening now and some kind of commentary on the culture at that moment. And while *Scream* wouldn't be *Scream* without the killers, at the end of the day they're survivor stories.

"Our movies, *5* and *6*, are nowhere remotely close to *1, 2, 3,* and *4* but they are inside very specific guardrails that are unwritten," says producer William Sherak. "One of the things I'm most proud of is that we actually care about what came before us. We don't look at the world and go,

'We're better than them.' We look at the world and go, 'How do we continue to make Kevin happy?' He's our barometer. All of us needed to be able to look at him at every stage and go, 'Are we doing it right?' As long as he says we're making a *Scream* movie, I feel like fans will at least recognize that's what we're trying to do."

"I think the trick is to never do what *Nightmare 2: Freddy's Revenge* did. Wes hated the wink of that movie," says *Scream* editor Patrick Lussier. "*New Nightmare* is a darkly serious movie because he didn't want it to laugh at itself. That's the way *Scream* can continue, if it stays true to who it is and never becomes the *Moonraker* of the franchise and never, *never* becomes so self-aware that it's its own joke."

"*Scream*, regardless of the visionary at the helm, is a horror movie at a fundamental basis," says Gooding. "Allow that movie to be scary, to be funny at times, to be violent. Just make 'em scary and make it full of passion and heart. Whoever needs to hear this, keep letting the people that have loved the franchise for as long as they have be at the helm of these movies. It is a long franchise and it has been made with a level of love that I don't think you find in most other franchises."

Sherak says *that* actually is a key ingredient, maybe *the* key.

"Don't let anybody in the circle who isn't a fan," says Sherak. "That doesn't mean you can't be creative and do new things, but everybody—*everybody*—should be a fan, from top to bottom. If there is one voice in the room that isn't a fan, it can derail every decision you make." Love for the genre is vital to nailing the tone and commentary as well.

"They've gotta be made by people who love horror movies but also are willing to critique horror movies," says *Dead Meat*'s Chelsea Rebecca. "Then it feels like a loving send-up versus someone feeling like they're above it and picking apart the genre."

Character development can't be overlooked either—which is where her partner James A. Janisse says *Scream* deviates from some of its peers. "It's so easy to look at most horror franchises and be like, oh, it's about Jason. It's about Freddy," he says. "It's *not* about Ghostface. You need the protagonists to be lovable and enjoyable to watch."

"When fans talk about the franchise, so much of it is about the characters," says director of photography Brett Jutkiewicz. "A lot of it is about how scary things are, or how bloody it is, or how brutal it is, but the core of it is how much they love these characters."

"The movies have been very clever about how external forces can influence characters' decisions and how it can shape their future, how past traumas are passed along, the lineage of that," says *Scream* producer Cathy Konrad. "The idea that you can't escape your past and there are certain people that are going to be in your history for the rest of your life to make sure you never forget it."

And, of course, they have to be murder mysteries.

"They're great whodunits," says James Vanderbilt. "The first *Scream* movie is up there with Agatha Christie. It's just so fucking great. It's one of the best mysteries written in the last hundred years, in my opinion."

"At a certain point, the hardest part is the villain and the motive. I think I'm out of villains and motives at this point. I want to see new blood. I want to see new ideas," says Guy Busick. "Be careful not to retread what has come before while still honoring the DNA of the thing. It's a meta slasher whodunit. Set it anywhere, have one Ghostface, ten Ghostfaces. You can do whatever you want as long as it makes sense, as long as you're not just throwing shit at the screen because it's different and you're breaking a rule just to break it."

And as much fun as they had filming Ghostface with a flamethrower in the fake *Stab 8*, that kind of thing wouldn't fly in *Scream*.

"You just can't do something that's not true to the grounded world it created. Things were a little bit too stabby at the end of *Scream 6*," says Blumhouse exec Ryan Turek. Real-world stakes and realistic reactions are a requirement for this kind of storytelling.

"I say this from a very biased perspective because the *Scream* movies for me are now cinematic experiences. You'll always have me. I'll always be there opening night."

"I think it's key never to remake it and never to reboot it," says *Heart Eyes* cowriter Michael Kennedy. "They always should be connected even if it's the idea that 'Oh, I'm the new main character and I know about these murders with these other people, but somehow now I'm the focus and I don't know any of these fuckin' people. I have nothing to do with that town.' People love that this is a soap opera. It's *Days of Our Lives* with a serial killer, and if you can continuously keep it in the same timeline that'll do nothing but benefit the franchise and keep its longevity going."

Horror filmmaker Eli Roth says making a sequel, and keeping a franchise alive, is a daunting challenge—and audiences showing up to theaters is more important than ever.

"What made *Scream* great is that people gave a new

franchise a chance in the theaters, and they supported it through word of mouth. I am very thankful that they did that with *Thanksgiving* and that I get to continue it," says Roth. "For that to continue, audiences need to keep showing up and filmmakers and writers need to keep giving them a good reason to. There is no experience like it. You remember where you were in that theater the way you remember a great sports event when you saw a goal or a home run or that touchdown, or when you were at that concert when that person came on stage. At that moment in time, you had to be in the room. That's what *Scream* was that first time. Then when *Scream 2* came out, we all saw it opening night and everybody had the best time. Every time the *Scream* movies open, everybody wants to be there in the theater. Having that experience is so important. That's how we'll keep more franchises alive."

As Roger L. Jackson put it: "Going to a theater to see a film is the closest thing we have to collective dreaming."

There's no guarantee *Scream 7* will be a box office smash, and no way to know how fans will respond, but so far *Scream* has defied the odds to succeed where other slasher franchises have failed.

"There's a lot of weight on this movie. There's pressure for it to be good, and I think the script delivers," says Lillard. "My only hope is that we're continuing to bring people whatever sick joy they get out of this story, that we're continuing that legacy. I want people to know we're trying our damnedest to deliver something that we care about as much as they do."

With nostalgia on its side, and Williamson at the helm, I'd say the odds are in its favor.

"I'm looking forward to recapturing the feeling I had when I read that first *Scream* and when I got to be on set making that first movie and how pure it was and how unencumbered it was. I really am excited about revisiting those characters and seeing where the story has taken them over the last thirty years," Julie Plec says. "As *Scream* is entering its fourth decade of success, to have put it in the hands of the person who created it in the first place is just a really smart move."

———

AS FOR WILLIAMSON—THE WRITER WHO CRAFTED THE *SCREAM* UNIVERSE, created one of the most iconic villains of all time, and changed the horror genre indelibly—the mere existence of a *Scream 7* is a dream come true.

"I'm so thrilled that the franchise is living on," Williamson says. "I'm so thrilled that every decade it seems like there's a new audience out there that's going to the theater. There are young people embracing *Scream* the way that the young people in the '90s did, and the people in the '90s who are now older are still embracing it."

The future of the franchise is still to be written and, regardless of where it goes from here, Williamson manifested the story he wanted to see—both *Scream*'s and his own.

"*Scream* is probably the thing I'll be most remembered for after I'm long gone, and I'm really happy about that," Williamson says. "I set out to write my *Halloween* and I feel like I did it."

ACKNOWLEDGMENTS

When I was eight months pregnant with my younger son, I got an email from a guy I didn't know at a literary agency I'd never heard of (sorry!) explaining that he was determined to find someone to write a book about *Scream*. What followed was maybe the warmest cold email in history, genuinely thoughtful and flattering enough to convince me I'm the writer who should tell the story of this franchise.

There's no not nauseatingly earnest way to convey this, so sorry in advance. As far back as I can remember, I felt like an author who hadn't yet written a book. Jon, because of you—and your truly remarkable email-pitching abilities—now I have. Thank you for believing in me, guiding me through the still surreal publishing process, being my sounding board, and at least feigning amusement when I communicate via ridiculous GIFs.

To my editor, Charlotte, for your insightful feedback, unwavering enthusiasm, and extraordinary patience as I kept chasing interviews and tinkering with this until the last possible second; to Lexy for seeing this book's potential from the start and taking a chance on a first-timer; to Abby for transcribing more than eighty hours of interviews and surviving through conversational detours like [talking about the dog] and [reality TV]; and to the Plume team who designed what is, in my opinion, one of the most iconic book covers of all time: Thank you for helping make this a reality.

To everyone who paused their busy lives to reminisce about all things *Scream*, this book wouldn't be what it is without you. Your stories, your energy, and your love for the franchise truly brought this to life. Every single conversation was a delight. How each of you could be so talented and also so grounded and truly nice is unreal—there really is something special about people who create horror. Thank you for being part of this.

To William, Matt, Tyler, and Guy: I hadn't ever met any of you before starting this, but from day one you've treated me like part of the *Scream* family. Thank you for the hours on Zoom—during which you were always engaged and never rushed despite everything you have going on—and for graciously responding to all my "quick question for you" emails and calls.

To the many people in my life who've helped by brainstorming, connecting me with interviews, and listening to me vent and celebrate and endlessly talk about *Scream*-related topics for the past three-ish years: Thank you for everything.

To the fans: This franchise would not be alive and well thirty years later without you. Your passion, dedication, and knowledge are unparalleled. Hundreds of people have been able to make these films, and do work they love, because you keep showing up to support them. Thank you.

To Kevin: You are the one person I couldn't tell this story without. Thank you for dreaming up *Scary Movie*, sharing your memories with me, trusting me enough to talk about the lows, and going out of your way to help me. It is an absolute joy to know you, and I will forever be grateful for your time and support.

No thanks whatsoever to the Santa Rosa City School District Governing Board.

SOURCE NOTES

INTRODUCTION

Author interviews with John Carpenter, Patrick Lussier, and Kevin Williamson.

CHAPTER ONE: REWRITING HORROR

Author interviews with John Carpenter, Cathy Konrad, Iya Labunka, Tony Magistrale, Julie Plec, Richard Potter, Jack Quaid, Eli Roth, Ryan Turek, and Kevin Williamson.

Archival author interview with Liev Schreiber (2021).

Quotes from Wes Craven: Terry Gross, "Wes Craven Discusses His Hybrid of Horror and Satire," NPR, February 18, 1998.

Robert Dole, "Hollywood Speech," transcript of speech delivered in Los Angeles, CA, May 31, 1995, https://www.presidency.ucsb .edu/documents/remarks-los-angeles-hollywood-speech.

"The First Horror Movie & the History of the Horror Genre," New York Film Academy, July 21, 2022, https://www.nyfa.edu /student-resources/how-horror-movies-have-changed-since -their-beginning/.

CHAPTER TWO: CONVINCING CRAVEN AND A CHARMED CAST
Author interviews with Lisa Beach, Neve Campbell, Roger L. Jackson, Sarah Katzman, Christopher Landon, Matthew Lillard, Marianne Maddalena, Rose McGowan, Julie Plec, Richard Potter, and Kevin Williamson.

Quotes from Courteney Cox: Ashley Cullins, " 'Faster, Better and More Blood': A 'Scream' Oral History," *Hollywood Reporter*, October 29, 2021, https://www.hollywoodreporter.com/movies /movie-features/scream-movie-cast-stories-1235038248/.

CHAPTER THREE: MUSIC, MAYHEM, AND THE MASK
Author interviews with Marco Beltrami, Stuart Besser, Ed Gerrard, Patrick Lussier, Marianne Maddalena, Nick Mastandrea, Bruce Alan Miller, Julie Plec, and Richard Potter.

Tina Anima, "School Board in Quandary over Gory Film," *Press Democrat*, March 28, 1996.

Quotes from Wes Craven: Tina Anima, " 'Scary Movie' Director: We'll Sue," *Press Democrat*, April 16, 1996.

Pete Golis, "The Compromise That Didn't Happen," *Press Democrat*, April 18, 1996.

Nick Cave and the Bad Seeds, *Let Love In*, Mute Records, 1994, vinyl.

Ryan Hills, "Loren's Ghost: The Haunted History of the SCREAM Mask," *Fangoria*, March 9, 2023, https://www.fangoria .com/lorens-ghost-the-haunted-history-of-the-scream -mask/.

CHAPTER FOUR: THIS ISN'T SCARY
Author interviews with Neve Campbell, Cary Granat, Mark Irwin, Roger L. Jackson, Jamie Kennedy, Cathy Konrad, Patrick Lussier, Nick Mastandrea, Greg Nicotero, Julie Plec, Richard Potter, and Kevin Williamson.

Quotes from Wes Craven: Joe Nation, "Wes Craven: Don't Trust Anyone!" Rogue Spotlight, September 20, 2010, YouTube, https://www.youtube.com/watch?app=desktop&v=gJPZRM5380M.

CHAPTER FIVE: WHAT'S THE MOTIVE?
Author interviews with Stuart Besser, Peter Deming, Mark Irwin, Patrick Lussier, Scott Ressler, Gary Ushino, Kevin Williamson, and Henry Winkler.

CHAPTER SIX: WINE COUNTRY
Author interviews with David Arquette, Stuart Besser, W. Earl Brown, Neve Campbell, Courteney Cox, Peter Deming, Dane Farwell, Jamie Kennedy, Cathy Konrad, Matthew Lillard, Marianne Maddalena, Nick Mastandrea, Rose McGowan, Julie Plec, Richard Potter, Eli Roth, Skeet Ulrich, and Kevin Williamson.

CHAPTER SEVEN: SELLING A HOLIDAY HORROR SHOW
Author interviews with David Arquette, Matt Bettinelli-Olpin, Guy Busick, Tyler Gillett, Cary Granat, Jamie Kennedy, Michael Kennedy, Cathy Konrad, Matthew Lillard, Patrick Lussier, Julie Plec, Richard Potter, Eli Roth, Gary Ushino, James Vanderbilt, Kevin Williamson, Henry Winkler, and Edgar Wright.

Wes Craven, Wes Craven to Motion Picture Association of America Ratings Board, September 30, 1996.

CHAPTER EIGHT: TAKING A STAB AT A SEQUEL
Author interviews with Lisa Beach, Marco Beltrami, Peter Deming, Sarah Michelle Gellar, Ed Gerrard, Cary Granat, Michael Kennedy, Cathy Konrad, Patrick Lussier, Julie Plec, Richard Potter, Eli Roth, and Kevin Williamson.

CHAPTER NINE: BUCKETS OF BLOOD
Author interviews with Tina Anderson, David Arquette, Peter Deming, Sarah Michelle Gellar, Roger L. Jackson, Jamie Kennedy,

Michael Kennedy, Christopher Landon, Patrick Lussier, Nick Mastandrea, Laurie Metcalf, Elise Neal, Richard Potter, Eli Roth, Ryan Turek, James Vanderbilt, and Kevin Williamson.

Archival author interview with Liev Schreiber (2021).

CHAPTER TEN: META
Author interviews with Tina Anderson, Lisa Beach, Stuart Besser, Scott Foley, Cary Granat, Sarah Katzman, Cathy Konrad, Patrick Lussier, Marianne Maddalena, Heather Matarazzo, Emily Mortimer, Greg Nicotero, Julie Plec, Parker Posey, Richard Potter, Ryan Turek, Skeet Ulrich, James Vanderbilt, Sheila Waldron, and Kevin Williamson.

Archival author interview with Liev Schreiber (2021).

Quotes from Laeta Kalogridis: *Still Screaming: The Ultimate Scary Movie Retrospective*, directed by Ryan Turek, Masimedia, 2011.

CHAPTER ELEVEN: THE END OF THE TRILOGY
Author interviews with David Arquette, Peter Deming, Scott Foley, Cary Granat, James A. Janisse, Michael Kennedy, Patrick Lussier, Bruce Alan Miller, Parker Posey, Chelsea Rebecca, Ryan Turek, and Sheila Waldron.

Wes Craven, "Nickisms," September 1, 1997.

Quotes from Wes Craven, Patrick Lussier, and Marianne Maddalena: Blu-ray commentary, *Scream 2*, Dimension Films, 2000.

CHAPTER TWELVE: A NEW NIGHTMARE
Author interviews with Marco Beltrami, Rory Culkin, Peter Deming, Dane Farwell, Carly Feingold, Ed Gerrard, Erik Knudsen, Cathy Konrad, Iya Labunka, Nick Mastandrea, and Kevin Williamson.

CHAPTER THIRTEEN: CRAVEN'S FINAL *SCREAM*
Author interviews with David Arquette, Rory Culkin, Peter Deming, Dane Farwell, Carly Feingold, Tyler Gillett, Roger L. Jackson, Mark Kligerman, Erik Knudsen, Cathy Konrad, Iya Labunka, Patrick Lussier, Nick Mastandrea, Hayden Panettiere, Julie Plec, Richard Potter, Jay Prychidny, and Edgar Wright.

CHAPTER FOURTEEN: WES
Author interviews with Tina Anderson, David Arquette, Stuart Besser, W. Earl Brown, Neve Campbell, John Carpenter, Courteney Cox, Rory Culkin, Peter Deming, Carly Feingold, Scott Foley, Sarah Michelle Gellar, Roger L. Jackson, Jamie Kennedy, Cathy Konrad, Iya Labunka, Matthew Lillard, Patrick Lussier, Marianne Maddalena, Nick Mastandrea, Bruce Alan Miller, Emily Mortimer, Elise Neal, Greg Nicotero, Hayden Panettiere, Julie Plec, Parker Posey, Eli Roth, Meryl Streep, Skeet Ulrich, Sheila Waldron, Kevin Williamson, Henry Winkler, and Edgar Wright.

CHAPTER FIFTEEN: SURPRISING BUT INEVITABLE
Author interviews with Matt Bettinelli-Olpin, Jasmin Savoy Brown, Guy Busick, Neve Campbell, Rich Delia, Kyle Gallner, Tyler Gillett, Mason Gooding, Chad Keith, Heather Matarazzo, Paul Neinstein, Richard Newby, Jack Quaid, William Sherak, Ryan Turek, Brian Tyler, Skeet Ulrich, James Vanderbilt, and Kevin Williamson.

CHAPTER SIXTEEN: *5CREAM*
Author interviews with David Arquette, Matt Bettinelli-Olpin, Jasmin Savoy Brown, Neve Campbell, Kyle Gallner, Tyler Gillett, Mason Gooding, Roger L. Jackson, Brett Jutkiewicz, Jamie Kennedy, Michael Kennedy, Iya Labunka, Matthew Lillard, Heather Matarazzo, Paul Neinstein, Richard Newby, Jack Quaid, William Sherak, Ryan Turek, Skeet Ulrich, and Kevin Williamson.

Quote from Jenna Ortega: Ashley Cullins, "Next Gen Talent 2022: Meet The Hollywood Reporter's 12 Rising Young Stars," *Hollywood Reporter*, November 17, 2022, https://www .hollywoodreporter.com/lists/next-gen-talent-2022-meet-the -hollywood-reporters-12-rising-young-stars/jenna-ortega-3/.

CHAPTER SEVENTEEN: GHOSTFACE TAKES MANHATTAN
Author interviews with Matt Bettinelli-Olpin, Guy Busick, Neve Campbell, Jack Champion, Rich Delia, Tyler Gillett, Michael Kennedy, Iya Labunka, Liana Liberato, Patrick Lussier, Dermot Mulroney, Devyn Nekoda, Jack Quaid, William Sherak, James Vanderbilt, and Kevin Williamson.

CHAPTER EIGHTEEN: A SECRET ACTION MOVIE
Author interviews with Matt Bettinelli-Olpin, Jasmin Savoy Brown, Guy Busick, Jack Champion, Tyler Gillett, Mason Gooding, Brett Jutkiewicz, Michèle Laliberté, Liana Liberato, Dermot Mulroney, Paul Neinstein, Devyn Nekoda, Avery Plewes, Jay Prychidny, William Sherak, and Kevin Williamson.

CHAPTER NINETEEN: HAM SANDWICH
Author interviews with Matt Bettinelli-Olpin, Jasmin Savoy Brown, Jack Champion, Courteney Cox, Rich Delia, Tyler Gillett, Mason Gooding, Liana Liberato, Patrick Lussier, Dermot Mulroney, Jay Prychidny, Jack Quaid, Tony Revolori, Eli Roth, William Sherak, Ryan Turek, and Kevin Williamson.

CHAPTER TWENTY: THE *SCREAM 7* THAT WASN'T
Author interviews with Matt Bettinelli-Olpin, Jasmin Savoy Brown, Guy Busick, John Carpenter, Tyler Gillett, Christopher Landon, William Sherak, and Kevin Williamson.

Melissa Barrera (@melissabarreram). "First and foremost I condemn Anti-Semitism and Islamophobia," Instagram, November 22, 2023.

CHAPTER TWENTY-ONE: A CRIME OF PASSION
Author interviews with Guy Busick, Neve Campbell, Brett Jutkiewicz, Iya Labunka, Christopher Landon, William Sherak, and Kevin Williamson.

Neve Campbell (@nevecampbell), "Hi All. I'm so excited to announce this news!!!" Instagram, March 12, 2024, https://www.instagram.com/p/C4bG052PMhE/.

CHAPTER TWENTY-TWO: FULL CIRCLE
Author interviews with David Arquette, Matt Bettinelli-Olpin, Guy Busick, Neve Campbell, Jack Champion, Rich Delia, Mason Gooding, Roger L. Jackson, James A. Janisse, Brett Jutkiewicz, Michael Kennedy, Cathy Konrad, Matthew Lillard, Patrick Lussier, Rose McGowan, Julie Plec, Parker Posey, Richard Potter, Chelsea Rebecca, Eli Roth, William Sherak, Ryan Turek, James Vanderbilt, and Kevin Williamson.

INDEX

ABOUT
THE AUTHOR

ASHLEY CULLINS is an award-winning entertainment journalist with more than a decade of experience. After graduating with a master's degree in journalism from Northwestern University's prestigious Medill School, Ashley began her career in broadcast news before making the jump to print. *Your Favorite Scary Movie* is her first book.